GREENFIELD PUBLIC LIBRARY

DATE DUE

4/16/04			

D1275367

A Fresh Look at

SAUCING FOODS

A Fresh Look at

SAUCING FOODS

DEIRDRE DAVIS

Addison-Wesley Publishing Company
*Reading, Massachusetts   Menlo Park, California   New York
Don Mills, Ontario   Wokingham, England   Amsterdam   Bonn
Sydney   Singapore   Tokyo   Madrid   San Juan
Paris   Seoul   Milan   Mexico City   Taipei*

Grateful acknowledgment is made to *Bon Appétit* magazine
for permission to reprint their recipe for Crab Cakes with Creole Sauce.
Copyright © 1984 by *Bon Appétit* magazine.
Reprinted with permission.

Many of the designations used by manufacturers and sellers to distinguish their products are claimed as trademarks. Where those designations appear in this book and Addison-Wesley was aware of a trademark claim, the designations have been printed in initial capital letters.

Library of Congress Cataloging-in-Publication Data

Davis, Deirdre.
    A fresh look at saucing foods / Deirdre Davis.
      p.   cm.
    Includes index.
    ISBN 0-201-57710-0
    1. Sauces. I. Title.
  TX819.A1D38 1992
  641.8′14—dc20   92-9717
                                 CIP

Jacket design and illustration by Diana Coe

Text design by Ruth Kolbert

Set in 11-point Bembo by Shepard Poorman Communications

1 2 3 4 5 6 7 8 9-VB-95949392

First printing, December 1992

To Chris

CONTENTS

ACKNOWLEDGMENTS

THIS BOOK HAS GROWN OUT OF ME WITH THE HELP, LOVE, ENergy, and support of many people.

A very special thank you to my husband Chris, my son Max, and my father Russell. Whether it was one of the many moments of doubt and frustration when I wanted to scrap the whole thing and switch careers, or when I was on such an intense testing schedule that I nearly killed everyone through force-feeding, my family supported me, tasted critically, shopped, cleaned, laundered, took over all child care, read the manuscript, and offered much feedback. I would also like to thank Chris for the many hours of computer advice he gave to me, my father for his patience, and Max for giving me privacy to "tap on my computer."

Thank you to Henry, Joan, Russell, Chris, and Owen Davis; Kelly and Amelia Davis; Patty Davis; Geoff and Yami Davis; and Sarah Cullen for many food discussions, tastings, and wonderful ideas.

Thank you to Madeleine Kamman for her inspirational teaching, thus opening my eyes to a world beyond tuna casserole.

Thank you to Faith Childs, my agent, for her enthusiasm and insight; to my Aris editor, John Harris, who had faith in my sauce-with-food idea and helped me keep my focus; and to my Addison-Wesley editors Elizabeth Carduff and John Fuller for their patience and understanding of my style.

A huge thank you to my neighbors, Sheila, Bob, Mark, and Amanda Bodwell, for their palates, critiques, and incalculable hours of loving child care, particularly by Amanda.

To my dear friend and colleague Linda Marino for her unwavering support through the hard times, impromptu brainstorming, and unparalleled technical advice.

To Kathy Gunst for her emotional support and thoughtful reading and editing of the manuscript.

Many thanks to my professional colleagues for the hundreds of times that I bugged them: Nancy Verde Barr, Judith Barrett, Laura Brennan, Jacqueline Cattani, Doe Coover, James and Alison Dodson, Lisa Ekus, June Ferris, Roberta Frechette, Linda Gervich, Ethel Goralnick, June Gosule-Zieff, Beth Gurney-Piskula, Patricia Kelly, Nancy Klavans, Richard Kzirian, Elaine O'Toole, Susan Peery, Denise Schorr, Nina Simonds, Drew Spangler, Ruth Tanner, P. T. Thorndike, and Paula Wolfert.

Thank you to all who contributed scientific advice regarding flavored oils: Professor David A. Evans at the University of Massachusetts, Amherst; *Gourmet* magazine; Sheryl Julian; Madeleine Kamman; the Fresh Garlic Association; Nancy C. Stutzman at the Cooperative Extension of the University of Massachusetts; Ruth Tanner; the Women's Culinary Guild of New England; and Nancy Young.

Thank you to everyone who diligently prepared recipes for their families, whose palates and tastebuds helped clarify and streamline these ideas, or who listened, advised, and picked me up when I needed it: Doug and Liz Babbitt; Liz and Terry Bartow; Sandy Bettencourt; Virginia Drachman and Douglas Jones; Martha Hayward; Tami Kaplan and Jonathan Lewis; Kate Kimball; the Malarkey family; Lynn Merz and Bill Kennedy; Deborah Moules; Lee Orloff; Harry Payne; the Playgroup testers and tasters of Pam Constantine, Betsy Friedman, Bev Harrison, and Leslie Sands; the Touisset, Rhode Island, tasting group; and Carol Williams and Ken Jackson.

Finally, thank you to the late Beverly Stobaugh and her husband Robert, catering clients of mine, for getting me started on this crazy idea in the first place. At countless dinner parties over nine years I explored different sauce and food combinations and honed my craft. Their continuous enthusiasm and excitement over my cooking has no peer.

Introduction

■ ■ ■ ■

A Passion for Sauces

When I was a child I ate Sunday roasts glistening with gravy made from pan drippings, leg of lamb with mint jelly, bright yellow mustard on franks, and soft spaghetti from a can with an orange-colored sauce. When I was about eight years old and just beginning to cook, my specialty was chicken breasts smothered in condensed cream-of-something soup. I loved these comforting dishes and I was intrigued with the idea of saucing food.

My love for food and sauces led me, fresh out of high school, to cooking school with Madeleine Kamman, an expert sauce-maker. There I savored a meal that I will never forget and can still taste today: French onion soup, boneless breast of chicken with sauce supreme, and an apple tart. The chicken dish astonished me. The sauce, lightened and smoothed by luxurious heavy cream, had been carefully composed of fresh ingredients and tasted exactly as it smelled—full of a deep, meaty flavor. I realized then that the baked cream-of-something-soup and chicken which I had loved as a child was a mere imitation of this authentic dish. I was shocked and elated to learn that another way to prepare the chicken existed. After finishing my professional chef's program and apprenticeship in Madeleine's restaurant, Chez La Mère Madeleine, I knew that sauce making would be an important part of my food career.

The dishes of my childhood are not so appealing to me today; my cooking has changed and grown up, but those dishes kindled the desire in me to consistently want a sauce with my food. This book is the culmination of the idea that sauces and food bring out the best in each other, whether it is a simple oil and vinegar dressing on lettuce or a complex reduction sauce over salmon.

Ever since the Greeks and Romans, and probably before, people have devised ways to embellish foods. Today the urge to sauce food is still strong and it is my hope that this book will help you pair ingredients and flavors that work together and enhance each other's qualities. But how is this done? How do we know that tomatoes and basil are a transcendent pair? That without pasta and Parmesan, Italy could not function? There are no easy answers to this question of combining ingredients to give us pleasure. Part of it is a combination of all our senses and another inner sense of knowing that some ingredient would be delicious with another simply by reading about it, seeing it at the market, or thinking and talking about food. For instance, one day I was struck by the beauty of a pile of red bell peppers and lemons on my counter and I felt compelled to make a dish with these two ingredients. Red Peppers and Peas with Lemon Zest Dressing (pages 80–82) is the result of my experiment. The dressing, a puree of lemon zest and mint, is poured over roasted red peppers, thin strips of lemon zest, and fresh sweet peas.

When I am putting a dish together, there are a few things I always consider: the texture of the finished dish, the taste, what ingredients are in season, and the cooking technique. For instance, when I make a crisp Waldorf Salad (pages 63–64), I prepare a smooth, creamy sauce. On the other hand, in a sauce for poached fish or roasted beef tenderloin, I would add ingredients with lots of crunch. But sometimes it is not enough merely to contrast textures; sometimes you must also contrast tastes. When making a dish, I like to use sweet, acidic, salty, bitter, or spicy elements in various combinations. If one ingredient is inherently sweet, such as red bell peppers, an opposing ingredient, such as vinegar, may be used to balance the dish. The recipe for Prune and Sekel Pear Sauce on Pork Tenderloin (pages 222–224) combines sweet fruit with an aromatic red wine and plenty of cracked black peppercorns for heat and spice.

Many ingredients are available year round, but it is best to use those that are in season. In her book, *Verdura* (New York: William Morrow & Co., 1991), Viana La Place has an interesting salad of tomatoes and peaches (the recipe idea is from an old Italian cookbook) with lemon juice, olive oil, and a scattering of walnuts. It is a wonderful blend of sweet, tart, smooth, and crunchy using two ingredients at their peak in the same season. There are countless combinations of seasonal ingredients that make great dishes, such as artichokes and peas, asparagus and salmon, strawberry and rhubarb, cranberries and orange, or corn and basil. The ingredients may be prepared in classic ways or given new twists, as in the recipe for Strawberry and Rhubarb Compote (pages 303–304). In this dish, thick rhubarb slices are poached in spiced wine and served with fresh berry slices.

Your choice of cooking technique—whether you plan to bake, saute, steam, or grill—will also help you balance textures and flavors. There is nothing like sinking your fork into deeply cooked lamb with a simple gravy (see pages 258–259). However, a crunchy fresh vegetable relish calls for something quickly cooked and succulent such as Cherry Tomato Salsa on Swordfish (pages 176–177). These are some of the elements I think about when putting dishes together. Most important, however, is your own personal preference and taste. If there is an ingredient that you love and want to use in some way, think about its natural taste and texture, how it might work in a sweet or savory setting, and have fun experimenting.

Sauces complement. They need food under them, over them, beside them, or dipped into them. Because of my interest in matching sauces with food, I have arranged the chapters in this book by food groups, rather than by sauce. This reflects my emphasis on complete dishes, not sauces in isolation. This organization should help you find interesting sauces for the food you plan to prepare, while making it easier for you to create everyday meals. I have included a glossary and master recipe chapter to explain basic recipes and their techniques. With each recipe I have given suggestions for using the sauces with other foods. The recipes range from such classics as Dad's Chocolate Sauce with Butterscotch-Praline Ice Cream (pages 180–182) and Fish and Chips with Tartar Sauce (pages 300–302) to innovative combinations like Roast Duck with Rhubarb and Leek Sauce (pages 210–211) and Cracked Wheat with Grape Sauce (pages 132–133). They also vary widely in formality. This book gives you my viewpoint on pairing sauces and foods, and I hope it encourages you to create and discover new combinations.

Sauce making is not a formidable task, and it will add an endless variety of tastes and pleasures to your meals. When I talk with people about making sauces, they often say that they are too intimidated to try. I think this fear stems from the legendary difficulty of classic French sauces based on mixtures of long-simmered stocks or the frightening combination of temperamental egg yolks and melted butter. Not all sauces, however, belong to the small group of French "mother" sauces, or base recipes, and not all sauces are hard to make. While it is true that some are difficult and time-consuming, most are not. Contemporary sauces include many quick and easy marinades, condiments, dressings, compotes, and dipping mixtures as well as the more challenging ones associated with French cooking. I hope you will use the ideas in my book as a starting point for exploring your own fresh ideas for combining sauces and foods.

Chapter 1

Master Recipes
with
Variations

*T*HIS CHAPTER ON MASTER RECIPES IS THE BACKBONE OF THE book; all the basics are here. Most books about sauces are organized by the type of sauce, such as mayonnaise or marinades. This book is arranged by food categories, making this chapter particularly helpful if you are looking for information about a specific sauce and its technique. In many of the recipes I refer to this chapter for a basic sauce such as reduced cream or a tomato sauce. Here you will find recipes for stocks, reduction sauces, tomato sauces, marinades, vinaigrettes and dressings, mayonnaise, compound butter, vegetable and fruit purées, yogurt or sour cream sauces, whipped cream, caramel sauce, and *crème anglaise.*

Think of these recipes as basics, but not as absolutes. There are hundreds of recipes for stock in the world and countless formulas for vinaigrette. Try these and others, then settle on a technique and finished taste that you prefer. I believe that technique is the foundation of all cooking, and that knowledge of the basics sets you free to create any dish imaginable.

STOCKS

An invaluable ingredient in sauce making, stock is a mixture of meat or fish, vegetables, herbs, and water simmered together for a long time to extract all the flavor and gelatin from the ingredients. In the French kitchen, stock is the strength and support of its cuisine and the connective ingredient of many dishes. In American cuisine, stock is used less often even though it is easy to make and store, full of flavor yet light and healthy, and can add complexity and texture to our foods.

There are two types of meat stock, white and brown. White stock is made with raw, unbrowned meats; brown is made with roasted meats and vegetables. Meat or poultry stock may take many hours to cook, but it does not require a lot of effort or care. With a little monitoring, stock can simmer at an unhurried pace while it literally makes itself. Fish stock takes only thirty minutes to cook.

The key to great stock is meat. A stock made only with bones will have plenty of gelatin, but will lack deep flavor. Use bones, preferably meaty ones, mixed with a cut of meat such as a veal breast, shank, or neck, shins or ribs of beef, a whole fowl, chicken drumsticks, or wings. The proportion of meat to bones should be at least equal; the more meat there is in stock, the richer, more textured, and more flavorful the finished sauce will be. About two pounds of meat and bones will yield about one quart of stock. Cut all meat and bones for stock into roughly four-inch pieces to have more surface area exposed to release gelatin. If the stock should jell completely when refrigerated this is a good sign and indicates that there is lots of gelatin in the stock. Gelatin is what gives stock texture and body. Without it, stock will be as thin as water.

I have found that the most versatile stock is a mixture of chicken and veal. It blends with all flavors while adding texture. I use plain chicken stock for lighter sauces, such as the Sweet and Sour Caraway Sauce served with pork tenderloin (pages 229–230), seafood dishes, and soups. Chicken stock requires a shorter cooking time so it is ideal if you are cooking something on the spur of the moment.

Keep in mind that stocks should be simmered slowly, not boiled for hours. If stock boils, it will become cloudy as the fat from the meat emulsifies in the liquid. Skimming is important for a clear broth. Impurities that rise to the surface, called "foam" or "scum," as well as the fat need to be removed. (Clarifying stock with eggshells is done for aspic or

A FRESH LOOK AT SAUCING FOODS

consomme; this is not necessary when you are using stock in sauces.) Evaporation will occur, so add more water as necessary to keep vegetables and meats covered. I prefer not to add salt to my stocks. In the final dish stock is often combined with other ingredients, some of which, such as soy sauce or anchovies, may be salty. Many sauces use stock reductions, which concentrate the natural salts in the liquid. For these reasons it is best to wait and season the sauce and the dish to be sauced shortly before serving.

Stock can be prepared in small or large quantities. I find it more useful to make a larger batch and freeze it in quart or pint containers. Using two twelve-quart stockpots (simply because I do not have a bigger stockpot), I make about six quarts of stock, which is a manageable amount to cook and store. Recipes for stock can easily be cut in half or increased. You can make stock in whatever pot you have—pasta pot, Dutch oven, stew pot, stockpot. Make sure that the pot is not too thin on the bottom, or the meats could stick and burn.

Stock can be refrigerated or frozen. Frozen stock keeps well for six months while refrigerated stock keeps for about ten days, but must be brought to a boil every three days to kill any possible bacterial growth. You can also reduce the stock to meat glaze and freeze or refrigerate that. Meat glaze keeps in the refrigerator for about two months and in the freezer for about a year. However you choose to store it, always bring stock to a full, rolling boil before using it.

 # All-Purpose Brown Chicken and Veal Stock

This stock takes several hours of cooking to release the gelatin in the veal, but very little tending. The veal and vegetables in this stock are browned. Ideally the chicken should be added to the pot, unbrowned, during the last hours of cooking because chicken takes less time to break down and release its gelatin, proteins, and flavors than veal does. Count on about three hours simmering time for the chicken and eight hours for the veal. If it is not feasible to add the chicken toward the end of the cooking process, add it at the beginning with the other meat and vegetables. The stock will be fine. Peppercorns should be added toward the end because if they are cooked for a long time they can give the stock a bitter taste. This stock really is all-purpose: Use for sauces, stews, braises, pot roasts, and meat soups.

MAKES ABOUT 6 QUARTS

6 pounds veal breast or shoulder, cut into 4-inch pieces
4 onions, peeled
2 carrots, peeled
2 leeks, trimmed, split, and washed of all grit
2 stalks celery
4 cloves garlic
2 bay leaves
8 sprigs fresh thyme or 2 teaspoons dried thyme
10 fresh parsley stems
4 whole cloves
3 pounds chicken parts (wings, carcasses, necks)
3 pounds chicken legs, cut in half, or drumsticks or thighs
1 teaspoon black peppercorns

Preheat the oven to 450 degrees F. Place the veal pieces in a roasting pan and brown for about 30 minutes, turning occasionally. Add the onions, carrots, leeks, celery, and garlic and continue roasting for another 15 minutes. Place the veal and vegetables in a pot (divide evenly if you are using two pots) and add about 1 cup water to deglaze the roasting pan. Scrape the pan to release all the drippings and browned pieces. If necessary, do this over heat to help dislodge any stubborn bits. Add to the pot. Cover the meat and vegetables with water and slowly bring just to a boil. Skim off any impurities (foam or scum) and the fat that rise to the surface as the stock comes to a boil. Add the bay leaves, thyme, parsley, and cloves and reduce the heat to a slow simmer. Cook the stock for 5 hours, stirring occasionally. To replace what is lost through evaporation, add water now and again to barely cover the meats and vegetables.

Add the chicken, slowly bring to a boil again, skim, and lower heat back to a simmer. Add the peppercorns (after skimming the stock so that you do not skim them away) and continue cooking for 3 more hours. When done, the meat will fall off the bones. If the stock is cooked too long, the bones will dissolve and calcify the broth, giving it a chalky taste.

Strain the stock through rinsed cheesecloth or a fine sieve. Refrigerate until solid. When the stock is cold, remove the layer of fat covering the surface. The stock can now be used or stored.

❦ *White Stock*

The ingredients for White Stock are the same as those used to make All-Purpose Brown Chicken and Veal Stock (pages 5–6), yet because they are not browned, this stock is less time-consuming, but has good body, texture, and taste. Rinse the chicken and veal well under running cold water. Set the chicken aside (refrigerated). Place the veal in a large pot and cover with cold water. Bring it slowly to a boil and skim off the impurities and fat that rise. Skim 2 or 3 times. Then add the remaining ingredients, except the chicken and peppercorns, and lower the heat to a simmer. Follow the recipe for All-Purpose Brown Chicken and Veal Stock (page 6), adding the chicken and peppercorns during the last hours of cooking.

Use for all sauces, stews, sautés, braises, pot roasts, or meat soups.

VARIATIONS

The following directions are all for variations on the basic, all-purpose stock given on pages 5–6. Except as noted, the ingredients, quantities, and cooking directions are the same, as is the yield.

Chicken Stock   Replace the veal with a stewing hen or fowl, omit the browning step, and cook the stock for 3 or 4 hours. Chicken has much less gelatin than veal. If you would like extra body in your chicken broth without the heavier flavor of veal, add a veal knuckle to your stockpot. Have the butcher saw the knuckle into 4 pieces.

Use plain chicken stock for light sauces, dipping sauces blended with other ingredients, soups, sautés, and pilafs.

Veal and Beef Stock   Replace the chicken with beef shin, cut in 4-inch pieces. Brown the meats and vegetables. Cook the beef and veal together for the entire 8 hours.

Use this stock for sauces, stews, braises, pot roasts, and beef or lamb soups.

Veal Stock   This stock includes a reduction step, which makes the preparation slightly different. Replace the chicken with additional veal meat and bones that are cut in 4-inch pieces. Brown the meats and vegetables, transfer them to the stockpot, deglaze the roasting pan with 1 cup of white wine, and add that mixture to the pot. The acidity of the wine helps to break down the meat and bones to release more gelatin. Cover the stockpot and place it over low heat for 20 minutes. This will draw out the meat juices, which contain gelatin. Uncover, raise the heat, and reduce the liquid to a glaze. The glazing technique produces a stock with more body and taste because the meat juices concentrate in flavor and thicken from the gelatin. The glaze will be sticky and will coat the back of a spoon. It will have the consistency of thick syrup. Watch the glaze carefully so that it doesn't burn. The time it takes for this step will vary according to the amount of stock you are making and the size of your pot. Add 1 more cup of wine and again reduce the liquid to a glaze. Add water to cover and continue cooking for 8 hours.

Use this stock for all sauces, stews, braises, and pot roasts.

 # Meat Glaze

Meat glaze is a homemade version of the bouillon cube without all the salt and preservatives. I call it black gold. Dark and reminiscent of caramel, meat glaze is made by reducing stock at a gentle boil until a thick, concentrated substance is obtained. The heat is lowered as the stock thickens so as not to burn the glaze. Generally stock is reduced by three-quarters (one quart down to one cup) to make glaze, but that ratio depends on the type of stock and the amount of gelatin it contains. Sometimes I reduce it by seven-eighths (one quart to one-half cup) for a more potent brew. When the stock has been reduced to one cup, taste it and judge for yourself. A finished glaze will have the consistency of thick syrup, be very sticky, and taste extremely strong. When refrigerated, meat glaze solidifies and turns rubbery.

Stock reduced to a glaze is easier to store and is also invaluable for strengthening the flavor of insipid sauces. Meat glaze is so powerful that a teaspoon or so will transform a sauce that needs something into a vastly improved creation. Simply add this glaze to a hot sauce and stir to melt. If you want to add meat glaze to a sauce that is not hot, such as hollandaise or mayonnaise, melt the glaze over low heat or add it to a bit of hot water, stir to melt, and then add it to the sauce.

If you want to make meat glaze for storage purposes but you plan to use it as stock, simply freeze or refrigerate the glaze until you are ready to use it and then add water to reconstitute it. Add the same amount of water that was lost to evaporation while the stock was reducing: If you reduced one quart stock to one cup glaze, add three cups of water to make stock again.

MAKES BETWEEN $^1\!/_2$ AND 1 CUP

1 quart stock

Strain the stock through rinsed cheesecloth or a fine strainer into a pan and bring it to a boil. Lower the heat so that the stock boils gently. Gradually decrease the heat as the stock thickens to avoid burning it. Reduce to 1 cup, approximately. The glaze is ready when it is very syrupy, quite sticky, and coats the back of a spoon without running off. You may need to reduce the stock to $^1\!/_2$ cup or less before the consistency is right. Transfer the glaze to a container and refrigerate until it is solid. Store the glaze in one piece or cut it into small chunks to use in sauces. Keep the chunks either refrigerated or frozen. You can also freeze glaze in ice-cube trays and, when the cubes are frozen, transfer them to a plastic bag or container to store.

Fish Fumet (Fish Stock)

Fish *fumet* is fish stock. It is made with fish heads and bones (often called frames), which are generally available at fish markets—sometimes they are happy just to give the frames away—and is quick and simple to make once the frames have been cleaned. You can ask the fishmonger to do this for you or you can do it yourself. Use a sharp knife or kitchen shears. First cut off the head and set it aside. Next, remove and discard the section containing all of the innards. Then rinse the fish head and bones well under cold water to remove the blood.

A good, all-purpose fish stock can be made with the heads and bones of sole, ocean perch, snapper, flounder, whiting, or other mild, not too oily, white fish. These fish have flavor and produce enough gelatin to make a tasty, full-bodied stock.

Fish stock will keep for only two or three days in the refrigerator and about two or three months in the freezer. If fish stock needs to be reduced for a sauce, it is best to simmer it with other ingredients, such as wine. *Fumet* alone does not make a good glaze; the taste is too fishy and chalky.

MAKES 2 TO 3 QUARTS

5 pounds fish bones and heads, cleaned
2 onions, sliced
1 carrot, sliced
1 large bouquet garni (parsley stems, bay leaf, and thyme)
2 cups dry white wine

Place the cleaned bones and heads in a large pot. Add the onions, carrot, bouquet garni, and white wine. Add enough cold water to cover the bones barely; they should not be flooded. Bring the mixture to a boil and lower the heat to a simmer. Cook the stock for 30 minutes.

Remove from the heat and strain through cheesecloth or a fine sieve. Refrigerate or freeze. Refrigerated or frozen stock should always be reboiled before it is used.

GRAVIES

A gravy is a sauce made from pan drippings or juices. Gravy makes itself while the food is cooking and needs only a few finishing touches before being served. A gravy can be made from the juices left in a roasting pan, from a sauté, stew, braise, or pot roast, or with the liquid in which food was poached. Once the food has cooked, remove it to a platter to rest.

If you are making gravy for a roast, pour off the excess fat, deglaze the roasting pan with liquid (stock, wine, citrus juices, cream), using between one and one and a half cups for four people, and reduce the liquid over medium-high heat by one half or until it is tasty. Thicken the reduction using one or two teaspoons of starch for each cup of liquid (see slurry, page 359), or using a tablespoon each of flour and unsalted butter for every cup of liquid (see *beurre manié,* page 357). Add flavorings like herbs, spices, mustard, and enrichments, like butter or cream.

If the gravy is being made from a dish that has been braised, stewed, pot roasted, poached, or sautéed, remove the food to an ovenproof platter or casserole and keep it warm. Strain the liquid into a pot. Taste the juices. If they are full of flavor and have some body, serve the gravy as it is. If they are well flavored but thin, thicken them with a slurry or *beurre manié,* using the proportions given in the preceding paragraph. If the juices taste a bit flat, reduce until they are tasty; the degree of reduction depends on the quality and quantity of the liquid. Let your palate be your guide. If you prefer to leave the gravy unthickened, at least reduce it to the texture of heavy cream. Add flavorings or enrichments.

REDUCTION SAUCES

A reduction sauce is a liquid that has been simmered down to intensify the flavor and increase the body. Reduction sauces do not need extra thickening with a starch because the cooking down, or reduction, creates the texture. The reduced liquid is garnished (with herbs, zest, vegetables, and so on) and often enriched (usually with butter) to round out the taste, thicken the sauce slightly, and smooth its texture. A reduced cream sauce already has a substantial amount of butterfat, however, and needs no further enrichment. Any more would create an overwhelmingly fatty sauce. If you want less fat in your diet, reduced sauces based on stock are fine even without the enrichment.

Straightforward reductions can be made with any stock: white or brown, chicken, veal, beef, game, or any combination. Fish *fumet* can taste chalky and "fishy" when reduced on its own, so it is best mixed with other ingredients, such as wine.

Veal stock or stock made from a combination of chicken and veal is the best stock for reduction sauces. It is not overpowering and blends well with other flavors. Because veal stock contains so much gelatin, a reduction sauce made with it is full of body. Plain chicken stock has less so it will not produce as textured a reduction. Brown and white stocks both reduce well with brown stock contributing more flavor and color to the sauce. (See pages 7–8.)

Once the stock is cooked, strained, and cleaned of the fat, it is ready for reducing. Every stock is different in texture, but in general plan to reduce by half. A light stock may need more concentration. Let the taste and texture be your guide. The sauce should taste meaty and flavorful, not watery, and it should coat the back of a spoon. When you taste it you should also notice a slightly sticky feeling. Bear in mind that the sauce will continue to reduce a bit even after you've taken the pan off the heat. If it reduces too much, add a bit of fresh stock to thin it.

A reduction sauce can be made with just about any liquid. In addition to stock, you may also use cream, wine, clam or mussel juice, fruit or citrus fruit juice, cider, and the cooking juices from poaching, braising, or stewing (see the discussion of gravies on pages 10–11). As you do with stock, reduce the liquid by half and then taste for flavor and texture. Experiment with combinations of flavors. Red wine reduced with fennel seeds and stock and finished with a bit of butter makes a good sauce for chicken breasts or lamb.

The recipes that follow are the basic reductions called for in many of the sauces in this book. Since reductions can be made ahead of time, you can incorporate them into sauces without having to take time out for reduction. That way, the food waiting to be sauced will not dry out, cool off, or overcook.

Use these recipes as a jumping-off point for creating your own sauces. For a list of recipes in which these reductions are used, see page 345.

♥ Reduced Stock

Stock can be reduced on its own or with flavorings such as herbs, mushrooms, or garlic. These are strained out after reducing and fresh flavorings may be added just before serving.

MAKES ABOUT 1 CUP

2 cups veal or veal and chicken stock (pages 8, 5–6)

Bring the stock to a boil in a pan. Lower the heat to a simmer and reduce the liquid to 1 cup. Check the texture; it should be thickened and coat a spoon lightly. The taste should be rich and flavorful with a slight feel of gelatin, but not extremely sticky or gummy. If it is too gelatinous, add a bit of fresh stock to thin it.

♥ Reduced Cream

Heavy cream makes the silkiest and simplest reduction sauce. Cream gradually becomes sweeter as it concentrates, a quality that makes it especially wonderful on desserts. Try it (reduced with cinnamon or nutmeg) over a warm apple pie instead of whipped cream. For savory dishes, the sweetness of the cream can be balanced with salt, pepper, herbs, or an acid such as lemon juice or sour cream.

Heavy cream can be reduced by between one-third and one-half. If cream is reduced by one-third, you can finish the sauce without overconcentrating the cream. Cream should be reduced to one-half if you are going to finish the sauce by adding a liquid, such as poaching liquid, liqueur, or a liquor that will thin and balance the texture.

Cream can be reduced on its own or with flavorings such as herbs, nuts, or citrus zest. These are strained out after reducing and fresh ones may be added just before serving.

1 cup heavy cream

Slowly bring the cream to a boil in a saucepan, whisking occasionally. Watch it like a hawk: heavy cream has a tendency to boil over in a split second. Lower the heat to a simmer and reduce the liquid to ²/₃ cup. The cream will be ivory colored and thickened to a coating texture. Overreduced cream is not only too thick, but it might separate, with little pools of butterfat breaking out from the cream. If this happens, whisk in some fresh heavy cream to bring back the texture. The cream is now ready to use.

❦ *Reduced Wine*

Wine, either red or white, makes another easy reduction. It can be reduced alone and then added to another reduction or combined with stock or other ingredients. (See Salmon Fillets with Saffron and Lemon, pages 172–174.) Fortified wines such as sherry do not reduce well by themselves because of their sweetness. It is best either to reduce a small amount in combination with table wine or to add them, unreduced, to the finished sauce.

Wine can be reduced on its own or with flavorings such as citrus zest, herbs, shallots, or vegetables. These are strained out after reducing and fresh ones may be added just before serving.

MAKES ³/₄ CUP

1¹/₂ cups red or white wine

Slowly bring the wine to a boil in a saucepan. Lower the heat and reduce the liquid to ³/₄ cup. It is best to simmer, rather than boil, the wine so that there is time to break down the acidity. Plan to reduce wine by half, but be sure to taste it. A lighter wine may need more reducing to concentrate the flavor; a heavier, more powerful wine may need less. In either case, the reduction should have a concentrated wine flavor, without the alcohol or acids.

▼ *Reduced Cider*

Reduced cider makes a surprisingly lovely sauce with a definite taste of apple and overtones of lemon. Try using it as a dip for apple or other fruit fritters, over pancakes or French toast, drizzling it over fruit tarts, or spooning it over a well-browned chicken breast.

Cider can be reduced on its own or with flavorings such as spices (ginger, cardamom, fennel seed, and so on) or citrus zest. These are strained out after reducing and fresh ones may be added just before serving.

MAKES 1 CUP

1 quart fresh apple cider

Place the cider in a saucepan and bring it to a boil. Lower the heat and simmer gently until the cider has reduced to 1 cup. Skim any foam that accumulates while reducing. When done, cool the reduction to room temperature and then refrigerate or freeze. Reduced cider keeps for between 2 and 3 weeks in the refrigerator or 6 months in the freezer.

Many reduction sauces given in this book are combinations of separate reductions or blends of ingredients reduced together. An example is the *Ravigote* Cream Sauce for mushrooms (pages 100–102), in which wine, vinegar, shallots, and herbs are reduced, cream is added, and then the whole mixture is reduced again. These sauces can be prepared quickly and go well with many foods. Wine, fortified wine, fish *fumet,* shellfish juices, cream, stock, citrus or other fruit juice, cider, vegetable juices, or mushroom juices are all possibilities. Let your imagination take over, but pair flavors that have a natural affinity with the food being sauced.

Pan Reductions

Pan reductions are sauces that are made right in the pan in which poultry, meat, or fish was cooked. They are quick, light, and easy to prepare as well as being delicious. Their savoriness comes from the bits of cooked food left behind in the pan after the fat has been poured off. Those bits are little explosions of concentrated flavor that, when mixed with a liquid, form the basis of a fine sauce. The technique is simple: Pan-fry or pan-roast a piece of poultry, meat, or seafood, spoon off the fat, deglaze the pan with liquid (stock, wine, cream, juices) or a prepared reduction (this makes it even faster and the food waiting to be sauced has less time to cool off), and reduce until the mixture is very flavorful. The sauce may be strained or not depending on how refined you want it to be. Enrich if desired, garnish, season, and serve. (See Pork Chops with a Caper and Tomato Sauce, pages 219–220, for an example of this technique.)

Essence

An essence is an elegant reduction sauce brought to another level of taste, texture, and intensity. The finished sauce is richer than one made with plain reduced stock, has considerable body, and a deep color with lots of sheen.

To make an essence, stock is reduced with browned meat. (In an essence for duck, for example, meaty duck bones and wings are chopped and used.) The technique for a successful essence is that the stock is reduced in installments, ladleful by ladleful. Each installment is reduced to a glaze before adding the next, and the final ladleful is reduced to about the consistency of heavy cream. The result is a glistening, complex-tasting, mirrorlike sauce. To enrich an essence, butter is whisked in at the finish in varying quantities. The amount depends on one's own taste as an essence is delicious with or without butter. An essence can also be enriched with plain or reduced heavy cream instead of butter. Plain cream will thin the sauce a bit so it may need further reduction.

Essences begin to appear in French cookbooks about the late seventeenth and early eighteenth century and continue to be seen in print until the early twentieth century. Although those early essences were thickened, the one given here is not.

I learned the following essence technique from Madeleine Kamman. The master recipe given here is particularly suited for meats, poultry, and game. For a list of other recipes incorporating an essence see page 347.

MAKES 1 TO 1¼ CUPS

2 teaspoons oil
½ pound meat or poultry, cut in 1-inch pieces
1 quart veal or veal and chicken stock (pages 8, 5–6)
4 tablespoons (or more to taste) unsalted butter or heavy cream
(plain or reduced) (optional)

Heat the oil in a skillet over high heat. Add the meat and brown it well on all sides. It is important not to crowd the pan or the meat will steam, not brown and caramelize. Do this step in two batches if you have a small pan and combine the batches before adding the stock.

Pour off the excess fat and add ½ cup of the stock. Deglaze the pan and bring the liquid to a boil. Gently boil or simmer the stock to reduce it to a glaze. Repeat another 6 times using ½ cup of stock each time and reducing it to a glaze before adding the next. Add the final ½ cup stock and reduce the liquid until the sauce coats the back of a spoon and has the texture of heavy cream. Strain the essence into a clean saucepan, bring to a boil, and whisk in the butter 1 tablespoon at a time. If using heavy cream, slowly pour in a steady stream, whisking to incorporate.

▼ *Beurre Blanc (White Butter Sauce)*

From the Loire in France comes *beurre blanc*, or white butter sauce, a velvety, creamy, ethereal sauce that has no peer. It is a reduction of shallots and an acid liquid—such as wine or vinegar—with butter whisked in. To obtain the proper texture, you should not melt the butter completely as you want to avoid separating the butter into liquid butterfat and milk solids. It should remain creamy, with enough consistency to coat a spoon. This consistency is key: it gives the sauce its seductive texture and surprising thickness.

To make variations of a basic *beurre blanc,* try using different liquids, such as fish *fumet,* juices from steamed shellfish, or fruit juices. Red wine and red wine vinegar will make a *beurre rouge.* The following master recipe is for a classic *beurre blanc.* (For a list of different sauces made by this method, see page 351.) Use it to make up your own sauces and garnish as you like. Serve a *beurre blanc* on fish or shellfish, poultry, or vegetables, particularly leafy greens and green vegetables.

MAKES ABOUT 1 CUP

2 large shallots, chopped
1/2 cup dry white wine
1/2 cup white wine vinegar
1 cup unsalted butter, softened
Salt
Freshly ground black pepper to taste

Combine the shallots, wine, and vinegar and bring to a boil. Lower the heat, simmer, and reduce the liquid to 2 tablespoons. Remove the reduction from the heat and allow it to cool a few minutes. Turn the burner to its lowest setting. With the pan still off the heat, whisk in the butter, 2 tablespoons at a time. If the mixture gets cold, put the pan back on the heat and continue adding butter. The sauce should remain warm, but not hot. Strain, season, and serve plain or with a garnish.

TOMATO SAUCES

Given the bounty of recipes for tomato sauce, who needs another? There is, however, more than one way to skin a tomato and even more ways to prepare a sauce. Here I have given you two basic recipes, one using fresh tomatoes, one using canned, and variations on both. I have not included uncooked tomato sauce such as salsa (see Cherry Tomato

Salsa, pages 176–177) in this section. Tomato sauces freeze very well. I like to make a big batch, divide it into containers, and then freeze it.

▼ Fresh Tomato Sauce

This is a particularly light, fresh-tasting sauce with lots of the natural sweetness that is lost in canned tomatoes. Use it as a sauce or add it to other sauces, such as vinaigrette, essence, and mayonnaise.

MAKES ABOUT 2 CUPS

2 pounds fresh, very ripe Italian plum tomatoes
Salt
Freshly ground black pepper

Cut the tomatoes in quarters and slice off the cores. Place in a nonaluminum pan with a heavy bottom. Simmer over medium to medium-low heat for about 1 hour, stirring and crushing the tomatoes occasionally. Purée in a blender, a food processor, or a food mill, and strain. Season with salt to taste and pepper, if desired, and store or use right away.

——— VARIATIONS ———

Vegetable Add 1 chopped onion, 1 chopped celery stalk, 1 chopped carrot, and 2 minced garlic cloves to the tomatoes and simmer together. Purée and finish as above.

Sautéed Vegetable Sauté the vegetables in olive oil rather than simmer them with the tomatoes. Sauté until they are just translucent, not browned, add the tomatoes, and continue with the recipe. This makes a heavier, less delicate sauce, but it has a more complex flavor.

Herb, Hot Pepper, or Anchovy Add about ¼ to ½ cup chopped fresh herbs (basil, rosemary, oregano, dill, or mint), cayenne pepper or hot pepper flakes (during the last 5 minutes), or minced anchovies or anchovy paste and garlic. You can add all together or each on its own.

Butter   Between 2 and 4 tablespoons unsalted butter may be added at the end of cooking for extra richness. The same quantity of olive oil may be used instead.

Citrus   Add ¼ to ½ cup citrus juice and 2 to 4 teaspoons grated zest and cook for a few minutes. The result is a good dipping sauce for grilled lamb, chicken, and shrimp.

Avocado and Lime   Add ¼ to ½ cup lime juice and 2 to 4 teaspoons grated lime zest and use for tortilla chips. Add a ripe avocado, mashed, to the finished sauce and use for tortilla chips, grilled beef kebabs, or chicken cut in pieces.

Fennel   Fennel seeds can be cooked in the sauce and grated orange rind added after the mixture has been puréed and strained. Beef steaks, veal chops, seafood, and poultry will be enhanced by this version.

Feta   See the variation suggested on page 21 for Winter Tomato Sauce and feta cheese.

Winter Tomato Sauce

Make this version when fresh plum tomatoes are not available.

M A K E S   4   T O   6   C U P S

2 tablespoons olive oil
1 onion, chopped
1 celery stalk, chopped
1 carrot, chopped
2 garlic cloves, minced
1 teaspoon salt
1 can (28 ounces) Italian plum tomatoes
1 can (28 ounces) Italian tomato purée
Freshly ground black pepper

Heat the oil in a large, heavy-bottomed pot over medium heat. Add the vegetables and salt and sauté until they take on some color, about

10 minutes. The sweetness from browning the vegetables will help balance the acidity of the tomatoes. Crush the tomatoes (I find it easiest to gently squeeze the tomatoes over the pot with my hand) and add, together with the juice from the can. Add the tomato purée. Bring the mixture to a boil, lower the heat, and simmer for about 1 hour, occasionally stirring and crushing the tomatoes further with the back of a wooden spoon or potato masher. Season with pepper and more salt if desired. Serve chunky or purée if you like a smooth sauce. Store or use right away.

VARIATIONS

Hot Pepper Add cayenne pepper or hot red pepper flakes to the sauce during the last few minutes of cooking.

Herb Chopped fresh herbs such as basil, Italian (flat-leaf) parsley, mint, rosemary, marjoram, dill, or sage are nice. The choice will depend on what you like and what you are using the sauce with. If the sauce is to be frozen, add herbs after the sauce has thawed and been reheated. This version is delicious with grilled sausage, egg pasta, macaroni, polenta, and gnocchi.

Sautéed Vegetable, Wine, and Stock After sautéing the vegetables, add 1 cup dry red wine and reduce the liquid to about ¼ cup. Then add about 1 cup chicken stock and reduce again, roughly by half. Add the tomatoes and tomato purée and continue with recipe. This is a full-bodied sauce that is good on all pasta, gnocchi, polenta, rice, meats, and poultry. For seafood, use white wine and clam juice or fish *fumet* instead of the chicken stock.

Meat Add ground pork, veal, meatballs, sausages, chicken wings, or pieces of pork or beef such as ribs (short ribs for beef). Brown the meat with the vegetables and continue with the recipe.

Feta Tomato sauce mixed with finely crumbled feta cheese and chopped fresh dill (or oregano and garlic) is delicious with grilled shrimp.

Bacon or Pancetta Cook bacon or *pancetta* (Italian unsmoked bacon), crumble it finely, and add it to the cooked tomato sauce together with chopped fresh parsley and scissored fresh chives. This is particularly good with cooked scallops or bluefish.

Olive and Garlic Add garlic, minced olives, and chopped fresh basil or parsley and serve with grilled turkey or lamb kebabs.

Barbecue Winter Tomato Sauce is the basis for the barbecue sauce given on pages 195–196 in which both ground and candied ginger are used. For an all-purpose barbecue sauce, follow that recipe but omit the candied ginger; use on ribs, chicken, chops, steak, and shanks.

Also, see the variations on Fresh Tomato Sauce for additions of avocado and lime and of fennel (page 20); both versions are suitable for winter tomato sauce.

MARINADES

An ancient means of preserving food, marinating also enhances the flavor of fruit, vegetables, seafood, meat, and poultry. There are liquid marinades (cooked and uncooked), dry marinades, pastes, purées, and dairy marinades with buttermilk or yogurt. As the flavors of the marinade are absorbed by the foods, the acids in it help soften the outer layer of the meat, poultry, or fish. Meat and unboned poultry can marinate the longest; fish, boneless poultry, vegetables, and fruit are delicate in texture and a long marination would soften the fibers excessively. I like to marinate meat for forty-eight hours, whole or cut-up poultry for between twenty-four and forty-eight hours, boneless chicken or turkey breast for between two and eight hours, fish for between two and four hours, vegetables for twenty-four hours, and fruits for a few hours.

Liquid marinades usually include three elements: acid, oil, and flavorings. The acid tenderizes just the exposed surface of the food, the oil prevents drying, and the aromatics give the finished dish its distinct character. The acids may be citrus juices, fruit juices, wine, vinegar, yogurt, or buttermilk. Oils can range from avocado to walnut; use any type you like. If you are interested in reducing the fat in your diet, try using smaller quantities of stronger oils such as sesame, walnut, hazelnut, and very fruity olive oils. Some marinades have no oil. The flavorings in a marinade can be fresh or dried herbs, whole or ground spices, or raw or cooked vegetables. It is not necessary to marinate food in a large quantity of liquid. Small batches, about 1 to 1½ cups are quite sufficient if the food is tossed often.

Dry marinades are spice and herb mixtures rubbed into the surface of a piece of meat, poultry, or seafood. The mixes penetrate and flavor the food, but they do not tenderize it. The simplest example of a dry marinade is the classic Steak *au Poivre* (page 284).

Pastes are thick mixtures of wet and dry ingredients that have been ground together. Spread on food, they can be left for between twelve and twenty-four hours, depending on what ingredients are used. If the marinade has an abundance of hot spices, marinate for less time. *Pesto* and *Tapenade* (pages 44–45) make good paste marinades for chicken, shellfish, or lamb.

A barbecue sauce with a tomato base may be used as a purée marinade (see Chicken on the Grill with Ginger Barbecue Sauce, pages 195–196) as may other vegetable or fruit purées. Try a spicy plum purée for duck, chicken, turkey, or shrimp.

Dairy marinades are made with yogurt, buttermilk, or soured milk. In Indian cuisine yogurt mixtures flavored with spices, chilies, and ginger are used for the classic *tandoori* dishes. Buttermilk with seasonings makes a good marinade for lamb, poultry, or vegetables.

You can marinate food in glass, enameled cast iron, ceramic, or stainless steel dishes, but you should avoid using aluminum. (Some cooks use self-sealing plastic bags.) Keep meat refrigerated while it is marinating, but take it out of the refrigerator about an hour before cooking to bring it to room temperature. Keep poultry and seafood refrigerated until ready to cook. Before cooking, drain and dry the food or wipe off excess paste or purée marinade.

When marinading poultry, pork, or seafood, remember that their raw juices are not safe for consumption. If you want to baste while cooking or serve the marinade as a sauce (or part of a sauce) at the table, then be sure to make an additional amount that will not come in contact with the uncooked food. In the case of liquid marinade, it is not necessary to make extra, but be sure to boil and strain it before using it to baste or to serve with the cooked food. Otherwise, discard used marinade at cooking time. Marinades that have been used with meats are fine for basting or for use in a sauce if boiled and strained first. Marinades that have been used with vegetables or fruits are fine to use for basting or with the finished dish without boiling.

For other ideas for marinades see the sections on Vinaigrettes and Dressings (pages 28–32), Flavored Oils, Vinegars, and Mustards (pages 32–39), Tomato Sauces (pages 18–22), Yogurt and Sour Cream Sauces (pages 49–50), and Herb, Vegetable, and Fruit Purées (pages

43–49). For lists of marinades and sauces that can be used as marinades, see pages 348–349 and the chapter on salads.

▼ Liquid Marinade

The recipe below is for a basic, generic liquid marinade. The main ingredient may be wine, fruit juice or citrus fruit juice, a vinaigrette, soy sauce, sherry, milk, buttermilk, yogurt, or oil, all of which may be used alone or in combinations of varying proportions. The flavorings are usually chopped aromatic vegetables such as onions, shallots, garlic, carrots, or celery, and condiments like mustard. The quantities given here make enough marinade for about two pounds of meat, poultry, seafood, vegetables, or fruit.

MAKES 1 1/2 TO 2 CUPS

1 cup liquid of choice
1/4 to 1/2 cup flavorings of choice
1 tablespoon ground spices (optional)
1/4 to 1/2 cup chopped fresh herbs (optional)

Mix the liquid and flavorings in a bowl. Add the spices and herbs and mix again. Pour the mixture over the food to be marinated and turn the food so that it is coated completely. Refrigerate, tossing the food often, until about 1 hour before cooking for meats or until ready to cook for seafood and poultry.

VARIATION

Teriyaki Used for poultry, pork, beef, seafood, and mushrooms that are to be grilled, *Teriyaki* marinade consists of equal parts *mirin* or sherry, soy sauce, and *sake* with a bit of sugar. Freshly grated ginger, minced garlic, or sliced scallions may be added.

▼ Dry Marinade

The quantities given make enough for two pounds meat, seafood, or poultry.

2 tablespoons spices, grated citrus zest,
   or chopped fresh herbs, mixed

Mix all the ingredients together in a bowl, rub the mixture over the entire surface of the food to be marinated. Set aside (refrigerated if seafood or poultry, room temperature for meat) for between 30 minutes and 1 hour.

VARIATIONS

Lemon and Pepper   Blend equal parts of grated lemon zest and coarsely ground black and white pepper. Rub the mixture into boneless chicken breast, pork cutlets, veal chops, or thick slices of turkey breast. Marinate for 30 minutes and then cook.

Mixed Spice   Two of my favorite spice mixtures make excellent rubs for meats, poultry, and seafood. One is *quatre épices* (four spices) from France, the other is *ras-el-hanout* from Morocco. There are countless recipes for these blends, so there is much room for interpretation. The *quatre épices* can be made up of any of the following: ground coriander, cinnamon, nutmeg, cloves, ginger, mace, mixed pepper (black, white, and cayenne), crumbled bay leaf, thyme, sage, basil, marjoram, or rosemary. For a simple version of *ras-el-hanout*, see the recipe for Moroccan Lamb Chops (pages 246–248).

Purée and Paste Marinades

One cup of paste or purée is enough to marinate about two pounds of meat, seafood, or poultry.

❦ *Tomato Marinade*

MAKES 1 CUP

¾ cup Fresh Tomato Sauce (page 19)
6 anchovy fillets packed in olive oil
¼ cup pitted black Greek or Italian olives
2 tablespoons chopped fresh herb or mixture of herbs

Purée all the ingredients together in a blender, spread the mixture on boneless chicken breasts, thick slices of turkey breast, shellfish, pork, beef, or veal. Refrigerate, tossing food often, for between 6 and 24 hours.

❦ *Vegetable and Yogurt Paste*

MAKES ½ TO ¾ CUP

1 tablespoon oil
1 onion, sliced
4 cloves garlic, minced
1 tablespoon fresh thyme leaves or 1 teaspoon dried thyme
1 bay leaf, crumbled
1 teaspoon ground coriander
1 teaspoon ground cumin
1 teaspoon paprika
¼ to ½ teaspoon cayenne pepper
¼ teaspoon freshly ground black pepper
¼ cup plain yogurt

Heat the oil in a skillet over medium heat, add the onion and garlic, and sauté for 3 or 4 minutes. Add the herbs and spices and cook for 1 minute. Remove the mixture from the heat, mix in the yogurt, and purée in a blender. Spread the paste on poultry, pork, lamb, or seafood and refrigerate for between 6 and 12 hours.

Yogurt   Mix yogurt and lots of chopped fresh mint or other herbs to make a marinade for boneless chicken breast. Refrigerate for between 6 and 12 hours.

Pesto or Tapenade   Use 1 cup of *Pesto* (pages 44–45) or *Tapenade* (page 44) on chicken, thick slices of turkey breast, lamb, pork, or seafood; refrigerate for between 4 and 12 hours.

Marinades for Fruit

Marinades for fruit (marinated fruit is properly called macerated fruit) are somewhat different from other marinades in that the fruit is first cooked, then marinated. Some fruit—such as berries—is marinated uncooked. Marinades are usually served with the fruit, and often the marinade is first reduced separately, then poured over the fruit. Essentially sugar syrups, fruit marinades may be made of fruit juices (such as raspberry, strawberry, or citrus), cider, dry or sweet wine, fortified wine such as port, or vermouth. The liquid is cooked with sugar, honey, or maple syrup. Spirits or liqueurs can replace up to one quarter of a cup of the liquid in a marinade. They can be flavored with sweet herbs or spices, such as mint and cinnamon, citrus zest, vanilla, and even crushed coffee beans. Apart from being used to macerate fruit, the syrups may be served over pancakes, waffles, or French toast, to embellish simple desserts such as pound cake, ice cream, sherbet, or unfrosted cakes, for soaking *savarins* and *babas*, or to flavor sparkling water.

 ## *Basic Fruit Marinade*

M A K E S   1   T O   1 ½   C U P S

1 cup liquid of choice
¼ to ½ cup sweetener of choice
1 tablespoon flavorings of choice

Combine the liquid and sweetener in a heavy pot. Bring the mixture to a boil over medium heat and add the flavorings. Simmer together for 5 minutes, add the fruit, and simmer until the fruit is tender. Remove the fruit to a flat dish and cool the syrup. Pour the syrup over the fruit and then chill the two together to marinate.

Alternately, simmer the syrup alone for about 10 minutes and pour it hot over uncooked fruit; marinate in the refrigerator.

VARIATIONS

Red Wine and Spice for Dried Fruit Bring a mixture of hefty red wine such as a Côtes-du-Rhone, sugar, vanilla, lemon zest, ginger, and ground coriander to a boil. Pour the mixture hot over prunes or other dried fruit or a mixture of dried fruits such as prunes and apricots or peaches and pears. Cover and steep for between 24 and 48 hours. Serve chilled with the syrup. You can also add a tablespoon or two of cognac or other brandy before serving.

Citrus, Banana, and White Chocolate Make a sugar syrup of orange juice, lemon juice, and sugar with strips of zest and bring it to a boil. Add Grand Marnier liqueur and pour the mixture over slices of ripe banana and peeled, sliced oranges. Marinate until cool. Top with toasted coconut and grated white chocolate and serve.

Fruit in Uncooked Wine Steep peeled peaches or nectarines, or unpeeled apricots or plums in Riesling, Muscat, Beaujolais, or Gewürztraminer. Sprinkle the fruit with a bit of sugar before dousing it with wine and add a vanilla bean if desired. Marinate for between 4 and 12 hours.

Cherries in Port Macerate pitted cherries in ruby port and maraschino liqueur with orange zest for 2 hours.

Blueberries in Rum Macerate blueberries in golden rum flavored with lime zest for 2 hours and serve topped with toasted coconut.

VINAIGRETTES and DRESSINGS

Vinaigrettes and dressings are uncooked sauces that are a mixture of an acid liquid, oil, and a flavoring. Vinaigrette is a type of salad dressing made with vinegar and oil; other mixtures used for the same purpose fall into the loose category of dressings. These sauces are wide open to interpretation and are among the few that need not be made according to fairly rigid formulas. Vinaigrettes and other dressings are quick and easy to prepare, can be served on hot or cold foods, are healthy, useful in all seasons, and keep for about two weeks when covered and refrigerated.

The standard ratio for a vinaigrette or dressing is three parts of oil to one part of acid. I like a tart sauce, especially with rich foods such as salmon, so most of the time I use a ratio of two to one, but you should always taste and increase the oil as needed. Vinegar tends to be stronger than citrus juices, so you may want to add more oil when using it. For those concerned with fats, the two to one ratio decreases the amount of oil needed. Basically, let your palate be your guide and make this sauce as assertive or mild as you want.

Since there are few ingredients in a dressing, they must all be of good quality. The oils I recommend include virgin or extra virgin olive oil, safflower, walnut, hazelnut, almond, dark sesame, grapeseed, avocado, and flavored oil (pages 33–36). Store oils in a cool, dark cupboard or in the refrigerator. Since nut oils are fragile and become rancid quickly in hot weather, they must be refrigerated. For vinegars I use balsamic, sherry, red or white wine, Japanese rice (which is low in acidity), champagne, cider, malt, and fruit- or herb-flavored vinegars (pages 37–38). For mustard in a vinaigrette or dressing, I prefer a Dijon-style or a grainy type, but there are many others available: spicy or sweet German mustard, mustard made with honey or other sweetener, hot Chinese, and dry English mustards. Flavored mustard is made with Dijon-style mustard mixed with herbs, spices, fruit, or honey. For a recipe, see page 39.

To make dressings with lots of flavor, reductions of vinegar, wine, fortified wine, stock, fish *fumet*, or citrus juices may be used as a base to which an acid or oils are added. Stock reduced to a glaze will add taste, creaminess, and richness to dressings (see Braised Leeks in a Tarragon Coat, pages 116–117). Reduce the liquid and let it cool. Add flavorings such as mustard and whisk in the oil. Add garnishes such as herbs, chopped vegetables, or diced fruit. Fruit and vegetable purées, either cooked or uncooked, may also be used for dressings (see Asparagus with Scallion Vinaigrette, pages 60–61, and Melon and Prosciutto with Strawberry Dressing, pages 65–67).

Make a dressing or vinaigrette about one hour before using and leave it at room temperature to allow the flavors to blend and develop. Because these sauces change dramatically in an hour or so, leave the final seasoning until just before serving. When seasoning, bear in mind that the taste of a dressing on a dish is very different from its taste in a spoon. If the dressing is for a salad, taste it with a leaf of something and then make changes. If it is for a piece of meat, seafood, or poultry, remember that the sharpness from acidity or the strong flavors of herbs, mustard, or garlic will calm down when the dressing is eaten on the food.

You can make vinaigrettes and dressings in a blender or with a whisk. The blender makes a creamier dressing and it stays emulsified longer. A dressing made by hand may separate on the plate, which can look very appealing. Add chopped ingredients, such as nuts, shallots, or herbs, to a blender dressing after blending so that they retain their shape and texture. If you want to purée the herbs for color or if you want to purée cooked garlic or shallots, add those ingredients to the vinaigrette or dressing before blending it.

Dressings and vinaigrettes are typically used with greens or tossed salads, but they also make wonderful sauces for composed salads (salads arranged on a plate) or hot main-course dishes of meat, seafood, poultry, or grilled foods. They can be served on fruit salads or on fruit mixed with meat, particularly smoked meat. Try them on grilled or roasted vegetables or slices of cold, cooked meat, poultry, or seafood. Gently toss them with a dressing and allow the mixture to steep in the refrigerator overnight. Vinaigrettes and dressings also make excellent marinades for uncooked foods. For a list of recipes using vinaigrettes and dressings, see pages 349–350.

▼ *Basic Vinaigrette*

In France, this dressing is made right in the salad bowl: Some of the oil is added to the greens first to coat the leaves, then the vinegar, salt, pepper, and remaining oil are mixed in as needed.

2 tablespoons vinegar
¹/₄ teaspoon salt
Freshly ground black pepper
4 to 6 tablespoons olive oil or other oil

Place the vinegar, salt, and pepper in a bowl. Whisk and let the salt dissolve. Whisk in the oil in a steady stream until all of it is incorporated. If the vinegar is particularly sharp, add a bit of water. The yield depends on the amount of oil that is added.

VARIATIONS

Vinaigrette and dressing may be flavored with a variety of ingredients:
Minced shallots with or without chopped fresh herbs, such as chervil, tarragon, basil, or parsley—added to a vinaigrette made with balsamic vinegar and olive oil—for smoked trout or other fish, poultry, beef, lamb, vegetables, salads, or shellfish
Sliced, cooked shallots (caramelized)—with balsamic vinegar, chopped fresh herbs, and olive oil—for meats, poultry, *foie gras*, calves' liver, and potatoes
Capers, olives, minced anchovies, and celery—for fish
Garlic
Ginger, dark sesame oil, and scallion
Mustard, especially when made with sherry vinegar
Plum tomato puréed in the blender either alone or with fresh herbs, garlic, scallions, capers, or anchovies
Chunky tomato with lemon juice, zest, and chopped fresh basil
Roasted peppers, hot and sweet, with lemon, lime, or orange juice
Black olive—for poultry, pork, shellfish, and oranges (see pages 78–80)
Diced red onion, julienne of lemon or lime zest, chopped fresh parsley—for poultry, seafood, or smoked trout
Cooked berries (see the recipe for Melon and Prosciutto with Strawberry Dressing on pages 65–67)
Cooked prunes, apricots, or other dried fruit, puréed and mixed with herbs or spices

Toasted nuts (see page 54)—lemon and walnut dressing for spinach or bitter greens; orange and hazelnut dressing for trout, chicken, turkey, wild rice, or slices of citrus

Ground coriander, diced red onion, garlic, and chopped fresh mint—for lobster, lamb, chicken, pasta such as *orzo*, or grains such as cracked wheat

Gorgonzola cheese and diced red onion—for steak

Mango and scallion puréed into a citrus vinaigrette—for chicken breast

FLAVORED OILS, VINEGARS, and MUSTARDS

The following recipes are for flavored ingredients to enhance your vinaigrettes and dressings. They are only suggestions; try them and then make up your own combinations. For example, try mixing herbs, garlic, and spices (such as basil, garlic, and cayenne pepper); combining oriental flavors (such as dark sesame and peanut oil, ginger, garlic, and scallions); or try spices and citrus fruit (such as orange, clove, and cinnamon). The inspiration for the following flavored oils comes from Jean-Georges Vongerichten's book *Simple Cuisine* (Englewood Cliffs, NJ: Prentice Hall Press, 1990).

When you make flavored oil it is imperative that the oil be refrigerated at all times after preparation. These oils should be used within forty-eight hours, preferably sooner. Clostridum botulinum—the bacterium that causes botulism—has been found in garlic oil, and because it thrives in anaerobic environments such as oil, it could grow in oil flavored with herbs, members of the onion family, or other plant-based ingredients. To be safe, before adding garlic, shallots, onions, scallions, or leeks to the oil, you should peel and then mince them, removing all roots. Herbs should be stemmed, carefully washed, blanched for fifteen seconds, refreshed under cold water, and then dried. Purée the herbs with the oil or chop them and add them to the oil to steep. When kept in the refrigerator, olive oil will partially solidify. Let it sit at room temperature for a bit and it will return to its liquid state.

Vinegar and mustard are high-acid foods; they can be stored much longer than oils. Vinegar may even be kept in a cool cupboard. The vinegars, together with the flavorings, should marinate at room temperature in a cool, dark place for the designated time. After the marination period they should be stored in the refrigerator. Mustards should also be kept refrigerated. Glass jars with lids or wine bottles with corks are good containers to use for storage. Always use very fresh ingredients. Making oil, vinegar, or mustard is a good way to use up herbs from your garden before winter sets in.

Flavored Oils

 *Hot Pepper Oil*

For this oil use the hot, long, red peppers that are available at Italian markets. Use the oil in vinaigrettes or dressings, or for sautéing and splashing on foods. Peeled, minced garlic cloves (all roots removed) may be added.

MAKES 1 CUP

6 dried hot peppers
1 cup olive oil

Crush the dried peppers and place them in a jar; cover the peppers with oil. Cover the jar and marinate the peppers in the refrigerator for at least 2 hours before using. Shake, taste, and let sit longer if the oil is not spicy enough. Keep refrigerated and use within 48 hours.

Herb Oil

Use a single herb or a combination of herbs, such as rosemary and thyme or bay leaves and savory. A mixture of parsley, thyme, and bay leaves will give you bouquet garni oil. Carefully remove all roots and stems from the herbs before measuring. Garlic—peeled, roots removed, and minced—may be added to any herb oil.

1 cup olive oil
½ cup herbs, all stems and roots removed

Carefully wash the herbs and dry them thoroughly. Bring a pot of water to a boil. Add the herbs and blanch, stirring for 15 seconds. Drain, refresh under cold water, and dry the herbs. Chop the herbs, place them in a jar, and pour oil over the top, making sure that all the herbs are submerged. Cover the jar and let the mixture sit, refrigerated, for no longer than 48 hours. Shake, strain, and use.

❦ Garlic or Shallot Oil

It is important that the roots and peel of the garlic or shallots be removed before making this oil. Add your favorite herbs to this oil if desired, making sure to blanch them first for fifteen seconds; then refresh them under cold water.

MAKES ABOUT 1 CUP

½ cup whole garlic cloves or shallots, peel and roots removed, minced
1 cup olive oil

Place the shallots or garlic in a jar and pour oil over them. Cover the jar and let the mixture sit, refrigerated, for no longer than 48 hours. Shake, strain, and use.

❦ Black Peppercorn and Lemon Oil

Orange, tangerine, grapefruit, or lime zest may be used instead of lemon. This oil is used in the recipe Skewers of Swordfish with Lemon and Herb Dressing, pages 165–166.

Grated zest of 1 lemon
1 tablespoon freshly ground black peppercorns
1 cup olive oil

Place the zest and pepper in a jar and pour oil over them. Cover the jar and let the mixture sit, refrigerated, for 1 day before using it. Keep it refrigerated and use it within 24 hours. Shake, strain, and use.

 # Emerald Oil

Use this oil for making mayonnaise as well as vinaigrettes and dressings. Use it also to make *pesto,* to sauté vegetables, or to toss with pasta. Use basil, mint, parsley, fennel greens, coriander, chives, dill, or tarragon. The stronger pungent herbs—rosemary, thyme, oregano, marjoram, or savory—are best for Herb Oil (see pages 33–34). Carefully remove all roots and stems from the herbs before measuring. For a recipe using flavored oil, see Parsnips with Orange-Basil Dressing, pages 105–106.

MAKES 1 CUP

½ cup tightly packed leaves (no stems) of a sweet herb
1 cup olive oil

Carefully wash the herbs and dry them thoroughly. Bring a pot of water to a boil. Add herbs and blanch, stirring for 15 seconds. Drain, refresh under cold water, and dry the herbs. Place them in the blender with the oil. Purée the mixture. Place the mixture in a jar, cover, and refrigerate for 1 day before using. Strain the mixture through cheesecloth, return the oil to the jar, and store it in the refrigerator for no more than 1 day. Use the strained herbs right away for *pesto,* in a compound butter, mixed with yogurt, to sauté cherry tomatoes, to toss with cooked vegetables, or added to soups or stews. Peeled and minced garlic cloves (roots removed) may be added.

Fresh Ginger Oil

MAKES 1 CUP

⅓ cup chopped fresh ginger (about a ¼ pound piece)
1 cup peanut, safflower, or olive oil

Place the ginger and ¼ cup of the oil in a blender. Blend until the mixture is grainy, almost a purée. Add the remaining oil and blend briefly to mix. Pour the mixture into a jar, cover, and refrigerate for 1 day before using. Strain the oil as necessary. Keep it refrigerated and use within 12 hours.

Fennel Oil

This is a most delicious oil on seafood, tomatoes, red peppers, or a citrus salad. It is used in the recipe for Fennel and Green Bean Salad, pages 85–86. This oil can also be made with other whole spices such as allspice, cloves, cinnamon sticks, coriander, cracked nutmeg, or anise seeds.

MAKES 1 CUP

½ cup fennel seeds
1 cup olive oil

Crush the fennel seeds with a mortar in a pestle or use a blender. Add the olive oil and blend to mix. Pour the mixture into a jar, cover the jar, and let it sit for 2 days, refrigerated, before using. Strain the oil, discard the seeds, and use the oil right away.

Homemade Vinegar

I make my own vinegar with leftover wine or from fresh cider in the fall. These liquids will turn to vinegar by themselves if left alone, but that takes months. Once a vinegar "mother" (a gelatinous disc of fungus that floats on the top or sinks to the bottom) has grown, however, you can make vinegar much more quickly.

Simply place wine or cider (without preservatives) in a crock or dark bottle. Cover the container with several layers of cheesecloth or foil in which you have poked a few holes. This allows air to circulate while preventing any bugs from flying in. Store the crock or bottle in a cool, dark place for four to six months. Check periodically for the mother and taste for acidity. If the vinegar is weak, let it sit longer, checking it every two weeks or so. When it's ready, strain off the vinegar and transfer it to a clean bottle. In the crock, add fresh cider or wine to your mother and start another batch of vinegar. Do not mix cider and wine in one crock; keep two separate batches going. If you are not ready to start another batch right away, leave some vinegar in the crock or bottle so that the mother remains submerged. It might keep growing, so check it from time to time and keep it covered with liquid.

Whether you make your own vinegar or not, try making your own flavored vinegars (see below); it is fun to experiment, and your own vinegar will be less expensive than store-bought vinegars.

Flavored Vinegars

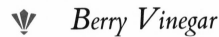 ## *Berry Vinegar*

Mix crushed ripe red raspberries, blueberries, or strawberries with an equal amount of red wine vinegar. Let the mixture sit in a cool, dark place for 4 weeks, strain, add a few fresh whole berries, and use.

Fruit Vinegar

Mix very ripe, peeled and diced pears, peaches, plums, or nectarines with an equal amount of white wine vinegar. Crush the fruit slightly with a fork. Let the mixture sit in a cool, dark place for 4 weeks. Strain when it is ready and use.

Herb Vinegar

Having removed the roots and large stems, pack sprigs of fresh herbs tightly into a 1-cup measure. Place the herbs in a bottle or jar, add 2 cups vinegar (red or white wine, champagne, or cider) and let the mixture stand in a cool, dark place for 4 weeks before using.

Shallot Vinegar

Peel and chop about 8 large shallots. Heat 2 cups vinegar (red or white wine or cider) to just below the boil and pour the vinegar over the shallots. Let cool, cover, and allow the mixture to sit in a cool, dark place for 4 weeks. Taste and strain the vinegar when it is ready.

Garlic Vinegar

Peel and crush about 25 garlic cloves (enough to make $\frac{1}{2}$ cup). Heat 2 cups vinegar (red or white wine or cider) to just below the boil. Pour the vinegar over the crushed garlic cloves. Let cool, cover, and allow the mixture to sit in a cool, dark place for 4 weeks. Taste and strain when the vinegar is ready.

Combination Vinegars

This is where you can experiment and have fun. Garlic, peppercorns, strips of citrus zest, cloves, allspice, bay leaves, shallots, or chili peppers are among the ingredients useful for making flavored vinegars. If you want to combine garlic or shallots with an herb, remove all roots, wash, dry, and add the herbs when the vinegar has cooled, cover, and allow the mixture to sit for 4 weeks.

Flavored Mustards

For flavoring you might consider tarragon with a few drops of lemon juice, rinsed and mashed green peppercorns, herbs (rosemary, oregano, chives, dill, basil, thyme, sage, chervil) used alone or mixed in varying proportions, horseradish, cooked and cooled fruit, such as rhubarb, prunes, pears, raspberries, strawberries, or pineapple.

The basic quantities for flavored mustard are ½ cup Dijon-style mustard and between 2 and 4 tablespoons flavoring. Flavored mustards can be used immediately or stored, covered, in the refrigerator for several weeks.

MAYONNAISE

Most of us rely on store-bought mayonnaise, but there are times when the flavor of homemade mayonnaise can really enhance a dish.

Most cooks do not realize how simple it is to make mayonnaise at home. Here is a basic recipe, along with variations, for easy-to-make, inexpensive, and fresh-tasting mayonnaise. The mayonnaise may be made with vinegar instead of lemon juice.

Homemade mayonnaise keeps in the refrigerator for about three days. If you want to make it in the blender, replace the egg yolks with one large whole egg.

 ## Basic Mayonnaise

MAKES ABOUT 1 ¼ CUPS

2 large egg yolks
1 teaspoon lemon juice, plus 1 to 2 extra tablespoons lemon juice
½ teaspoon salt
Freshly ground black pepper (to taste)
1 cup oil of choice

Place the egg yolks and 1 teaspoon of the lemon juice in a bowl along with the salt and pepper. Whisk to mix. Slowly add the oil, drop by drop, whisking continuously. As the mixture thickens and emulsifies, increase the flow of the oil to a steady stream. After adding 1/2 cup of the oil, add 1 tablespoon of the lemon juice to thin the mayonnaise. Continue to whisk in the remaining 1/2 cup oil in a steady stream. Add the remaining tablespoon of lemon juice to taste and correct the seasoning. Refrigerate until ready to use. If the sauce should separate, add a teaspoon or 2 of water, lemon juice, stock, or other liquid.

▢ **NOTE**
You can cut the sweetness of store-bought mayonnaise by adding lots of lemon juice and pepper. The lemon juice thins the mayonnaise and creates a lighter, more saucelike texture.

VARIATIONS

Once you have made your own mayonnaise, you can experiment with many garnishes and variations. Here are a few of my favorite combinations, both classic and new. I have suggested foods to serve with the mayonnaises as well, but all of them can simply be used on sandwiches or as dressing for salads made with vegetables, meat, seafood, or poultry. For a list of other mayonnaises, see pages 39–41.

Aioli   See pages 74–75.

Green Goddess   See page 149.

Remoulade   A mayonnaise flavored with mustard and other seasonings. In Cajun cooking the sauce is made hot with cayenne pepper or Tabasco and usually contains horseradish. The French version uses gherkins, capers, parsley, chervil, tarragon, scallion, and mashed anchovy. Whatever you decide, try it on fried fish or shellfish, hard-cooked eggs, cold cooked shellfish (especially crab), cold baked or poached fish such as salmon, cold chicken, potato salad, or other vegetables.

Rouille   See page 192.

Sauce Gribiche   A chunky French classic used on cold fish and meat. To regular mayonnaise or mayonnaise with hard-cooked egg yolk add mustard, chopped sour pickles (cornichon, gherkins, dill), capers, tarragon, chervil, chives, and parsley.

Tartar Sauce   See pages 180–181.

Nut This sounds rich—and it is. It is also intriguing and delicious. Toast nuts (page 54), chop, and add to mayonnaise made with some nut oil. Serve with poultry or grilled fish, or with hard-cooked eggs. See Artichokes with Hazelnut Mayonnaise, pages 59–60.

COMPOUND BUTTER

A compound butter is a flavored butter, either sweet or savory, that makes a versatile topping, stores well in the refrigerator or freezer, and can liven up a dish without a lot of elaborate preparation, making for delightful, spur-of-the-moment meals. Ingredients are mixed into softened butter and left to sit and marinate. Use it on top of, or mixed into, cooked food. As the butter barely melts on the food, it makes its own sauce, without becoming oily or greasy.

The master recipe for compound butter is simple: Mix enough unsalted butter with whatever flavoring you choose. Use about four tablespoons butter to serve six or eight people. The butter must be soft enough to be creamed with the ingredients. Place it in a bowl or on a plate large enough to allow you to mix all the ingredients well, or use a food processor. Add whatever seasonings or foods you want (along with salt and pepper if you are making a savory butter), mix well, cover, and let the butter sit for about one hour to marinate.

At this point you can leave it in the bowl or make a log. To make a log, place a piece of plastic wrap on a counter and spread the butter into a loglike shape in the center. Fold the plastic all the way over the butter to cover it completely. Using your hands, shape the butter into a log and roll it smooth. Twist the ends of the plastic and store the log in the refrigerator or freezer.

When you want to use the butter, whether it is refrigerated or frozen, simply slice off disks, let them sit at room temperature for about fifteen or twenty minutes, and then place them on the hot food. Recipes for compound butter can easily be doubled and stored in the freezer.

VARIATIONS

Variations are based on 8 tablespoons (1/2 cup) of unsalted butter. The quantities given are suggestions. Use more or less to taste. Add 1/4 teaspoon of salt to all savory butters and a pinch of salt to all sweet butters. Season savory butters with black pepper to taste.

Savory Compound Butters

Nuts ($^1/_2$ cup), toasted (page 54) and ground

Minced hot chilies (1 to 2), lime juice (2 tablespoons), zest (2 teaspoons), and garlic (1 to 2 cloves)

Minced garlic (1 to 2 cloves), anchovies (6 mashed), and fresh parsley (2 tablespoons)

Chopped fresh herbs ($^1/_2$ to 2 tablespoons) and lemon juice (1 to 2 tablespoons)

Mustard (2 to 4 tablespoons) either alone or with chopped fresh herbs

Mashed avocado (1), garlic (1 to 2 cloves), and lemon juice (1 tablespoon); wonderful on steak or hamburgers, cauliflower, corn on the cob, or rice

Minced shallots (2), garlic (1 to 2 cloves), and fresh parsley (2 tablespoons); this is the classic snail butter

Garlic (4 cloves)

Sun-dried tomatoes (1 ounce, minced) and chopped fresh herbs (2 tablespoons)

Chopped fresh basil (2 tablespoons), cayenne pepper, and Tabasco sauce; delicious on corn on the cob

Indian butter: fresh minced ginger (1 tablespoon), garlic (1 to 2 cloves), paprika (1 teaspoon), cumin ($^1/_2$ teaspoon), coriander ($^1/_2$ teaspoon), cardamom ($^1/_2$ teaspoon), cayenne pepper ($^1/_4$ teaspoon), cinnamon ($^1/_4$ teaspoon), and cloves (1 pinch)

The flavors of a compound butter may be varied to complement specific vegetables. Here are a few ideas:

Dill butter, for carrots and cucumbers

Shallot butter, for broccoli

Lemon and Black Olive Butter (page 119) for fennel and green beans or peppers and squash

Anchovy butter, for peppers and squashes

Soy-garlic butter, for snow peas and radishes

Toasted sesame seed butter, for asparagus

Basil butter, for zucchini and mushrooms

Hazelnut butter, for zucchini and mushrooms, cornmeal or fresh corn pancakes, sautéed red peppers, sautéed red pepper and savoy cabbage, cut tomatoes sprinkled with breadcrumbs and baked, or popcorn

Ginger and scallion butter, for carrots and Jerusalem artichokes

Lime butter, for red cabbage

Sweet Compound Butters

Berries (¼ pound) cooked 3 to 5 minutes with maple syrup (3 tablespoons) and
        mashed with a fork; may be used on pancakes, warm cakes, muffins,
        scones, toast, or other breakfast breads

One or two peaches, nectarines, plums, or apricots mashed, honey and liqueur or
        flavoring extract to taste; may be used with pancakes, warm cakes,
        muffins, scones, toast, or other breakfast breads

Orange juice (¼ cup) and maple syrup (¼ cup) reduced to 3 tablespoons and
        cooled

Confectioner's sugar (½ cup) and melted and cooled bittersweet chocolate
        (2 ounces); may be used with croissants, French toast, muffins, or
        flavored scones

Confectioner's sugar (½ cup) and brandy (1 to 2 tablespoons); this is hard sauce

Confectioner's sugar (¼ to ½ cup) and nuts (½ cup), toasted (see page 54) and
        ground

For a list of recipes using compound butter, see pages 350–351.

HERB, VEGETABLE, and FRUIT PURÉES

The vibrant colors, soothing textures, and intense flavors of vegetable
and fruit purées will heighten a dish. Vegetable purées are traditionally
eaten as side dishes, but they can be used as sauces, either for dipping
or topping, or added to sauces (tomato purée may be added to a vinaigrette or compound butter; *crème anglaise* may be enhanced by peach
purée). If the purée is too thick to be used as a sauce, it may be thinned
with a liquid (such as stock or cream) so that it will coat the food. If it
is to be added to a sauce, a thicker mixture (such as apple butter or a
thick tomato purée) is better; cook the purée over medium-low heat to
reduce it.

Just about any vegetable, herb, nut, or fruit can be cooked and
puréed and the results served on pasta, polenta, *gnocchi*, seafood, meat,
poultry, vegetables, fruit, cakes, waffles, French toast, steamed puddings, soufflés, tarts, crisps, cobblers, and crêpes. For a list of sauces
based on vegetable and fruit purées, see pages 351–352.

Tapenade

Tapenade is a spread traditionally used in Provence as a dipping sauce for raw vegetables or served with hard-cooked eggs. *Tapenade* may be used as a dipping sauce for lamb kebabs or alongside a lamb or veal shank that has been slowly grilled. Use as a topping on cooked chicken breasts or whole roasted chicken, spread on flavorful fish, such as fresh tuna or swordfish, on grilled or raw vegetables, on veal *scaloppine* or chops, or on roasted or grilled duck. It may be used to fill an omlette, to toss with egg noodles or pasta, to spread on toast or garlic bread, or to liven up a vinaigrette. The basic recipe includes black olives, anchovies, capers, and olive oil, but I have come across recipes that include canned tuna, basil, parsley, lemon juice, mustard, and cognac.

MAKES 1 1/2 CUPS

1 cup black, brine-cured olives, preferably from Nice, pitted
8 anchovy fillets
2 cloves garlic, minced
1 tablespoon drained capers, rinsed and drained again
1/2 cup olive oil

Using a knife, a mortar and pestle, a food processor, or blender, purée the olives, anchovies, garlic, and capers to a smooth paste. Add the oil in a steady stream and mix until smooth. If you prefer a thinner sauce, use more olive oil. Store *tapenade* in the refrigerator; it will keep for several months.

Pesto

Traditionally, *pesto* is made with fresh basil and pine nuts. Inventive cooks have scrambled the combination of herbs and nuts using mint, sage, and coriander with walnuts or almonds. Sometimes they have omitted the cheese. Here is a basic formula. Serve *pesto* on pasta, vegetables such as steamed summer squash, baked or steamed potatoes, potato *gnocchi*, pasta and potatoes mixed, with soft-cooked or poached eggs, as a filling for an omlette, with fish, poultry, and meat, on bread, toast, garlic bread, or as a dip for apple slices or carrots and cauliflower.

MAKES 1 TO 1 $\frac{1}{2}$ CUPS

3 cups torn basil leaves
2 cloves garlic
¼ cup toasted pine nuts (page 54) or 2 tablespoons each toasted walnuts
* and toasted pine nuts*
½ cup olive oil
¼ cup grated Parmesan cheese
¼ cup grated Romano cheese
Freshly ground black pepper
Pinch of salt

Place the basil, garlic, and nuts in a blender or food processor and blend to a purée. Add the oil and blend just to mix. Transfer the mixture to a bowl and stir in the cheeses, pepper, and salt.

Pesto keeps for several weeks in the refrigerator. To store it longer, cover the *pesto* with a ¼-inch layer of olive oil. To use, drain off the oil, take out the amount of *pesto* you want, top the remainder with oil again, and store, refrigerated. *Pesto* also freezes well. Frozen or covered with oil, *pesto* will keep for the winter.

VARIATION

Herb and Chili A combination of fresh parsley, coriander, and hot chilies with lemon juice, garlic, and, if you like, toasted (page 54) and ground almonds, may be puréed together and served with steamed, poached, or grilled fish, especially swordfish, stir-fried shrimp or tofu, grilled tenderloin of beef or pork, roasted duck, or pan-fried duck breast.

❦ Red Pepper Purée

MAKES ABOUT ³/₄ CUP

2 large red peppers
1 tablespoon olive oil

Preheat the broiler. Quarter, seed, and trim the peppers. Brush the skin side with oil and place the peppers on a baking sheet or jelly-roll pan skin-side up. Broil them as close to the heat as possible without turning for between 10 and 12 minutes, until they are black and blistered. Remove them from the heat and let them cool on the pan; there is no need to place the peppers in a paper bag, as is sometimes suggested. Peel off the skin and discard it. Purée the peppers in a blender or food processor until smooth.

Vegetable Purées

Usually vegetables to be puréed are simmered in liquid; they can, however, be braised (cooked in butter, covered, without liquid) or grilled. They are then puréed in a food mill, food processor, or blender until smooth, and placed back into a pot to be rewarmed and seasoned. Only tomato purée needs to be strained unless you use a food mill. Thin the purées (with cream, stock, wine, water, citrus or other fruit juice, or cider) to give them a spreading consistency, use them as they are, or cook them over low heat to thicken.

❦ Basic Vegetable Purée

MAKES ABOUT 2 CUPS

2 cups diced vegetables
¹/₂ to 1 cup liquid of choice

2 tablespoons unsalted butter (optional)
Salt
Freshly ground black pepper to taste
2 tablespoons chopped fresh herbs or other flavorings (optional)

Place the vegetables in a saucepan with enough liquid barely to cover them. Bring the liquid to a boil, lower the heat, and cook until the vegetables are soft. Purée, add butter if you wish, and season with salt and pepper. Add herbs or other flavorings and serve warm.

VARIATIONS

Leek   A purée of leeks, stock, cream, unsalted butter, and thyme may be used for pasta, mashed potatoes, poultry, or white fish, or may be added to other sauces, such as reductions, essences, white butter, sour cream or yogurt sauces (for a topping on vegetable pancakes), and vinaigrette.

Spinach or Chard   A purée of cooked spinach or chard, unsalted butter, cream, raisins, toasted (page 54) pine nuts, and a pinch of nutmeg goes well with a pork or chicken stir-fry, other poultry such as duck, or a cheese soufflé.

Fruit Purées

Fruit purées may be cooked or uncooked: Raspberries, strawberries, papaya, and mango need not be cooked; blueberries, cherries, pears, apples, apricots, grapes, peaches, nectarines, plums, rhubarb, and cranberries are best when cooked to soften the fruit. It is not absolutely necessary to strain the purées. Add citrus juices, zest, spices, sweeteners, and liqueurs and serve as a sauce. Fruit purées can be added to custard sauces, compound butters, vinaigrettes, mayonnaises, white butter, reduction sauces, and sugar syrups.

◆ *Basic Fruit Purée*

MAKES ABOUT 1 TO 1½ CUPS
using fresh berries or fruit,
¾ TO 1 CUP *using frozen berries*

1 pint fresh berries, 1 bag (12 ounces) frozen berries, or ½ to
  1 pound fresh fruit
Sugar to taste, about 1 to 2 tablespoons (use about ⅓ cup with
  rhubarb or cranberries)
Few drops lemon juice
1 to 2 tablespoons liqueur to taste (optional)

If you are using berries, place them in a blender or processor and purée until smooth. Flavor with sugar (the amount depends on the tartness of the fruit) and lemon juice and strain if desired. Stir in the liqueur, if you are using it, and chill the purée until ready to use it. If using frozen berries, purée them with the juices, then strain. Add sugar and lemon juice to taste.

If you are using other fruit, you may want to trim and peel them. Cut the fruit into chunks. Add sugar and lemon juice and heat slowly to draw out the juices, stirring often. When liquid is visible in the saucepan, turn up the heat and bring fruit to a boil. Lower the heat and boil gently until the fruit is tender when pierced with the tip of a knife. Cooking time varies, but should be between 3 and 5 minutes, unless you are using dried fruit. Purée the cooked fruit in a blender and flavor it with more sugar, lemon juice if needed, and the optional liqueur. Serve warm, or chill the purée until you are ready to serve it.

VARIATIONS

Italian Prune Plum   A purée of plums, sugar, and lemon juice may be used for duck and venison, added to custard sauce, or poured over cakes or steamed puddings.

Rhubarb   A purée of rhubarb, red wine, sweetener, and grated orange zest may be used for steamed pudding, cakes, cobblers, and strawberries, or added to *crème anglaise*, sour cream or yogurt sauces, and vinaigrettes.

Cranberry   A purée of cranberries, sweetener, and the juice and grated zest of any citrus fruit may be used for cheesecake, cakes, tarts, cobblers, crisps, steamed pudding, and ice cream, or added to vinaigrettes or *crème anglaise*. With less sugar cranberry purée may be used as a savory sauce on pork, turkey, chicken, or fish.

YOGURT and SOUR CREAM SAUCES

Yogurt is an ideal ingredient for making a creamy sauce without the fat of heavy or sour cream. Try it as a topping for hot food as you would a compound butter or as a dipping sauce. Many ingredients may be used to flavor yogurt, particularly herbs and members of the onion family. Try some of the flavor combinations described in the sections on mayonnaise, vinaigrette, or compound butter. To make a richer sauce, use sour cream or a mixture of sour cream and drained yogurt. For a list of recipes see pages 352–353.

♥ *Drained Yogurt (Yogurt Cheese)*

I like to drain the yogurt a little to make it slightly thicker and less acid.

MAKES   1 ¹/₂   CUPS

2 cups plain, unsweetened low-fat or regular yogurt

Place a paper towel in a strainer, add the yogurt, and let it drain for between 1 and 1¹/₂ hours. For savory mixtures season with salt (optional) and pepper and combine with whatever flavoring you have chosen.

—————— **VARIATIONS** ——————

Savory Coconut   Mix shredded coconut, lime juice and zest, minced garlic, and chopped fresh mint into drained yogurt. Season with salt and pepper and use with poultry, a mixture of melons, or shellfish, particularly shrimp.

Roasted Pepper   Mix drained yogurt with 1 large roasted red pepper (see Red Pepper Purée, page 46), chopped. Add cayenne pepper or hot pepper flakes, if desired, and season with salt and pepper. Use with lamb, poultry, seafood, vegetables, and baked or steamed potatoes.

Orange Yogurt   Reduce ½ cup orange or tangerine juice to 2 tablespoons. Cool and add the reduction to drained yogurt, together with 1 tablespoon grated zest. Serve orange yogurt with fruit, pound cake, almond cake, pancakes, waffles, French toast, crêpes, steamed puddings, crisps, or cobblers.

Sweet Banana   Mash a banana and add it to drained yogurt together with lemon juice, vanilla, and honey or sugar; mix well. Use banana yogurt with fruit, pancakes, waffles, French toast, crêpes, cakes, or steamed puddings.

Raita   *Raita* is an Indian condiment made with yogurt and used to temper the fieriness of spicy food. *Raitas* may be made of drained yogurt and any of the following combinations of ingredients:

Mashed banana and lemon juice

Grated cucumber and chopped fresh mint

Minced hot chilies and ground cumin

Roasted and chopped tomato, with or without garlic

Roasted or grilled and mashed eggplant, cumin, and garlic

Scallions, garlic, and chopped fresh basil (especially good with a mixed pasta and potato salad)

Shredded coconut, garlic, hot chilies, and chopped fresh coriander

Shredded coconut, grated fresh ginger, and freshly chopped coriander

Serve *raitas* as dipping sauces or as toppings for grilled, roasted, or baked poultry, grilled, stir-fried, sautéed, or poached seafood, grilled or roasted lamb or beef kebabs, grilled pork tenderloin, steamed or baked potatoes, or cooked or raw vegetables.

WHIPPED CREAM

Everyone knows how to whip cream, but not everyone knows its stages of thickness. Chantilly cream is a cream beaten until it just forms soft peaks. Not at all stiff, it flows, more like a sauce. A stiffly beaten cream is thicker. Avoid overbeating it. If cream is overbeaten, tiny particles of butter will be evident on your tongue.

Chill the cream, bowl, and whisk beforehand. Whip the cream and store it in the same bowl until you are ready to serve it. It will keep for a few hours in the refrigerator when whipped ahead of time, but it will separate a little. If you see liquid at the bottom of the bowl, give the cream a few extra beats to rehomogenize it and then serve. All-purpose and heavy or whipping cream can be used interchangeably. Light cream will not whip; it does not have enough butterfat. If you like your cream sweetened, add powdered sugar. Granulated sugar does not always dissolve and may make the cream gritty. To avoid overbeating, add the sugar when the cream starts to thicken, but before it is completely whipped. I like to add sour cream or *crème fraîche* to whipped cream and use anywhere between two tablespoons and half a cup per cup of cream. Gently beat in the sour cream as the heavy cream starts to mound. Other flavorings such as vanilla, liqueur or brandy, and a pinch of salt may be added at the same time as the sugar.

Whipped cream is used as a sauce, usually a sweet one, but may be served with cold meats or vegetables (unsweetened and flavored with a savory ingredient such as mustard or horseradish) or added to a mayonnaise or hollandaise to lighten the texture.

CARAMEL SAUCE

Caramel is simple to make, but in a split second the sugar can turn from deep brown to black and burned. Do not stray too far from the saucepan. Caramel is ready when it is caramel colored. I prefer a caramel that is a dark reddish brown, not one that is pale and golden, whether it is destined for praline, candy, or sauce. The darker the color, the more bitter the taste. Yet, without some bitterness, caramel will taste too bland and lack its special character. A deeply colored caramel has a complex, bittersweet flavor as well as a gorgeous sheen.

The liquid used may be cream, juice of any kind, cider, liqueur, water, or a mixture of liquids.

MAKES 1 TO 1 ½ CUPS

1 cup sugar
½ cup water
Few drops lemon juice
⅔ to 1 cup liquid

Place the sugar, water, and lemon juice in a heavy, nonaluminum saucepan. Slowly bring the mixture to a boil over medium heat. Boil until the mixture turns a deep, reddish brown, between 5 and 10 minutes. Do not stir the mixture while it is cooking, but you may swirl it in the pan. The caramel will be thick. Remove the pan from the heat and let the caramel cool for a minute, swirling the pan. Place a strainer over the pan and pour in whatever liquid you have chosen. (The strainer will help prevent spattering.) Once the caramel has stopped bubbling, stir it to dissolve and incorporate the liquid. If the caramel does not dissolve completely, return the pan to the heat and stir constantly until it is smooth. Remove the pan from the heat and allow the caramel sauce to cool to room temperature. Transfer it to a pitcher, cover, and keep at room temperature until you are ready to serve it. The sauce can be refrigerated overnight or for 3 to 4 days. Before serving, heat it slowly over a pan of warm water.

For recipes using Caramel Sauce, see page 354.

CRÈME ANGLAISE

A stirred custard sauce, made with egg yolks, sugar, and warmed milk or cream, *crème anglaise* is a soothing and delicious dessert sauce. It may be served warm, at room temperature, or cold, on tarts, cakes, pies, pastries, fresh or cooked fruit, soufflés, steamed or bread puddings, fruit upside-down cakes, crisps, or cobblers. With fresh fruit, you might want the sauce cold; with a warm cake or tart, a warm or room-temperature sauce is better.

 Basic Crème Anglaise

MAKES 1 TO 1 ¼ CUPS

3 large egg yolks
Pinch salt

¼ cup sugar
1 cup light cream or milk,* warmed
1 teaspoon vanilla extract or other flavoring

Place the egg yolks, salt, and sugar in a saucepan and whisk lightly, just to mix. Slowly whisk in the warmed cream or milk. Place the saucepan over medium-low heat and cook the mixture for between 3 and 5 minutes, stirring constantly with a wooden spoon until the custard thickens and coats the back of the spoon and the surface of the custard is smooth. As it cooks steam will rise from the mixture and the sweet smell of the sauce will change to a stronger smell of egg. Remove the pan from the heat, strain the custard (to remove any bits of egg that may have just begun to curdle and the *chalazae*, the white, spiral cords that keep the yolk centered and connect it to the lining of the shell), and whisk vigorously to cool it and stop the cooking. Add the flavorings.

For a list of recipes using *crème anglaise*, see page 354.

VARIATIONS

Caramel Place 4 tablespoons sugar in a heavy pot with 2 tablespoons water and a drop or two of lemon juice. Cook over medium heat to caramelize (see the recipe for Caramel Sauce on pages 51–52). Remove the pan from the heat and cool the caramel slightly. Place a strainer over the pan and add the 1 cup light cream. Stir to dissolve all the caramel, placing the pan back on the heat if large pieces of caramel will not melt. Cool the caramel cream until it is warm. Mix 1 tablespoon sugar with the 3 egg yolks and salt in a bowl. Whisk in the caramel cream and place the mixture back into the heavy pot. Cook according to the directions for Basic *Crème Anglaise*. Serve Caramel *Crème Anglaise* as it is or flavor it with a liqueur like Grand Marnier or a brandy like cognac, and serve it on cakes, tarts, cooked or uncooked fruit (it is delicious on poached pears), soufflés, crisps, cobblers, or puddings.

Chocolate For the quantities given in the basic recipe for *crème anglaise*, chop up between 2 and 4 ounces of bittersweet chocolate. Melt the chocolate

---

*If you are using milk, add 1 more large egg yolk, making a total of 4.

with the warmed cream, whisk until smooth and proceed with the recipe. Or add the chocolate to the finished custard, off the heat, and whisk until smooth. Strain the custard and serve. Try this sauce on a coffee soufflè or a mousse cake.

Coffee Scald the cream and infuse in it ¼ cup ground coffee, covered, until the cream has cooled; about 1 hour. Strain and rewarm cream before proceeding with the recipe. Pour Coffee *Crème Anglaise* over chocolate cake or mousse cake.

Nut For this variation, an infusion of milk or cream is made with toasted nuts. To toast nuts, preheat the oven to 350 degrees F. Spread nuts (¾ to 1 cup for *crème anglaise*) in a cake pan or on baking sheet. Toast 7 to 15 minutes, depending on the nuts. (Toasted hazelnuts should be skinned: Place them in a clean dish towel while they are still hot and rub them together in the towel. Discard the skins.) To make the *crème anglaise* place the nuts in a blender or food processor. Scald the milk or cream and add ¼ cup of it to the nuts. Carefully grind the nuts, gradually adding the remaining milk or cream and blending until the nuts are ground. Pour the mixture into a bowl, cover, and infuse the ground nuts in the warmed milk or cream until it has cooled; about 1 hour. Strain, heat again, and proceed with the recipe.

Butterscotch Replace the white sugar with dark brown sugar and add a few drops lemon juice to the sauce before straining it.

Simple Flavorings Add 2 tablespoons of your favorite liqueur or liquor, spices to taste, or between 1 and 2 tablespoons of grated citrus zest to the finished, strained sauce.

Chapter 2

Salads, Sauces, and Dressings

*S*ALADS CAN RANGE FROM A SIMPLE DISH OF LETTUCE, LEMON juice, and oil, to an elaborate arrangement of greens, meat, vegetables, nuts, herbs, and cheeses with a complex dressing. Depending on your preferences, salads may be served hot, warm, or chilled, or as a main course, first course, or side dish. Because of their versatility, salads offer a great deal of freedom when you are planning a meal.

When it comes to salads (all foods, actually), I enjoy complexity, but not to the extent that there are so many ingredients on the plate that no distinct flavors shine through. However, a basic salad can be varied each time it is prepared by adding one or two different ingredients, perhaps nuts one time and cheese another. For instance, I love a simple tomato salad the way Ali, my niece from Costa Rica, prepares it: she uses salt, pepper, and fresh-squeezed lemon juice, nothing more. To vary this simple salad you might want to add basil, or toasted hazelnuts, or crushed fennel seeds, or slices of fresh mozzarella. Perhaps you have olives, anchovies, or capers in the cupboard. By changing the ingredients and by mixing and matching, you can come up with many variations.

Varying the sauce or dressing can give a salad a new life. The sauce for tomato salad can be made very simply with just lemon juice, or it can include oil, cream, soy sauce, or other ingredients, depending on what's in the salad. For a salad of sliced tomatoes and sliced fennel, you can create a stronger flavor by making Fennel Oil Dressing (pages 85–86), or you can crush toasted fennel seeds and add them to the dressing. For the Asparagus with Scallion Vinaigrette (pages 60–61), instead of scattering the scallions over the salad they are puréed into the dressing, which creates a vibrant green sauce that gives a decided bite. For salads containing lots of uncooked ingredients, the dressing can be smooth and uncomplicated. If the ingredients are cooked and soft, add some texture to the sauce. (See Artichokes with Hazelnut Mayonnaise, pages 59–60.) Feel free to experiment. Just about any food can be used in a salad.

❦ *Broccoli and Cauliflower à La Grecque*

Vegetables *à la grecque* are marinated vegetables. The following recipe demonstrates the technique for cooking the vegetables in the same liquid in which they will then be marinated. These vegetables can also be served as an hors d'oeuvre or first course. They are at their best when marinated overnight, but may be allowed to steep for up to three days.

▮ *MARINADE À LA GRECQUE*

S E R V E S   8

1½ cups dry white wine
1½ cups water
½ cup olive oil
½ cup lemon juice
6 parsley sprigs
1 bay leaf
2 cloves garlic, crushed
2 teaspoons fresh thyme leaves or ½ teaspoon dried thyme
1 teaspoon salt
½ teaspoon black peppercorns
Hot red pepper flakes (optional)

▮ *VEGETABLES*

1 small head cauliflower, about 1 pound florets
1 small head broccoli, about ½ pound florets

Place all the marinade ingredients into a saucepan, bring them to a boil, add the cauliflower, and cook, stirring often, for between 5 and

10 minutes or until the vegetable is tender yet still crisp. Transfer the cauliflower to a nonaluminum baking dish. Add the broccoli to the marinade and cook until it too is tender yet crisp; about 5 minutes. Remove and add it to the cauliflower. Cool the marinade until it is only warm, pour it over the vegetables, cover, and refrigerate. Marinate overnight, or for up to 3 days.

Transfer the vegetables to plates or bowls and keep them refrigerated. Bring the marinade to a boil and reduce it to about ¾ cup. Chill. Spoon the sauce over the vegetables and serve.

VARIATIONS

Red Cabbage à La Grecque   Cut a red cabbage into quarters and then into very thin slices. Replace the lemon juice in the marinade with lime juice and add thinly sliced red onion. Cook the vegetables in the marinade.

Other vegetables and combinations of vegetables that may be used include artichokes, beets, mushrooms, green or red peppers, green and wax beans, parsnips, carrots and celery or celery root, baby onions and halved Brussels sprouts, fennel alone or with red peppers, green and yellow summer squashes, savoy cabbage and red peppers, or baby white turnips and small leeks. Vary or add additional herbs and spices to suit the particular vegetables.

 Artichokes with Hazelnut Mayonnaise

Artichokes are delicious with hazelnuts (see also Veal Chops in Hazelnut and Artichoke Cream, pages 264–265). The flavor of the hazelnuts is accentuated here by the use of hazelnut oil in the mayonnaise. Try these artichokes with a hazelnut vinaigrette, also made with hazelnut oil.

SERVES   6

6 large artichokes, stems and tips trimmed

■ *HAZELNUT MAYONNAISE*

MAKES ABOUT 1 ½ CUPS

1 recipe Basic Mayonnaise (pages 39–40) made with lemon juice,
  ½ cup hazelnut oil, and ½ cup safflower or vegetable oil
⅔ cup whole toasted hazelnuts (page 54), chopped

Steam the artichokes until they are tender, about 45 minutes, checking the water level occasionally. Transfer the artichokes to a plate and allow them to cool to room temperature. Cover and refrigerate until you are ready to serve them.

Make the mayonnaise and add the chopped hazelnuts. Correct the seasoning and refrigerate the mayonnaise until you are ready to use it.

To serve, spoon some mayonnaise into each of 6 ramekins or custard cups. Serve the artichokes with the mayonnaise as a dipping sauce.

VARIATIONS

Hazelnut Mayonnaise may be varied with the addition of herbs, such as chervil, tarragon, chives, or parsley, grated orange or lemon zest, or sliced scallion greens and coarsely cracked black peppercorns.

■

HAZELNUT MAYONNAISE may be

> Served with turkey, chicken, fish, or veal, hot or cold, or as a spread for sandwiches made from these meats and fish
> Lightened with yogurt, as a dip for carrots, apple slices, red peppers, or chilled asparagus

 Asparagus with Scallion Vinaigrette

This is a delicious and different green-on-green combination that goes well with all grilled dishes. The total preparation time is about five to ten minutes.

▪ *SCALLION VINAIGRETTE*

MAKES ABOUT ½ CUP

2 tablespoons lemon juice
¼ teaspoon salt
Freshly ground black pepper
4 large scallions, green part only
4 tablespoons olive oil

SERVES 4

1 pound asparagus, ends snapped off

Make the sauce by placing the lemon juice, salt, pepper, scallions, and olive oil in the blender and blend until the mixture is completely smooth. Transfer the vinaigrette to a bowl and set it aside.

Steam the asparagus for between 3 and 5 minutes, depending on its size, until it is tender. Transfer to 4 plates, spoon scallion vinaigrette over the warm asparagus, and serve.

———— VARIATIONS ————

Crumble feta cheese over the asparagus before spooning on the sauce.
Add dark sesame oil to the dressing.
The asparagus may also be served chilled.

▪

SCALLION VINAIGRETTE is delicious
   On cold or hot beef steak
   Spooned over grilled potato slices
   Used as a dip for artichokes, hot or cold
   Spooned over a salad of sliced tomatoes and combined with endive or
      with avocado, or with feta, black olives and cucumbers, or with a
      very fine julienne of blanched lemon zest and black olives
   Served on stir-fried tofu or shellfish
   Spooned over baked, grilled, broiled, or pan-fried tuna, swordfish, or
      salmon
   On steamed greens, such as spinach or escarole
   Served on a Greek salad
   Made with lime juice and served on grilled duck

❦ Smoked Turkey Salad with Mango Dressing

▪ *MANGO DRESSING*

MAKES ABOUT 1 ¼ CUPS

1 ripe mango, peeled
⅓ cup orange juice
3 tablespoons lime juice
2 tablespoons avocado or olive oil
1 clove garlic, sliced
¼ teaspoon salt
Freshly ground black pepper

▪ *SMOKED TURKEY SALAD*

SERVES 6 TO 8

1 pound smoked turkey or chicken, cut in ¼-inch slices
1 bunch radishes, trimmed and sliced
1 cucumber, cut in half lengthwise and then cut in slices
1 papaya, peeled, seeded, and sliced
2 scallions, trimmed and sliced

To make the dressing, cut the mango from the pit and place it in a blender or food processor. Add the remaining ingredients and blend until smooth. Transfer the dressing to a bowl and refrigerate until you are ready to serve it.

To make the salad, cut the slices of smoked turkey into ¼-inch julienne strips. Pile them onto the center of a platter. Scatter the radishes around the turkey, then the cucumber, and finally the slices of papaya. Top with the sliced scallion.

To serve, pass the salad and dressing separately.

▪

MANGO DRESSING may be
Served with fruit salad
Used as a sauce for cold artichokes or asparagus

Served as a dipping sauce for grilled pork skewers
Served on grilled or roasted chicken, duck, or turkey
Served with cold, cooked shrimp—a different shrimp cocktail

❦ *Waldorf Salad*

Here I've used Parmesan cheese and sour cream as the basis for a new dressing for Waldorf Salad.

▪ *WALDORF DRESSING*

MAKES ABOUT 1 ¼ CUPS

½ cup sour cream or Drained Yogurt (page 49)
½ cup grated Parmesan cheese
2 tablespoons apple cider vinegar
1 tablespoon grainy mustard
¼ cup safflower or other vegetable oil
Salt
Freshly ground black pepper

▪ *WALDORF SALAD*

SERVES 4

3 large, tart apples, quartered, peeled, cored, and sliced crosswise
3 long stalks celery, trimmed and thinly sliced
1 cup whole toasted walnuts (page 54), coarsely chopped

Make the dressing by combining the sour cream or yogurt with the cheese in a bowl. Add the vinegar and mustard and mix until smooth. Add the oil in a steady stream. Add the salt and pepper and refrigerate.

When you are ready to serve the salad, combine the apples, celery, and walnuts in a bowl. Add the dressing and toss well to coat. Correct the seasoning and serve.

▪

WALDORF DRESSING may be
Used as a dip for cooked artichokes, broccoli, cauliflower, carrots, beans, and sugar snap or snow peas

 # *Fruit Salad with Pineapple Dressing*

Although this dish might sound like a dessert, I prefer to serve it as a salad; it makes a nice contribution to a brunch or buffet menu. There are, however, suggestions below for serving this sauce as a sweet.

▍ *PINEAPPLE DRESSING*

MAKES ½ TO ¾ CUP

1 cup pineapple juice
2 tablespoons lemon juice
1 tablespoon honey
1 tablespoon minced fresh ginger

▍ *FRUIT SALAD*

SERVES 6

1 cantaloupe, seeded and peeled
2 cups seedless green grapes, stemmed
1 pint blueberries, rinsed and picked over

Combine the pineapple juice, lemon juice, honey, and ginger in a small saucepan. Bring the mixture to a boil, lower the heat and reduce the liquid gently to between ½ and ¾ cup; about 10 to 15 minutes. Transfer the dressing to a bowl and cool it to room temperature. Chill the dressing in the refrigerator until you are ready to serve it.

To make the salad, cut the cantaloupe into 1-inch chunks. Place them in a bowl and add the grapes and blueberries. Pour on the cold dressing and toss the fruit gently until it is coated. Serve immediately.

You may add other fruit to this salad or change the fruit altogether.
Nectarines and pitted cherries together make a beautiful color and wonderful
flavor combination.
Try papaya, mango, strawberries, plums, or peaches.

∎

PINEAPPLE DRESSING may be
    Served on melon and prosciutto
    Spooned over a pan-fried duck breast that has been cut into ½-inch
        slices and seasoned with salt and pepper
    Drizzled on pancakes, waffles, or French toast
    Spooned over slices of grilled pineapple or banana
    The fruit salad and the dressing may be served over cakes or ice cream

Melon and Prosciutto with Strawberry Dressing

This is an unusual technique for making a salad dressing. The fruit is
cooked with some of the ingredients, puréed with oil and seasonings,
and chilled. The vanilla extract accentuates the fruit flavor and blends
with the fruit in the salad itself. The idea for adding vanilla to a salad
dressing came from a fellow cooking-school student.

   The salad itself is a variation of the classic combination of melon and
prosciutto. The variation below of combining prosciutto, strawberries,
and cucumber is an idea that comes from my good friend and colleague
Linda Marino.

∎ *STRAWBERRY DRESSING*

MAKES ABOUT 1 ½ CUPS

4 ounces ripe strawberries, quartered
2 cloves garlic, crushed
1 teaspoon honey

¹/₄ cup port or orange juice
3 tablespoons balsamic vinegar, lemon juice, or strawberry vinegar
¹/₄ teaspoon vanilla extract
¹/₂ teaspoon salt
Freshly ground black pepper
¹/₂ cup safflower or other vegetable oil

▮ *MELON AND PROSCIUTTO SALAD*

S E R V E S   8

1 very ripe honeydew melon
8 slices prosciutto
1 pint strawberries

To make the dressing, place strawberries, garlic, honey, port, and vinegar in a small saucepan. Bring the mixture to a boil, lower the heat, and simmer for between 3 and 4 minutes to soften the fruit. Transfer the contents of the saucepan to a blender and purée them. Add the vanilla, salt, and pepper and blend. With the blender running, pour in the oil in a steady stream. Transfer the dressing to a bowl, cover it, and refrigerate until cold.

To make the salad, cut the honeydew into 8 portions and remove the seeds. Cut away the rind, then cut each portion into slices. Arrange the pieces of melon on plates and drape a slice of prosciutto over each. Scatter a few strawberries on each plate and spoon the chilled dressing over the fruit.

VARIATIONS

Add sliced cucumber to the salad.
Substitute peaches or apricots for the strawberries in the dressing and white wine for the port; serve with a salad of smoked turkey garnished with slices of fennel, red onion, celery, and oranges, or serve with any of those ingredients on its own.

▮

STRAWBERRY DRESSING is wonderful
>   On grilled chicken breasts or on turkey
>   Served on a cucumber and red onion salad
>   Spooned over cooked asparagus

❦ Egg and Red Pepper Salad with Sherry Vinegar Dressing

This salad is made with red peppers, but green, orange, yellow, or a combination of the colors would also work very well. Serve the salad with a loaf of warmed bread and pass grapes for dessert.

▮ SHERRY VINEGAR DRESSING

MAKES ABOUT ½ CUP

*1 recipe Basic Vinaigrette (page 31), using twice as much olive oil
   (Spanish, if available) as sherry vinegar*
2 tablespoons Fresh Tomato Sauce (page 19)

▮ EGG AND RED PEPPER SALAD

SERVES 4

4 large eggs
4 red peppers, roasted and peeled (page 46)
⅓ cup slivered almonds, toasted (page 54)

Make the vinaigrette, add the tomato sauce, and set aside to allow the flavors to blend.

To make the salad, place eggs in a saucepan, cover them with cold water, and bring the water to a boil over medium-high heat. When the water is boiling, remove the pan from the heat, cover, and let the eggs sit for 17 minutes. Drain and rinse the eggs under running cold water. Cover them with cold water and let them sit for a few minutes. When they are cool enough to handle, peel the eggs, and cut them in wedges. Cover and refrigerate.

Arrange the peppers on 4 plates, top with egg wedges, and scatter the almonds over all. Season the salad with salt and pepper. Give the dressing a few whisks and spoon it over the salad.

■

SHERRY VINEGAR DRESSING may be

Used to top slices of cooked beef or lamb: Let the meat marinate in the dressing for 1 hour or overnight—good picnic or lunch-box food
Served on cauliflower or other cooked vegetables
Spooned over poultry, veal, or seafood
Used to dress a potato salad

Shredded Parsnip and Ginger Salad

This unusual salad is made with raw, finely grated parsnips. Use spring-dug parsnips if they are available. They are mildly sweet, with a hint of parsley and a slight bite.

Serve the salad with a grilled veal chop and wilted spinach.

■ *GINGER VINAIGRETTE*

MAKES ABOUT 1/2 CUP

1 recipe Basic Vinaigrette (pages 30–31), using twice as much safflower oil as lemon juice
1/4 cup orange juice
1 tablespoon (packed) minced fresh ginger; a piece weighing about 1 ounce

■ *PARSNIP SALAD*

SERVES 4 TO 6

1 pound parsnips, peeled and finely shredded
Salt
Freshly ground black pepper

Make the vinaigrette and set it aside. Place the orange juice in a small saucepan and reduce it to a tablespoon. Add to the vinaigrette with the ginger and mix well.

Place the shredded parsnip in a bowl and add the dressing. Toss the vegetable well with a fork to coat the shreds evenly. Let the salad marinate in the refrigerator for about 1 hour. Correct the seasoning, toss again, and serve.

VARIATIONS

Add a pinch of cinnamon and nutmeg or mace, mustard, or parsley.

Add cumin, hot chilies, and chopped fresh coriander; serve on macaroni with any combination of peas, radishes, broccoli, snow peas, sugar snap peas, toasted walnuts, raisins, or currants—a good picnic or lunch-box dish.

GINGER VINAIGRETTE may be

Served on a salad of raw shredded carrots or beets, or on slices of cooked carrots or beets

Poured over a tofu, snow pea, cucumber, and radish stir-fry

Served with poultry, seafood, veal, pork, beef, or lamb

Tossed with cooked vegetables or served on potatoes, pasta salad, rice, or a grain

Spinach Salad with Hot Bacon Dressing

In this salad I have taken the basic idea of a spinach and bacon salad and added a few ingredients. The radishes replace the more traditional mushrooms and add color and crunch. I have also added currants, which taste delicious with spinach.

SERVES 4 TO 6

10 ounces fresh spinach, washed, stemmed, and dried
8 slices pancetta or bacon

1 bunch radishes, trimmed and sliced
2 large cloves garlic, sliced
¼ cup red wine vinegar or flavored vinegar (pages 37–38); basil vinegar
    is particularly good
¼ cup currants
1 teaspoon Dijon-style mustard
Salt
Freshly ground black pepper
2 tablespoons safflower or other vegetable oil

Place the spinach in a bowl and set it aside.

Cook the *pancetta* or bacon over medium heat until it is crisp and browned. Drain it on paper towels, crumble it, and set it aside.

Pour off all but 2 tablespoons of fat from the pan. Raise the heat to medium-high. Add the radishes and garlic and stir-fry for 1 to 1½ minutes. Add the vinegar, currants, mustard, and salt and pepper and stir to blend. Add the oil and pour the hot mixture over spinach. Toss all the ingredients together to coat them with the dressing. Scatter the crumbled *pancetta* or bacon over the salad and serve.

--- **VARIATIONS** ---

This salad may be made with a mixture of greens such as chard, Romaine, chicory, escarole, *frisée*, cabbage, mustard greens, or dandelion greens.

▼ *White Bean and Smoked Turkey Salad with Cream Dressing*

In the north of France the local cooks use a salad dressing, called a *daussade,* of heavy cream thickened with vinegar and mixed with scallions that is tossed with greens. Lemon juice may be used in place of the vinegar. Here it is tossed with cooked small white beans and surrounded by a julienne of smoked turkey.

▮ WHITE BEANS

MAKES ABOUT 3 CUPS

1 cup small white beans, soaked overnight
1 onion, cut in half
4 cloves garlic
1 tablespoon fresh summer savory leaves or 1 teaspoon
    dried summer savory
1½ teaspoons fresh oregano leaves or ½ teaspoon dried oregano
¾ teaspoon fresh thyme leaves or ¼ teaspoon dried thyme
1 tablespoon olive oil
Salt
Freshly ground black pepper

▮ CREAM DRESSING

MAKES 1 ½ CUPS

¾ cup heavy cream
4 tablespoons cider vinegar or flavored herb vinegar (page 38)
1 bunch scallions, trimmed and chopped
Freshly ground black pepper
Salt

▮ WHITE BEAN AND TURKEY SALAD

SERVES 6 TO 8

6 to 9 leaves Boston lettuce
1 bunch watercress, coarsely chopped
3 cups cooked beans, approximately
1 pound smoked turkey, cut in ¼-inch slices and then diced

To cook the soaked beans, drain and rinse them. Place them in a large pot and cover with water. Add the onion, garlic, and herbs and bring the liquid to a boil over medium heat. Reduce the heat to medium-low and cook the beans for about 40 or 45 minutes or until they are tender. Drain the beans and place them in a bowl. Add the oil, salt, and pepper and toss to coat. Cover the beans and refrigerate them.

To make the dressing, pour the cream into a bowl and stir in the vinegar, which will thicken the cream. Add the scallions, lots of pepper, and salt. Mix well and keep the dressing refrigerated until you are ready to serve it.

To assemble the salad, place the lettuce on a platter. Mix the watercress with the beans, adding enough dressing to coat them. Mix the beans well and pile them in the center of the platter. Scatter the smoked turkey around the beans and drizzle some dressing over the meat. Pass the remaining dressing in a bowl.

VARIATIONS

Add fresh peas, radishes, or sliced tomatoes.
Substitute smoked chicken for the turkey.
Substitute balsamic vinegar for the cider vinegar and toss the dressing with fresh
       strawberries; serve on pound cake, almond cake, or other unfrosted cake.

CREAM DRESSING may be
       Served on mixed greens
       Tossed with cooked fresh peas or a mixture of snap and fresh peas
       Served on hot or chilled fish, chicken, turkey, or veal
       Spooned over cooked vegetables
       Served over a salad of sliced tomatoes and hard-cooked eggs

Vegetable Salad with Buttermilk Dressing

This is a wonderful springtime salad with an abundance of color and texture. Serve it on its own with a loaf of warmed bread or with beef, fish, lamb, or poultry.

Buttermilk is an underutilized ingredient which is most typically found in baking. However, it is perfect for making a creamy dressing with fewer calories.

∎ *BUTTERMILK DRESSING*

M A K E S   A B O U T   2   C U P S

½ cup buttermilk
2 tablespoons grainy, Dijon-style mustard
Salt
Freshly ground black pepper
1 teaspoon grated lemon zest
1 teaspoon lemon juice
1½ cups olive oil
Pinch grated nutmeg
2 tablespoons chopped fresh parsley

∎ *VEGETABLE SALAD*

S E R V E S   6

4 small red new potatoes
2 medium beets
4 radishes, trimmed and cut into wedges
1 small zucchini, halved lengthwise and cut into thin slices
1 small summer squash, halved lengthwise and cut into thin slices
4 carrots, halved lengthwise and cut into thin slices
1 cucumber, quartered lengthwise, seeds removed, and cut in thin slices
2 scallions, trimmed and cut in thin slices
12 brine-cured black olives, pitted

To make the salad dressing, place the buttermilk, mustard, salt, pepper, and lemon zest in the blender. Turn on the motor and add the lemon juice. With the machine still running, slowly add the olive oil and blend until the mixture is smooth. Add the nutmeg and parsley and taste for seasoning. Add more salt and pepper as needed. This dressing can be made quite peppery. Chill the dressing until you are ready to serve it.

To make the salad, steam the potatoes until they are tender. Cool them, cut into wedges, and set aside. Steam the beets in the same pan, peel them, cut into wedges, and set aside. Keep all the vegetables separate.

Remove the dressing from the refrigerator and whisk to rehomogenize it. In a large bowl, toss the potatoes and radishes in some of the dressing and arrange them as a border on a platter. Next, toss each of the remaining vegetables separately with some dressing and set them within the potato border, arranging them diagonally across the platter in ridges. Scatter the sliced scallions and black olives over the top and serve. Pass the remaining dressing in a bowl.

■

BUTTERMILK DRESSING may be

Used on spinach or mixed greens, with freshly cooked peas
Served over asparagus, fiddleheads, or artichoke hearts
Served over fish or poultry
Spooned over slices of cooked cold meats, such as lamb or beef
Used as a marinade for chicken, turkey, lamb, or veal

Seafood with Aïoli

Aïoli is a pungent garlic sauce from Provence. It is traditionally made in a mortar and pestle by working the garlic with the salt and pepper to a purée and then adding the olive oil slowly until the mixture thickens like mayonnaise. It should be powerful, with lots of garlic. For this recipe I have suggested a sauce with between one and one and a half cloves per person, quantities that may be revised up or down.

The sauce can be made up to two days in advance. The fish can be poached up to one day ahead or early in the morning so that it can chill.

■ *AÏOLI*

MAKES ABOUT 1 1/2 CUPS

4 to 8 large cloves of garlic, minced
1 recipe Basic Mayonnaise, made with lemon juice and olive oil
(pages 39–40)

▪ SEAFOOD PLATTER

SERVES   4   TO   6

Salt
2 halibut steaks, each about 1-inch thick
1 pound sea scallops, tough membrane removed and scallops cut
  into ¼-inch slices
24 large shrimp in the shell
2 large shallots
1 quart mussels, scrubbed
½ cup white wine
8 small red new potatoes
Young, washed salad greens of any type
4 tablespoons chopped fresh parsley

To make the aïoli, mash the garlic with the side of a knife blade until a purée has almost formed. Place in a bowl and add the mayonnaise. Mix well and correct the seasoning. Chill in the refrigerator for at least an hour to blend the flavors.

Make the fish salad. Fill a skillet with water to a depth of 3 inches. Place a rack in the pan. Place the pan over high heat and bring the water to a boil. Lower the heat to simmer and salt the water. Poach the halibut steaks in the simmering water for between 5 and 7 minutes, until they are firm and completely opaque. Remove the halibut with a slotted spoon and place it on a plate to cool. Remove the rack. Add the scallops, poach them for 1 or 2 minutes, and remove them to a plate. Poach the shrimp for 5 minutes and remove them to a plate. Set aside ¼ cup of the poaching liquid and discard the rest. When all the fish has cooled, skin and bone the halibut and break it into flakes. Peel the shrimp. Keep all the fish separate, covered, and refrigerated until you are ready to serve.

Peel and coarsely chop the shallots. Place them in a large pot with the mussels and wine. Cover, place the pot over high heat, and steam for 3 to 5 minutes to open the mussels. Shake the pot to redistribute the mussels so that they cook evenly. When the mussels are open, remove them to a plate to cool. Discard any that failed to open.

Strain the cooking juices into a small, clean pot, add the reserved 1/4 cup fish poaching liquid and reduce to ½ cup. Cool the reduction and add between 2 and 4 tablespoons of this reduction to the reserved aïoli, 1 tablespoon at a time, and taste for saltiness and flavoring. The fish juices will thin the aïoli to a nice coating consistency. Taste for seasoning and correct with lemon juice or salt although the fish juices will be salty. Keep the aïoli in the refrigerator until you are ready to serve. When the mussels are cool, remove and discard the beard and shell. Chill in the refrigerator.

Steam the red potatoes until they are tender, cool, and cut into wedges. Refrigerate them until you are ready to serve.

To serve, arrange the greens on plates. Arrange the scallops, halibut, shrimp, and mussels on the plates and surround them with potato wedges. Place spoonfuls of aïoli on the plates and sprinkle the salads with the chopped parsley.

■

Aïoli (without the reduced fish juices) may be
    Served with cooked vegetables, particularly artichokes, broccoli, or
      cauliflower
    Used as a dip with apple wedges
    Used as a dressing for potato salad
    Served with other seafood, lamb, or poultry

■

SEE ALSO SPICY LEMON AÏOLI FOR ROAST CHICKEN (PAGES 191–192)

▼ Roasted Lamb Salad with Garlic Dressing and Spring Garnishes

Whole mint leaves are mixed with greens to form the bed for this colorful and substantial salad. The lamb is to be marinated; allow time for that step.

1½ to 2 pounds trimmed weight, boneless leg of lamb, with all fat and fell removed, butterflied

▌ *MARINADE*

M A K E S ²/₃ **C U P**

⅓ cup olive oil
⅓ cup white wine
6 very large or 8 medium cloves garlic, peeled and crushed
1 onion, sliced
2 tablespoons chopped fresh oregano or 1 teaspoon dried oregano
1 tablespoon chopped fresh thyme or 1 teaspoon dried thyme
1 tablespoon chopped fresh rosemary or 1 teaspoon dried rosemary

▌ *GARLIC DRESSING*

M A K E S 1 ½ **C U P S**

6 tablespoons lemon juice
2 tablespoons lime juice
1 tablespoon anchovy paste
3 large cloves garlic, sliced
1 cup olive oil
Salt
Freshly ground black pepper to taste

▌ *SALAD*

S E R V E S 6

1 pound asparagus, ends trimmed
12 ounces baby carrots, peeled and ends trimmed
1 small head red-leaf lettuce, washed, dried, and torn into pieces
2 cups packed, stemmed spinach leaves, washed, dried, and
    torn into pieces
½ cup whole mint leaves, washed and dried

To marinate the lamb, place the meat in a glass or enamel baking dish or a large bowl. Mix together the ingredients for the marinade and pour it over the lamb, turning the meat to coat it. Cover and marinate the lamb for between 24 and 48 hours, turning twice a day.

To make the dressing, place the lemon and lime juice in a blender with the anchovy paste, garlic, and olive oil. Blend until smooth. Season to taste with salt and pepper. This can be made 1 or 2 days ahead and kept refrigerated. It will be very tart, but will taste mellower when served with the lamb.

Steam or blanch the asparagus until it is just tender. The amount of time depends on the size of the spears. Drain and rinse the asparagus under cold water, drain again, pat dry, and transfer it to a board. Cut the spears into 2-inch pieces on the bias. Place them in a bowl, cover, and refrigerate until you are ready to serve.

Cut the carrots in half lengthwise and blanch them in boiling water until they are just tender, about 7 or 8 minutes. Drain the carrots, rinse them under cold water, drain again, and pat dry. Place them in a bowl, cover, and refrigerate until you are ready to serve.

To cook the lamb, preheat the oven to 400 degrees F. Remove the lamb from the marinade, leaving the herbs clinging to it, and place it on a rack in a roasting pan. Fish out the crushed garlic cloves from the marinade and dry them off. Chop them fine and rub the chopped garlic all over the surface of the meat. Roast the lamb for between 20 and 25 minutes, to an internal temperature of about 130 degrees F. in the thickest muscle. The meat will be rare in spots and medium rare in the thinner areas. Allow the meat to rest for 10 minutes. Slice the meat across the grain and set it aside. This can be done ahead.

To assemble the salad, place the lettuce, spinach, and mint leaves in a bowl. Toss them with the garlic dressing and arrange them on plates or a platter. Arrange the lamb slices over or around the salad and season with salt and pepper if desired. Place the asparagus and carrots in the bowl, toss them with more dressing, and scatter them over the lamb and lettuce. Pass the remaining dressing separately.

Beef Salad with Green and Black Olive Dressing

The flavors in this salad are bitter, sweet, and salty. The dressing needs to be made one day ahead so that the olives have time to color and flavor the sauce. In fact, the peppers, chicory, and meat can all be prepared the day ahead. Just assemble and serve the salad the next day.

▮ GREEN AND BLACK OLIVE DRESSING

MAKES 1 ½ CUPS

1 tablespoon red wine vinegar
4 tablespoons lemon juice
1 tablespoon fresh thyme leaves or 1 teaspoon dried thyme
1 clove garlic, minced
¾ cup olive oil
12 imported green olives, pitted and quartered
12 Greek black olives, pitted and quartered
2 tablespoons chopped fresh parsley
Freshly ground black pepper

▮ BEEF SALAD

SERVES 6

1 small head chicory
Olive oil for pan-frying
4 beef tenderloin steaks, each weighing about the same, between 6
    and 8 ounces
2 peppers of different colors, red, yellow, orange, or green, roasted and
    peeled (page 46)

To make the salad dressing, combine the vinegar, lemon juice, thyme, and garlic in a small bowl. Whisk in the oil slowly. Stir in the olives and parsley and flavor with a good amount of pepper. Refrigerate the dressing overnight.

To make the salad, wash the chicory and dry it well. Tear it into medium pieces and store them in a plastic bag in the refrigerator until you are ready to serve.

Heat some oil in a skillet over high heat and pan-fry the tenderloins until they are rare or medium rare. Set them aside on a plate to cool, then cover and refrigerate them until you are ready to serve.

Leave the peppers in quarters and set aside or refrigerate until you are ready to serve.

To assemble the salad, arrange the chicory on 4 plates. Slice the steaks into ¼-inch slices and drape them over the greens with the peppers. Spoon some dressing over the salad and pass the extra dressing on the side.

VARIATION

To the dressing add grated orange zest, substitute 1 tablespoon of orange juice for the lemon, and add a few fennel seeds, crushed with a mortar and pestle.

▪

GREEN AND BLACK OLIVE DRESSING may be
 Served with seafood (a salad of shrimp and oranges with this dressing is terrific), poultry, or lamb, hot or cold
 Served on a vegetable salad (it is particularly good with artichoke hearts)
 Served with a *salade Niçoise*
 Served on a wild, brown, or white rice salad
 Served on a potato or pasta salad

❦ *Red Peppers and Peas with Lemon Zest Dressing*

I have always wanted to make a dish of red peppers and lemon zest. In their natural state, the two look so striking. Here I have cut some of the zest in a fine julienne to capture that color combination and to enhance the texture of the salad.

▪ *RED PEPPER SALAD*

S E R V E S   4

4 large red peppers, roasted and peeled (page 46)
1 pound fresh peas in the shell

▌ *LEMON ZEST DRESSING*

MAKES ABOUT 1 CUP

5 strips lemon zest, measuring 1/2 an inch by 2 to 3 inches
2 cloves garlic, sliced
1/4 cup whole mint leaves
1/2 teaspoon salt, or to taste
Freshly ground black pepper
1/3 cup lemon juice
2/3 cup olive oil

To make the salad, arrange the peppers on four plates, cover them, and refrigerate.

Shuck the peas. Bring a pan of water to a boil and blanch the peas for 2 minutes. Drain and rinse them with cold water, drain again, and pour the peas into a bowl. Cover the bowl and refrigerate it.

To make the dressing, chop 4 strips of lemon zest and set them aside. Cutting at an angle, slice the remaining strip of lemon zest into very thin julienne strips and place them in a small bowl. Cover the bowl and refrigerate it until you're ready to serve.

Place the garlic, chopped lemon zest, mint leaves, salt, pepper, and lemon juice in a blender. Start to blend and then add the oil in a stream. Continue blending until the garlic and lemon zest are smooth and the mint is finely chopped. Pour the dressing into a jar and refrigerate it.

When you are ready to serve, spoon some dressing over the peppers. Toss the peas in a bit of dressing and scatter them over the peppers along with the reserved lemon zest julienne. Pass extra dressing separately.

VARIATIONS

When peas are out of season during the late summer and early fall, this salad is delicious with corn kernels, plain or mixed with 1 tablespoon of rinsed green peppercorns, scattered over the red peppers.

Add slivers of red onion to the salad.

Baby frozen peas, thawed, can be used to replace the fresh peas.

The dressing is also delicious when made with lime juice and zest in place of the lemon.

Instead of mint leaves, you might try dill, basil, tarragon, or parsley.

▌

Lᴇᴍᴏɴ Zᴇꜱᴛ Dʀᴇꜱꜱɪɴɢ may be

> Served as a substitute for butter over corn on the cob; mix the sauce well and brush it over the ears
>
> Served with assorted steamed vegetables such as carrots, green beans, summer squashes, snow peas, broccoli, cauliflower, or Brussels sprouts
>
> A nice change on grilled salmon or halibut
>
> Used as a dipping sauce for shrimp or scallops
>
> Served on roast chicken, poached or grilled chicken breasts, or lamb of any description
>
> Used for a salad of fresh crabmeat or strips of cooked chicken breast arranged on a bed of spinach

 # Caesar Salad

This lemony version of the classic is refreshing. The croutons are large and may be served whole, as they are here, or crumbled over each plate of salad.

S E R V E S   8

8 slices of French bread, cut 1-inch thick
3 large cloves garlic
½ can anchovies in olive oil, about 4 or 5
1 teaspoon Dijon-style mustard
Juice of 2 lemons
1 to 1½ cups olive oil
1 large head romaine lettuce
1 large egg
½ cup grated Parmesan cheese
Freshly ground black pepper

> Preheat the oven to 350 degrees F. Arrange the bread on a sheet and dry it in the oven for about 20 or 30 minutes. Cut one clove of garlic in half. Rub each side of the croutons with the cut garlic and set them aside.

Mince the remaining 2 cloves of garlic and place them in a bowl. Mince the anchovies and add them to the garlic, together with the mustard. Slowly add the lemon juice to the garlic mixture, whisking it in. Continue whisking and add 1 cup oil in a stream. Taste the dressing and add more olive oil if it is too tart, bearing in mind that it will mellow with the addition of the egg and when it's on the salad. Set the dressing aside.

Clean the lettuce, dry it, tear it into small pieces, and place them in a bowl. Boil the egg for 1 minute and rinse it under cold water to cool it. Break it open and scrape the contents into the dressing. Whisk to combine. Immediately pour the dressing over the lettuce, sprinkle on the cheese and lots of pepper, and toss everything together to incorporate the dressing. Arrange on plates and top each serving with a crouton.

▼ Sweet Potato Salad with Honey and Lemon Dressing

▮ SWEET POTATO SALAD

SERVES 4

3 large sweet potatoes, peeled and cut in 1/2-inch cubes
1 cup tiny peas, fresh or frozen
1 small red onion, finely diced

▮ HONEY AND LEMON DRESSING

MAKES ABOUT 3/4 CUP

1/4 cup lemon juice
2 teaspoons honey
2 tablespoons scissored fresh chives or chopped fresh mint, or 1 to 2
    teaspoons ground cumin

Pinch cayenne pepper
Salt
Freshly ground black pepper
½ cup olive oil

Steam the sweet potatoes for between 8 and 10 minutes, until they are tender when pierced with a knife. Place them in a large bowl. If you are using fresh peas, blanch them for 1 or 2 minutes, depending on their size, rinse them under cold water, drain again, and add them to the bowl. (If you are using frozen tiny peas, simply thaw and add them to the salad.) Add the onion and set the bowl aside.

Make the dressing by whisking the lemon juice and honey together. Add the chives, mint, or cumin, and the cayenne, salt, and pepper. Whisk in the oil in a steady stream. Taste the dressing for seasoning and pour it over the salad. Toss the salad gently with rubber spatulas (this will help prevent the potatoes from breaking up) until it is well mixed. Taste for seasoning; if you like more heat, add more cayenne. Serve at once or let the salad marinate (for between 2 hours and all day) in the refrigerator until you are ready to serve.

VARIATIONS

You can experiment with the ingredients in this salad by adding or subtracting flavors that go well with sweet potatoes: ham, spinach, avocado, apples, pears, scallions, Parmesan cheese, anchovies, and toasted pecans, pistachios, and almonds.

The dressing, too, may be varied with additions that complement sweet potatoes: lime juice, sherry, cream, garlic, ginger, horseradish, cinnamon, ground coriander, curry powder, cilantro, thyme, or red pepper flakes.

■

HONEY AND LEMON DRESSING is versatile and blends well with sweet or savory ingredients. Try it over

Slices of melon or fresh pineapple

A fresh pineapple and ham salad, pan-fried slices of ham, cold roast pork, pan-fried pork cutlets, or pork stir-fry with eggplant

Slices of grilled eggplant with toasted walnuts, or grilled eggplant and olive salad

Slices of fresh tomato

Browned and sliced boneless chicken breasts, sliced turkey breast, sliced smoked turkey breast, or a salad of smoked turkey, toasted almonds, and cucumber on a bed of spinach
Cold lamb salad

▼ Fennel and Green Bean Salad

The dressing for this wonderful crisp salad is made with a flavored oil. Serve it with a loaf of bread and a mild goat cheese.

▌ GREEN BEAN SALAD

SERVES 8

1 pound green beans
2 fennel bulbs
2 tablespoons chopped fresh fennel greens, tarragon, basil, or chives
2 tablespoons chopped fresh parsley

▌ FENNEL OIL DRESSING

MAKES ABOUT 1 CUP

2 tablespoons Dijon-style mustard or 1 tablespoon grainy mustard and 1
    tablespoon smooth mustard
1 clove garlic, minced (optional)
1/4 cup lemon juice or herb vinegar such as tarragon
1/2 cup Fennel Oil (page 36)
Salt
Freshly ground black pepper

Trim the beans and blanch them for between 5 and 7 minutes in boiling, salted water. Drain them, run them under cold water to cool and set the color, drain again, and dry.

Trim the fennel, cut the bulbs in half through the root, and remove cores. Slice the fennel thinly crosswise, pile it into a large salad bowl, and add the green beans and the herbs. Set this aside.

In a small bowl whisk the mustard, garlic, and lemon juice. Slowly whisk in the oil. Add salt and pepper to taste. Pour enough dressing over the vegetables and herbs to coat them and toss well. Marinate the salad in the refrigerator until you are ready to serve, between 2 and 8 hours.

FENNEL OIL DRESSING may be

Served on warm baby red potatoes

Used as a marinade for cooked artichoke hearts or whole baby artichokes

Poured over sautéed red peppers (marinate overnight in the refrigerator)

Tossed with uncooked vegetables, such as grated carrots, zucchini, beets, thinly sliced celery, sliced cucumber, or snow peas

Tossed with hot cooked green beans, asparagus, fiddleheads, wax beans, fresh peas, snow peas blanched for just 1 minute, carrots, cauliflower, or cooked *cannellini,* or navy beans

Added to a salad of uncooked sugar snap peas and yellow summer squash

Mixed with cooked grains, such as cracked wheat, white, brown, or wild rice, or a mixture of rices

Served on poached fish or chicken breasts or pan-fried pork tenderloin

Mixed Greens, Mint, and Sage Leaf Salad

Salads made with whole herb leaves were very popular in early New England. Mint and sage add a welcome surprise to the ubiquitous green salad.

▌ *APPLE CIDER VINAIGRETTE*

M A K E S   A B O U T   1   C U P

2 recipes Basic Vinaigrette (pages 30–31), using apple cider vinegar
Large pinch sugar

∎ *SALAD*

Half a small head or bunch of at least 4 different greens such as red-leaf
*   lettuce, Boston lettuce, arugula, spinach, chard, frisée and* raddi-
*   chio, cleaned, dried, and torn into pieces*
1 bunch young radishes, trimmed and sliced
2 scallions, trimmed and sliced
½ cup whole mint leaves, washed and dried
2 tablespoons whole small fresh sage leaves, washed and dried

Make the vinaigrette and add the sugar. Set the dressing aside at room
temperature to allow the flavors to blend.

Mix the greens, radishes, scallions, mint leaves, and sage leaves in a
bowl. When you are ready to serve, toss the greens with the dressing.
Correct the seasoning and serve.

VARIATIONS

Sliced cucumber, handfuls of currants, or nasturtium flowers are tasty additions
to this salad.

▼ *Chick-Peas and Vegetables with a
Cinnamon Dressing*

This Moroccan-inspired salad can be served as a main dish (especially
for lunch) with fruit, such as apricots or sliced oranges, or as a side
dish. It complements all grilled meats, fish, and vegetables, and
roasted meats. You can serve the salad as it is or in cups made from the
small interior leaves of soft lettuces such as Boston or Bibb lettuce, or
surround the salad with orange slices scattered with chopped dates.

■ *CINNAMON DRESSING*

MAKES ABOUT ½ CUP

¼ cup lemon juice
1 teaspoon honey
1 tablespoon ground cinnamon
¼ teaspoon paprika
Pinch cayenne pepper
½ teaspoon salt
Freshly ground black pepper
1 small clove garlic, minced
¼ cup olive oil

■ *CHICK-PEA AND VEGETABLE SALAD*

SERVES 6 TO 8

4 cups freshly cooked chick-peas or 2 19-ounce cans chick-peas,
    rinsed and drained
6 carrots, grated on a medium- to large-sized grater
1 bunch radishes, trimmed and quartered

Make the dressing first to allow the flavors to blend. Whisk the lemon juice and honey together and then whisk in the cinnamon, paprika, cayenne, salt, and black pepper. Add the garlic and then slowly whisk in the olive oil. Set the dressing aside.

Prepare the ingredients for the salad and combine them in a bowl. Whisk the dressing again and correct the seasoning. Add it to the vegetables and toss them well. Let the salad marinate at room temperature for about an hour, tossing once in a while. If you are serving it the next day, refrigerate the salad, stirring it occasionally, and then let it warm up about 1 hour before eating, so that you may enjoy the full flavors at room temperature.

■

CINNAMON DRESSING may be
    Served on a salad of sliced navel oranges and thinly sliced red onion, or
        slices of fruit such as melon or pineapple
    Used as a dip for sliced apples
    Served on chicken breasts, lamb, or shellfish

Lentil Salad with Apples, Walnuts, and Watercress

Serve this salad with grilled chicken or lamb. It also makes a delightful picnic or lunch-box dish.

▌ APPLE AND WALNUT DRESSING

MAKES ABOUT 2 CUPS

1/4 cup cider vinegar
2 tablespoons grainy mustard
1/2 teaspoon salt
Freshly ground black pepper
1/2 teaspoon ground coriander
1/4 teaspoon ground nutmeg
1/4 teaspoon ground cinnamon
1/4 teaspoon ground allspice
1/8 teaspoon ground cloves
1/8 teaspoon ground cardamom
1/2 cup walnut oil
3 tart apples, such as Granny Smith, quartered, peeled, cored, and cut
    into small pieces

▌ LENTIL SALAD

SERVES 6 TO 8

1/2 pound lentils
1 bay leaf
1 teaspoon fresh thyme leaves or 1/2 teaspoon dried thyme
1/2 teaspoon black peppercorns
1 bunch watercress, coarsely chopped
1 1/2 cups toasted walnuts (page 54), chopped

To make the dressing, place the vinegar and mustard in a bowl and whisk until they are smooth. Add salt and pepper and all the spices.

Mix well and then slowly whisk in the oil. Add the pieces of apple and let the dressing sit for 1 hour at room temperature for the flavors to blend.

While the dressing sits, cook the lentils. Wash and pick them over. Place them in a saucepan and cover with water. Add the bay leaf and thyme. Place the peppercorns in a cheesecloth bag or tea strainer with a lid and add that to the pot. Bring the water to a boil, lower the heat, and boil gently for 20 minutes or until the lentils are tender but not mushy. Remove the peppercorns and drain the lentils. Discard the bay leaf.

After 1 hour, pour the dressing over lentils and add the watercress and nuts. Stir the salad well to combine the ingredients and serve warm or chilled.

--- **VARIATION** ---

You can change the nuts in this salad. Try toasted almonds or pecans.

▪

APPLE AND WALNUT DRESSING may be
      Served on a mixed green salad to which bitter greens have been added
      Tossed with julienne ham strips for a salad
      Served on other grains or on potato salad

❦ *Fiddlehead Salad with Red Onion Dressing*

The onion in this dressing gives it a delicate pink tint that looks lovely against the background of bright green fiddleheads and shiny oranges. Fiddleheads have a very short season in the early spring. (When they are unavailable, use asparagus.) Serve this salad as a meal with warmed bread or as an accompaniment for grilled meats, seafood, or poultry.

▪ RED ONION DRESSING

MAKES ABOUT 1 ½ CUPS

3 tablespoons lemon juice
2 tablespoons balsamic or red wine vinegar
1 large clove garlic, sliced
2 strips orange zest, 3 inches long, sliced
½ teaspoon salt
Freshly ground black pepper
½ cup olive oil
¼ cup safflower oil
½ cup red onion, diced
2 tablespoons chopped fresh parsley

▪ FIDDLEHEAD SALAD

SERVES 6

1 pound fiddleheads
3 navel oranges, peeled to remove all white pith
2 cucumbers, peeled and quartered lengthwise, seeds removed
6 leaves red-leaf or Boston lettuce
Salt
Freshly ground black pepper

To make the dressing, combine the lemon juice, vinegar, garlic, orange zest, salt, pepper, and oils in a blender and blend until smooth. All of the garlic and orange zest should be puréed. Add the red onion and blend for between 15 and 20 seconds—do not purée the onion. The dressing should turn pink, but the onion should remain in small pieces. Put the dressing in a bowl and add the parsley. Taste for seasoning and refrigerate.

To make the salad. Clean the fiddleheads well by washing them and removing the brown paperlike covering (known as scale). Soak them in cold water if necessary to loosen the scale, then drain. Fiddleheads that are hard to clean may be wiped with a damp cloth. Blanch the fiddleheads in boiling salted water for between 5 and 10 minutes, depending on their size, until they have softened, yet are still crisp.

When they are done, drain them, and run them under cold water to stop the cooking. Dry them well and refrigerate them.

Cut each orange into 8 slices and chill them on a plate. Slice the cucumbers on the bias into ½-inch pieces. Refrigerate.

To assemble the salad, arrange the lettuce on 6 plates. Toss the fiddleheads and cucumbers in a bowl with some of the dressing. Season with salt and pepper to taste. Fan out 4 slices of orange on each plate. Season the oranges with pepper. Divide the fiddlehead mixture among the 6 plates, arranging them next to the orange slices. Spoon some dressing over the oranges and serve the salad. You may pass the extra dressing in a bowl.

∎

RED ONION DRESSING may be
>   Served with poultry, beef, lamb, seafood, or smoked trout
>   Tossed with grain, potato, or rice salads
>   Spooned over sautéed calves' liver

 ## *Warm Carrot Salad with Walnut Dressing*

SERVES 4

1 pound carrots, peeled and cut in half lengthwise

∎ *WALNUT DRESSING*

MAKES ½ CUP

¼ cup toasted walnuts (page 54), coarsely chopped
3 tablespoons walnut oil
1½ tablespoons lemon juice
1 tablespoon chopped fresh parsley
½ teaspoon salt
Freshly ground black pepper

Cut the carrot halves in 1/4-inch slices on the diagonal to make half moons. Blanch in boiling salted water until the carrots are crisp-tender; about 5 minutes. Drain and place them in a bowl. Place all the ingredients for the dressing in a small bowl and mix together well. Pour over the carrots and toss everything together. Serve warm.

■

WALNUT DRESSING may be

Served on spinach or other bitter greens or on fish, poultry, or cold slices of beef

Tossed with a potato, pasta, grain, or rice salad

Chapter 3

VEGETABLES

and

SAUCES

*T*HERE SEEMS TO BE NO END TO THE SPECTACULAR COMBINA-tions of vegetables and sauces that can be put together. They can be altogether new like Wilted Spinach with Avocado Sauce (pages 99–100), or they can combine cultural traditions, like Corn on the Cob with *Pesto* (page 109). I like to serve vegetables and sauces as a first course, main course, or a side dish.

In this chapter I have used a number of different vegetable cooking techniques to highlight different sauces. For instance, the recipe for Braised Leeks in a Tarragon Coat (pages 116–117) shows how to use the liquid in the pan as the basis for a flavorful and rich sauce.

When I think about which sauces might be suitable for a particular vegetable, a lot of variables play a role, as with salads. The most important are taste and texture. How does the flavor and consistency of the vegetable change when it is cooked? Is it sweeter? Is it different when baked, boiled, steamed, or braised? The recipe for Ginger Beets (pages 111–112) is a good example of how the cooking technique can affect a vegetable's flavor. Raw beets, delicious as they are when shredded in a salad, lack the sweetness of cooked beets. Baked beets, however, are much sweeter than steamed or boiled beets. For the Ginger Beets recipe, the sweetness of the baked beets is balanced by the heat and intensity of the ginger. Other sauces with acidic, salty, or spicy ingredients would also counter the sweetness of the beets.

The seasons are important in deciding what sauce to use. During the winter you may want a homey, soft dish without a lot of contrasting texture, perhaps the Buttercup Squash Purée with Honeyed Tomato Sauce (pages 102–103) or one with a rich cream sauce such as Mushrooms with *Ravigote* Cream Sauce (pages 100–102). Other sauces work best in other seasons. Whichever one you choose from this chapter, bear in mind that it can be used on many vegetables, alone or in a combination.

▼ *Steamed Snow Peas with Yogurt-Curry Sauce*

This delicious sauce will add an alternative low-fat method of creaming vegetables to your repertoire. The flavorings may be changed to suit the vegetable.

▮ *YOGURT-CURRY SAUCE*

MAKES 1 CUP

1 tablespoon unsalted butter
1 tablespoon curry powder
1 cup Drained Yogurt (page 49)

▮ *PEAS AND GARNISH*

SERVES 4

1 pound snow peas, trimmed and washed
1/2 cup slivered almonds, toasted (page 54)

Melt the butter in a small skillet over medium heat. Add the curry powder and sauté, stirring, for about 1 minute. Transfer the curry mixture to a bowl using a rubber spatula to scrape out the pan, let it cool, then add the yogurt and mix well. Set the sauce aside to let the flavors blend.

Place the snow peas in a steamer basket and steam for 3 to 5 minutes, until tender but still crisp and bright green. Transfer the peas to a bowl, pour the curry sauce over them, and toss them gently. Scatter the almonds over the peas and serve immediately.

∎

YOGURT-CURRY SAUCE may be
>Used to top lamb, chicken, or seafood
>Mixed with cooked potatoes, grains, or rice
>Tossed with other cooked vegetables such as carrots, baby onions, eggplant, green beans, broccoli, or cauliflower
>Mixed with cooked *cannellini,* navy, or pea beans

Wilted Spinach with Avocado Sauce

The very creamy consistency of avocado makes this a wonderful sauce on greens such as spinach. The colors of the two greens together are striking on the plate. Serve this vegetable with grilled chicken and corn on the cob.

∎ AVOCADO SAUCE

MAKES ABOUT 1 TO 1 1/2 CUPS

1 ripe avocado, preferably the smaller variety that has a textured skin
2 tablespoons lemon juice
1/4 cup plain yogurt
Salt
Freshly ground black pepper
2 tablespoons chopped fresh herbs, such as basil, dill, tarragon, or parsley

∎ SPINACH

SERVES 4

2 tablespoons oil
1 pound fresh spinach, washed, stems trimmed

∎ ∎ ∎ ∎ ∎ ∎ ∎ ∎ ∎ ∎ ∎ ∎ ∎ ∎ ∎ ∎

Peel and pit the avocado. Push it through a strainer with a spoon, then scrape off the outside of the strainer with the spoon or a rubber spatula. Add the lemon juice and mix. Add the yogurt, salt, pepper, and herbs. Mix well and set aside at room temperature. (You can also do this in a blender or food processor: Purée the avocado with the lemon juice until it is smooth. Transfer the purée to a bowl and add the yogurt, salt, pepper, and herbs.)

Heat the oil in a large skillet over medium-high heat. Add the spinach (it is fine if water is still clinging to it) and toss it frequently until it has barely wilted. Transfer the spinach to plates and top it with a good spoonful of the avocado sauce.

■

AVOCADO SAUCE may be
Spooned on baked tomato halves
Spooned over grilled or steamed vegetables, such as yellow summer squash, onions, fresh corn, or peppers
Served with chicken, turkey, beef, or fish
Spooned into a baked sweet potato or on rice

▼ *Mushrooms with Ravigote Cream Sauce*

The French verb, *ravigoter*, means to "sharpen the appetite." A *ravigote* sauce is a French *velouté* (flour-bound sauce) to which a reduction of wine, vinegar, and shallots is added. The sauce is finished with cream, butter, and cayenne pepper. The sauce given here is based on that wine reduction, but cream is added, instead of a *velouté*, and the sauce further reduced—a simple, yet versatile technique that can be used for all types of food.

Make this sauce with stock instead of the cream and it will resemble the original *velouté* and wine reduction mixture. It may be served on meat, poultry, vegetables, eggs, potatoes, grains, or pasta.

■ *RAVIGOTE CREAM SAUCE*

MAKES ABOUT ³/₄ CUP

½ cup white wine
½ cup white wine vinegar

6 shallots, chopped
1 cup heavy cream
1 tablespoon scissored fresh chives
1 tablespoon chopped fresh chervil (if unavailable,
   increase the tarragon to 2 tablespoons)
1 tablespoon chopped fresh tarragon
1 tablespoon chopped fresh parsley
Salt
Freshly ground black pepper

▮ MUSHROOMS

S E R V E S   6

2 tablespoons unsalted butter
1½ pounds cultivated mushrooms, trimmed and cut in wedges

For the sauce, combine the wine, vinegar, and shallots in a saucepan. Bring the mixture to a boil, lower the heat, and reduce the mixture to ¼ cup liquid (measure by squeezing the shallots to the edge of the pot and pouring off the liquid). Add the cream and again reduce the mixture to between ⅔ and ¾ cup liquid. Strain out the shallots and add the herbs. Season the sauce with salt and pepper to taste and set it aside.

For the mushrooms, heat the butter in a skillet over high heat. Add the mushrooms, salt, and pepper and toss to coat. Sauté the mushrooms until their liquid evaporates and they are browned and tender, about 10 minutes. Add the reserved sauce and heat through. Correct the seasoning and serve.

VARIATIONS

Different types of wild and cultivated mushrooms may be mixed in this dish. Different flavors may be added to the reduction and to the finished sauce: different herbs, ginger, mustard, horseradish, curry powder, cheese, or citrus.

▮

RAVIGOTE CREAM SAUCE may be
   Served on chicken, pork tenderloin, veal, sweetbreads, fish, carrots, peas and baby onions, green beans, pasta, potatoes, rice, artichoke

hearts, leeks, Brussels sprouts, or Brussels sprouts mixed with chestnuts and baby onions

Served, together with the mushrooms, on fish, chicken, veal, pasta, rice, potatoes, or toast

❦ Buttercup Squash Purée with Honeyed Tomato Sauce

This sauce's unique blend of lime, tomato, and honey provides an interesting taste balance for the squash. The bright red and orange colors make it visually appealing. The tomato sauce called for in this recipe can be made one or two days ahead and refrigerated.

SERVES   4   TO   6

1 buttercup or butternut squash weighing about 2 to 3 pounds

▮ HONEYED TOMATO SAUCE

MAKES   ABOUT   1   TO   1 ¼   CUPS

¾ cup Winter Tomato Sauce (pages 20–22)
6 tablespoons fresh lime juice
¼ cup honey
Salt
Freshly ground black pepper
4 tablespoons unsalted butter

Preheat the oven to 375 degrees F. Place the whole squash on a baking sheet and prick it with the tip of a knife. Bake until it is very tender, about 1 hour.

While the squash cooks, make the sauce. Heat the tomato sauce and add the lime juice and honey. Season with salt and pepper.

When it is done, remove the squash from the oven and cut it in half. Remove the seeds and scoop out the flesh into a food processor or heavy saucepan. Purée the squash in the processor or mash it with a potato masher. Add the butter, season with salt and pepper, and keep the purée warm.

Reheat the sauce. Spoon the squash onto plates and top it with sauce.

VARIATION

Squash Parmesan   You will need a double recipe of sauce for this dish. Spread half the squash purée in a baking dish. Spoon half the sauce over it and top with a mixture of Italian Fontina and Parmesan cheeses. Repeat with another layer of squash, sauce, and cheese. Bake at 350 degrees F. for between 20 and 30 minutes, until bubbly and golden brown. (This dish may also be made with thin slices of squash.)

∎

HONEYED TOMATO SAUCE may be
> Used on seafood, poultry, lamb, or pork
> Spooned on grains, legumes, rice, or sweet potatoes
> Served on a vegetable terrine, timbale, custard, or soufflé made with spinach, zucchini, or carrots

❦ *Zucchini and Currant Compote with Red Wine Sauce*

In this compote, the vegetables cook slowly with stock and red wine, making their own sauce. The dish is a delicious accompaniment to fried rice and all meats, game, poultry, and fish.

SERVES 4 TO 6

2 tablespoons currants or yellow raisins
1 to 1¼ pounds small zucchini, trimmed

2 tablespoons unsalted butter or olive oil
Salt
Freshly ground black pepper
¾ pound small to medium whole shallots, peeled
Large pinch cinnamon
Large pinch nutmeg
½ cup chicken and veal stock (pages 5–6)
1½ cups red wine
1 to 2 tablespoons lemon juice or red wine vinegar
2 tablespoons chopped fresh basil, marjoram, savory, or parsley

Soak the currants or raisins in water to cover for 1 hour. Quarter the zucchini and cut them into 1-inch pieces. Melt 1 tablespoon of butter in a large skillet over medium-high heat. Add the zucchini, season with salt and pepper, and brown it well. Remove the zucchini to a plate and reduce the heat to medium. Add the remaining tablespoon of butter to the pan and add the shallots, salt, and pepper; toss to coat, and cook until the shallots are golden brown, tossing them often. Add the cinnamon and nutmeg and stir. Add the stock and scrape to deglaze the pan. Cook until the liquid is reduced by half. Add the wine and lemon juice and stir to mix. Bring the wine to a boil, lower the heat, and simmer the shallot and wine mixture for 20 minutes.

Drain the currants or raisins and add them to the shallots with the zucchini; mix well and cook 10 minutes more, stirring often. The vegetables should be well coated with sauce. Add the herb, correct the seasoning, and serve.

VARIATIONS

Top the dish with chopped toasted pine nuts or hazelnuts.
Add saffron to the wine with the vegetables.

∎

ZUCCHINI AND CURRANT COMPOTE may be
Served over eggplant, egg noodles, polenta, grains, rice, browned tofu, fish, eggs, poultry, beef, lamb, liver, or pork

Parsnips with Orange-Basil Dressing

When combined, parsnips and oranges yield a rich, luscious flavor. Pan-frying the parsnips brings out their natural sweetness. Serve this hot or at room temperature as a side dish with a simply prepared piece of fish, poultry, or meat, or serve it with a green salad.

This recipe calls for basil oil, which greatly enhances all that it touches.

∎ ORANGE-BASIL DRESSING

M A K E S   ³/₄   C U P

½ cup orange juice
¼ teaspoon salt
Freshly ground black pepper
2 to 3 tablespoons lemon juice
¼ cup basil oil (see Emerald Oil, page 35) or olive oil mixed with
    1 tablespoon chopped fresh basil

∎ PARSNIPS

S E R V E S   4

1 pound parsnips, peeled and trimmed
1 to 2 tablespoons vegetable or olive oil

To make the dressing, place the orange juice in a small saucepan and bring it to a boil. Lower the heat to a gentle boil and reduce the liquid to 2 tablespoons. Transfer the juice to a bowl and add salt, pepper, and lemon juice. Whisk in the oil. The sauce will be sweet. Set it aside at room temperature to allow the flavors to blend.

Bring a large pot of water to a boil. Cut the parsnips into ¼-inch slices lengthwise and boil them for 8 to 12 minutes, until they are just soft. Gently remove them with a slotted spoon and place them on towels to drain. Heat the oil in a large skillet over medium-high heat. Add the parsnip slices and brown them well on both sides. Transfer the parsnips to plates and season with salt and pepper. Whisk the dressing and spoon it over the parsnips.

∎

ORANGE-BASIL DRESSING may be

> Served on cooked chicken, particularly grilled or pan-fried breasts
> Poured on fennel, artichoke hearts, asparagus, broccoli, or roasted peppers
> Served with any fish or shellfish or on seafood salad with sliced avocado
> Spooned over crab cakes (pages 169–171)
> Used as a dressing for any salad; try it with spinach
> Served with grilled or pan-fried lamb chops, a leg of lamb, or braised shanks

Baked Zucchini and Feta with Dill-Tomato Sauce

These zucchini are delicious when served at room temperature as part of an *antipasto* platter.

SERVES 4

Vegetable or olive oil for the pan
4 small zucchini, trimmed and split in half lengthwise
Salt
Freshly ground black pepper
¹/₃ cup bread crumbs
¹/₃ cup feta cheese, well crumbled
1 clove garlic, minced
¹/₄ cup chopped fresh dill

1 cup Fresh or Winter Tomato Sauce (pages 20–22)

Preheat the oven to 350 degrees F. Lightly grease a baking dish large enough to hold all the zucchini in one layer. Season the zucchini with salt and pepper and place them in the baking dish. In a bowl, combine the bread crumbs, feta cheese, garlic, half the dill, and some black pepper, mixing well with a fork. Top zucchini with this mixture, pressing it down slightly. Cover the dish with foil and bake for 45 minutes. Uncover and bake for another 15 minutes, or until the zucchini is tender. If the top is not browned, broil the zucchini for 1 or 2 minutes.

Just before serving, heat the sauce and add the remaining dill. Correct the seasoning and spoon the sauce over the zucchini.

■

DILL-TOMATO SAUCE may be
    Served with shrimp, chicken, or lamb
    Served on eggs, especially on omlettes
    Served over cooked cauliflower or broccoli
    Tossed with a mixture of pasta and wilted spinach
    Served over slices of vegetable terrine, timbale, or quiche

A Bagna Cauda Dipping Sauce for a Vegetable Platter

This sauce, from the Val d'Aosta region in northern Italy, is made of olive oil, butter, garlic, and anchovies. There it is served with raw and cooked vegetables. This recipe, when served with a loaf of crusty Italian bread, makes a wonderful appetizer, or it can stand alone as a great lunch.

■ *VEGETABLE PLATTER*

SERVES 6

6 large outer leaves of cabbage
1 head broccoli, divided into florets

2 bulbs fennel, halved
2 red peppers, raw or roasted (page 46)
6 stalks celery, trimmed
6 carrots, trimmed and peeled

▪ BAGNA CAUDA

MAKES ABOUT 1 CUP

1 cup olive oil
2 tablespoons unsalted butter
8 anchovy fillets packed in olive oil, minced
4 cloves garlic, minced
Freshly ground black pepper

Bring a large pot of water to a boil. Add the cabbage leaves and cook them for 2 or 3 minutes. Drain them, rinse under cold water, drain again, dry, and refrigerate the cabbage.

Steam the broccoli for 3 minutes. Transfer it to a bowl and refrigerate to chill.

Cut the fennel lengthwise through the core into thin wedges. Cut the peppers into strips. Cut the celery and carrots into 3-inch julienne strips. Keep all the vegetables separate.

To make the sauce, place the oil, butter, anchovies, and garlic in a saucepan and heat over medium heat until the mixture is well warmed, stirring often. Add pepper and keep the sauce warm.

Roll the cabbage leaves into cigars and place 1 on each of 6 plates. Arrange all the vegetables on the plates, dividing them evenly. Pour the warm dipping sauce, stirred to distribute the anchovy and garlic, into small ramekins or bowls, 1 for each person, and serve with the vegetables.

▪

BAGNA CAUDA may be
Served with grilled seafood, poultry, lamb, veal, or beef
Tossed into pasta, particularly spaghetti or *linguine*; add freshly chopped parsley
Tossed into potatoes, or rice or other grains
Spooned over a stir-fry of vegetables

Corn on the Cob with Pesto

The *pesto* is used here in place of butter on the corn. Serve this with grilled chicken, sliced tomato salad, and blueberry muffins.

SERVES 6 TO 8

1 recipe Pesto *(pages 44–45)*
6 to 12 ears corn *(1 or 2 per person)*

Have the *pesto* made and ready at room temperature.

Bring a large pot of water to a boil. Add the corn and bring the water back to a boil. Once the water boils again, cook the corn for between 1 and 3 minutes, depending on the size of the kernels. Drain cobs and place them on a platter. Pass the *pesto* instead of butter.

VARIATIONS

Instead of *pesto,* you might like to spread a compound butter (pages 41–43) on the cob. I also like my corn brushed with a vinaigrette (pages 28–32).

PESTO is a versatile sauce. For suggestions, see the master recipe (pages 44–45) and the index.

 # Cayenne Onion Rings with Tempura Dipping Sauce

Onion rings are one of my weaknesses, and these have satisfied me on many occasions. It is not customary to serve onion rings with a sauce, but they are perfect for a classic *tempura* dip.

■ TEMPURA DIPPING SAUCE

M A K E S   A B O U T   ³/₄   C U P

¼ cup dashi *or chicken stock (page 7)*
2 tablespoons mirin *or sherry*
2 tablespoons soy sauce
⅓ cup *finely grated daikon or other radish*
1 teaspoon *minced fresh ginger*
Half a hot red pepper, seeded and minced

■ ONION RINGS

S E R V E S   4

2 Spanish (mild) onions
1 cup flour
½ teaspoon salt
¼ teaspoon baking soda
1 large egg
1¼ cups buttermilk
2 tablespoons vegetable oil and additional oil for frying
½ teaspoon cayenne pepper
Freshly ground black pepper

Make the sauce by combining all the ingredients in a small bowl and mixing them. Divide the sauce among 4 small bowls, custard cups, or ramekins. Keep the sauce at room temperature if you will be using it soon, or refrigerate it until you are ready to serve.

To prepare the onions, cut them into ⅓-inch-thick slices and separate the slices into rings. Soak the rings in cold water to cover for 1 hour. Drain and pat the onion dry.

Mix the flour, salt, and baking soda in a large bowl. Make a well and add the egg, buttermilk, and 2 tablespoons of the oil. Whisk the flour into the liquid ingredients, forming a batter. Add the cayenne and black pepper and set the batter aside.

Set the oven at low heat. In a large skillet heat 1 or 2 inches of oil to 360 degrees F. over medium-high heat. If you do not have a thermometer, take a small onion, coat it with batter, and dip it into the oil. When the temperature is right, the onion should sizzle in a lively manner. Place a quarter of the onions in the batter, stirring gently to coat them. With tongs or a long fork, lift the rings one at a time from the batter, draining the excess back into the bowl. Place the onions in the oil and fry them, turning once, until they are golden (about 5 minutes). Transfer the rings to paper towels to drain. Keep them warm in the oven with the door ajar. Coat, fry, and drain the remaining onions. Sprinkle the onion rings with salt and pepper and serve them with the dipping sauce.

▢ **NOTE**
If you prefer crispier onion rings, omit the egg and dust the rings lightly with flour before dipping them into the batter.

VARIATIONS

Coat other vegetables, such as summer squash, carrots, broccoli, eggplant, pumpkin or winter squash, turnip, rutabaga, cauliflower, or squash blossoms with this batter, fry them, and serve with the dipping sauce.

▪

TEMPURA DIPPING SAUCE may be
Served with savory vegetable fritters, such as fennel or corn
Spooned over crab cakes (pages 169–171)
Served over grilled fish (especially shrimp), poultry, pork, or beef (try it with shish kebab)
Used for other fried foods, such as fish, chicken, or potatoes
Used for raw carrots, celery, broccoli, cauliflower, or snow peas
Mixed with dumplings, rice, or noodle dishes
Used as a marinade for beef, pork, poultry, or fish
Served with *sushi* or *sashimi*

 Ginger Beets

This must be an unusual dish. Four years ago I took it to a baby shower for a friend. Recently, I was with my son at a birthday party for the same baby. As introductions were being made, a woman exclaimed,

"The beets! I remember those beets!" Many thanks to my friend and colleague Richard Kzirian for this inspirational dish.

SERVES 4

8 medium beets

▌ GINGER CREAM

MAKES ABOUT ⅔ CUP

1 ounce fresh ginger, a piece about 2½ inches long and 1½ inches wide
1 cup heavy cream
Salt
Freshly ground black pepper (optional)

Preheat the oven to 350 degrees F.

Cut the greens off the beets (save for another use) leaving 2 inches of stem. Scrub the beets, prick the skin in a couple of places, and bake them on the oven rack for an hour or until the vegetables are tender when pierced with the tip of a knife. Cool them until you are able to handle, and then peel the beets and cut them into wedges. Place them in a bowl, cover, and refrigerate until you are ready to use them.

While the beets cook, peel and chop the ginger. Combine the cream and ginger in a saucepan, bring the mixture to a boil, lower the heat to a simmer, and reduce the cream until ⅔ cup is left. Strain and cool. The cream may be refrigerated for up to 2 days.

When you are ready to serve, place the beet wedges and cream in a saucepan. Reheat together over low heat and season with salt and pepper to taste. The beets will add a deep shade of pink to the cream sauce.

--- **VARIATION** ---

Add ½ cup orange juice and two thin strips of orange zest to the cream together with the ginger and reduce to ⅔ cup liquid.

▌

GINGER CREAM may be
    Served with carrots, sweet potatoes, baked winter squashes, parsnips, rice, poultry, and fish—it goes particularly well with these foods
    Served over fruit tarts, poached fruit, steamed puddings, or cakes

Spring Roast: Onions and Peas with Curry Butter

In this recipe, the sweetness of spring vegetables is combined with the heat of curry. The curry butter can be made well ahead of time and should be brought to room temperature before serving. I have used Vidalia onions here; combinations of Vidalia and red onions or of Spanish and red onions work as well and the colors are beautiful. There will be extra compound butter, so you may freeze it for another meal.

SERVES 4

Unsalted butter for the dish
4 Vidalia onions, weighing between ½ and ¾ pound each
Salt
Freshly ground black pepper

▎CURRY BUTTER

MAKES ½ CUP

½ cup unsalted butter, softened
1½ teaspoons curry powder
2 tablespoons scissored fresh chives
⅛ teaspoon cayenne pepper, or to taste; about 2 pinches

1 pound fresh peas in the shell

Preheat the oven to 350 degrees F. Lightly butter a baking dish that will hold the onions snugly.

Peel the onions, leaving the root intact, and place them on a board, root-side down. Cut through each onion from the top with 4 crosswise cuts making wedges, being careful not to cut through the root. When cooked, the onions will fall into sections. Place the onions (root-side down) in a pot that will hold them snugly. Cover the onions with cold water and bring them to a boil. Lower the heat and simmer for 5 minutes. Carefully remove each onion with a slotted spoon, place them in the prepared dish, and season with salt and pepper. Do not bother to drain off the small quantity of water that will be in the dish. Cover the dish with foil and bake the onions for 45 minutes. Uncover the onions and continue baking them for between 30 and 45 minutes longer, basting them occasionally, until they are tender when pierced with a knife. Keep the onions warm in the oven until you are ready to serve.

While the onions bake, make the curry butter. Heat 1 tablespoon of the butter in a small skillet. Add the curry powder, cook it for 1 minute, remove it to a bowl, scraping the skillet well, and allow it to cool. Then add the remaining butter, the chives, cayenne, salt, and pepper and mix well. Set the butter aside to give the flavors time to blend.

Just before serving time, shuck the peas. Bring a small pot of water to a boil. Add salt and peas and blanch them for 2 minutes. Drain the peas and place them in a bowl. Toss the peas with a bit of the curry butter.

To serve, transfer the onions to 4 plates. If you are using a combination of red and white onions, put some of each color on each plate. Dot the onions with the curry butter so that it will melt and spoon the peas over the top. Pour over the onions any cooking juices that have accumulated in the baking dish and serve.

VARIATION

These onions may be served cold on a bed of Boston lettuce with cold, blanched peas and a curry-tomato vinaigrette.

■

CURRY BUTTER may be

    Served on corn on the cob or baked tomato halves
    Served over lamb chops or chicken breast
    Served on crab cakes, grilled shrimp, or other shellfish
    Mixed with rice or noodle dishes
    Spooned into a baked white or sweet potato

▼ *Cauliflower with Red Pepper Butter*

Many people seem to be passionate about cauliflower: they either love it or hate it. The complaint I hear most often is that it is so bland and boring. Together, cauliflower and roasted red peppers offer an unusual combination of flavors and might go a long way to change such sentiments. There will be extra compound butter, so freeze any that is unused for another meal.

∎ RED PEPPER BUTTER

MAKES   ABOUT   ³/₄ TO 1 CUP

1 large red pepper, roasted and peeled (page 46)
½ cup unsalted butter, softened
Salt
Freshly ground black pepper

SERVES   6

1 head cauliflower, trimmed into florets

Place the peppers in a food processor or blender and process until they are chopped fine. Add the butter and process until the mixture is smooth. (If you are using a blender to chop the peppers, transfer them to a bowl before adding the butter.) There will be some flecks of pepper still visible and the butter will turn red. Season it to taste and set it aside to allow the flavors to blend. (If you are using it that day, keep the butter at room temperature, otherwise keep it refrigerated. If you are planning to use it more than a day or two later, wrap it tightly in plastic and freeze it.)

To serve, steam the cauliflower to the desired texture and transfer it to a bowl. Season it with salt and pepper and toss it. Add some Red Pepper Butter and toss the cauliflower so that it is completely coated. Serve hot.

∎

RED PEPPER BUTTER is very versatile and may be
> Served with baked potato or potato *gnocchi*, sautéed savoy cabbage, braised or sautéed fennel, wilted spinach, grilled jumbo shrimp, salmon fillet or steaks, roast lamb, pan-fried chicken breasts, or veal *scaloppine*
>
> Spread on corn on the cob; add a dash of cayenne pepper or some Tabasco sauce to the butter before using it

Braised Leeks in a Tarragon Coat

The sauce in this dish is really a variation on a vinaigrette made with the braising juices reduced to a glaze. This is a wonderful technique for making sauces for stewed or pan-fried meats or poultry. A variation of this dish was created by my friend and teacher Madeleine Kamman and was served at her Massachusetts restaurant, Chez La Mère Madeleine.

Serve this dish alone as an appetizer or with steaks, roasted meats and poultry, or baked fish.

▮ BRAISED LEEKS

S E R V E S   4

8 large or 12 medium leeks
1 teaspoon unsalted butter
2 cups chicken stock (page 7)
2 cloves garlic, crushed
1 teaspoon fresh thyme leaves or 1/4 teaspoon dried thyme

▮ TARRAGON DRESSING

M A K E S   A B O U T   1   C U P

2 tablespoons lemon juice
1 tablespoon water
1 teaspoon Dijon-style mustard
2 tablespoons chopped fresh tarragon or 1 teaspoon dried tarragon
1/4 cup vegetable oil
1/2 cup olive oil
Salt
Freshly ground black pepper

Preheat the oven to 325 degrees F. Trim the roots from the leeks and cut off the dark green tops (save for stock). Slice the leeks in half starting at the green end and stopping about 1/2 inch before the root end so that the leek stays in one piece. Wash the leeks thoroughly under running cold water to remove any grit and drain them. Butter a baking dish that is just large enough to hold the leeks in 1 layer and arrange the leeks in it. Pour the stock over the leeks and add the garlic and thyme. Cover the dish with foil and bake for 30 minutes. Gently turn the leeks over and bake for another 15 to 30 minutes (depending on their size) until they are soft and offer no resistance when pierced with a skewer or knife.

When they are done, remove the leeks to a platter and keep them warm. Place the juices with the garlic and thyme in a saucepan and bring them to a boil. Reduce the liquid by about 3/4 or until it is thick and glazed. Add the lemon juice and water and transfer the mixture to a blender or a bowl. Add the mustard and tarragon and blend or whisk until smooth. Slowly add the oils and blend to homogenize.

Season the dressing with salt and pepper to taste. Reduced stock is quite salty, so taste it before seasoning. Pour the dressing over the leeks and serve the dish warm.

VARIATIONS

Zucchini, fennel, cabbage, or onions all braise well and may be used in this recipe instead of the leeks.
Replace the tarragon in the dressing with thyme.

TARRAGON DRESSING may be
Served with poultry, fish, lamb, veal, or beef
Served on egg noodles, potatoes, or rice

Asparagus with Green Peppercorn Sauce

This sauce is a vinaigrette with a little mayonnaise added for creaminess. Sweet red pepper strips are included to contrast with the hot green peppercorns. Make the dressing a day ahead to allow the flavors to blend.

The asparagus can be served warm as a side dish for chicken, fish, or meat, or served cold as a salad.

▪ GREEN PEPPERCORN SAUCE

MAKES   ABOUT   1   CUP

1 red pepper, roasted and peeled (page 46)
2 tablespoons Basic Mayonnaise (pages 39–41)
2 tablespoons red wine vinegar
1/4 cup olive oil
1 tablespoon drained green peppercorns, rinsed and drained again
Salt
Freshly ground black pepper to taste

SERVES   6

1½ pounds asparagus

Cut the roasted red pepper crosswise into ¼-inch strips and set them aside.

Place the mayonnaise in a bowl and whisk in the vinegar until the mixture is smooth. Slowly pour in the oil in a stream, whisking well. Mix in the peppercorns and strips of red pepper. Cover the sauce and refrigerate it overnight. Taste for seasoning and add salt and pepper if you like.

Snap off the ends of the asparagus and steam the spears until they are tender, but not mushy. Arrange the asparagus on plates and spoon the sauce over them.

▪

GREEN PEPPERCORN SAUCE may be
Served on other steamed vegetables or a mixture of vegetables; green beans, wedges of red potato, carrots, broccoli, cauliflower, or any combination of those make a colorful salad or side dish
Spooned over boneless chicken breasts, either poached or browned
Spooned on poached brisket or grilled steak
Served with cold roasted leg of lamb
Served with eggs, particularly hard-cooked
Used on fish of all types

Vegetable Stir-Fry with Lemon Zest and Black Olives

Although summer squashes and carrots are available year-round, they are at their peak during the spring and summer months. The black olives in the butter make this a beautifully colored dish.

▮ LEMON AND BLACK OLIVE BUTTER

MAKES ABOUT ⅓ CUP

4 tablespoons unsalted butter, softened
20 brine-cured black olives, pitted and chopped
2 teaspoons grated lemon zest
¼ teaspoon salt
Freshly ground black pepper

▮ VEGETABLE STIR-FRY

SERVES 6 TO 8

4 carrots, peeled and cut in half lengthwise
3 small zucchini, trimmed
3 small yellow summer squash, trimmed
Vegetable or olive oil

Place the butter in a small bowl, cream until it is smooth, and add the olives, lemon zest, salt, and pepper. Set the butter aside at room temperature to allow the flavors to blend.

Cut the carrot halves on the diagonal into half-moon slices ¼-inch thick. Bring a pot of water to a boil. Add salt and the carrots and cook them for 5 minutes. Drain the carrots and set them aside.

Cut the zucchini and squash in quarters lengthwise. Cut them on the diagonal into ¼-inch-thick slices.

Heat the oil in a skillet over high heat and add the squashes. Season with salt and pepper and toss them well. Cook until they are slightly soft, but still crisp, about 2 or 3 minutes. Add the carrots and cook for

1 or 2 minutes more. Remove the vegetables to a bowl and toss them with the flavored butter until they are well coated. Correct the seasoning and serve.

──────── VARIATIONS ────────

In the spring add baby peas and tiny red radishes to this dish.
Try substituting minced shallots for the olives or chopped garlic and parsley for the lemon zest.

■

LEMON AND BLACK OLIVE BUTTER may be
>   Used on poultry, seafood, lamb, egg pasta, potatoes, rice, grains, eggs, spinach, or green beens
>   Spread on toast and topped with poached eggs

 ## *Steamed Vegetables in Harissa Dressing*

Harissa is a very hot Moroccan chili pepper paste sold in tubes. It can also be made from scratch. This dish can be served hot as a vegetable or cold as a salad. Change the vegetables for this dressing to match the seasons.

■ *HARISSA DRESSING*

MAKES ABOUT ³/₄ CUP

¼ cup lime juice
1 to 2 teaspoons Harissa
½ teaspoon salt
½ teaspoon paprika
½ cup olive oil

▎ STEAMED VEGETABLES

SERVES 6 TO 8

1 smallish head cauliflower
4 carrots
3 purple-topped turnips

For the sauce, whisk the lime juice, 1 teaspoon of the Harissa, salt, and paprika in a small bowl. Slowly pour in the oil, whisking. Set the dressing aside and taste it for spiciness after it has rested.

Cut the cauliflower into florets. Peel and cut the carrots in half lengthwise, then into 1/2-inch slices on the diagonal. Peel the turnips, cut them in half, slice in 1/4-inch-thick slices, and cut the slices into wedges. Steam the vegetables separately and place them in a large bowl as they are finished. Remove the cauliflower and carrots when they are tender, but still a bit crisp. Steam the turnips until they are just tender. Sprinkle the vegetables with salt and pepper and toss them gently.

Whisk and taste the dressing, adding more Harissa if you prefer a spicier sauce, and pour it over the vegetables. Toss them gently and serve.

▪

HARISSA DRESSING may be
Used on beef, lamb, chicken, slices of turkey, all kinds of seafood, or a mixture of fish and shellfish
Served on hard-cooked eggs for lunch with olives and crusty bread
Used as a marinade
Served with sweet potatoes

Cider-Glazed Apple Wedges

Rosemary and apple (or pear) is one of my favorite combinations. The pinelike aromatic herb balances the sweetness of the fruit for a delicious savory dish. I have made this dish with reduced cider, thereby cutting the total preparation time.

This dish is delicious served alongside poultry, duck, goose, pheasant, pork, ham, sausage, veal, game, or lamb. The recipe can be easily doubled.

S E R V E S   4

4 Granny Smith apples, quartered, cored, and peeled
2 tablespoons unsalted butter
1 tablespoon chopped fresh rosemary
Pinch sugar
2 tablespoons cider vinegar
1/4 cup reduced apple cider (page 15)
Salt
Freshly ground black pepper

Cut each apple quarter into 3 wedges.

Melt the butter in a medium sauté pan over medium-high heat. Add the apples and toss to coat them with butter. Sauté the apples for 5 minutes, tossing frequently. Lower the heat to medium, add the rosemary and sugar, and continue cooking until the apples begin to soften and caramelize to a deep brown, about another 5 or 10 minutes. Raise the heat to high, add the vinegar and let it evaporate. Then add the cider. Stir gently to coat the apple wedges with the glaze and remove them from the heat. Season with salt and pepper and serve.

VARIATION

Make this dish with 1 pound of carrots cut in julienne sticks 3 inches long. Change the herb from rosemary to chives and add them just before serving. Replace the vinegar with cognac or Calvados for a change.

Cook the carrots, covered, over low heat for about 15 to 20 minutes. Stir occasionally. Serves 4.

 # *Black-Speckled Green Beans*

The speckles in this dish come from the olives in the *tapenade*. The beans may be blanched ahead of time and refrigerated. Reheat them in a dry skillet over medium-low heat when you are ready. Serve these beans as a side dish or as a sauce for pasta.

S E R V E S   4

1 pound green beans, trimmed
⅓ cup Tapenade (page 44), at room temperature
Freshly ground black pepper

Blanch the beans in boiling salted water until they are tender yet crisp. Drain and place them in a bowl. Add the *tapenade,* toss the beans to coat them evenly with the mixture, and serve.

––––––––––––––––––––––– **VARIATION** –––––––––––––––––––––––

To make a richer sauce, and mellow the flavor somewhat, add 4 tablespoons softened butter to the *tapenade* before tossing it with the beans. (Because it is richer, you may want to use a smaller portion of the *tapenade*-butter mixture.)

TAPENADE is delicious with
Many other vegetables or starches, particularly cauliflower, artichokes, grilled eggplant, rice, potatoes, or baked tomatoes.
Other uses for *tapenade* are suggested on pages 44, 140, and 243.

Fennel and Red Pepper Sauté

In this recipe, the orange juice is reduced with the vegetables and orange zest into a slightly bitter sauce for the sweet vegetables. Serve with seafood, lamb, or poultry, and any rice dish.

SERVES 4

3 tablespoons olive oil
2 large fennel bulbs, halved, cored, and thinly sliced (crosswise)
Salt
Freshly ground black pepper
3 large red bell peppers, cored, seeded, and cut into thin strips
1 teaspoon grated orange zest
3/4 cup orange juice
1 tablespoon lemon juice

Heat the olive oil in a large sauté pan over medium-high heat. Add the fennel, salt, and pepper, and toss to coat it with oil. Sauté the fennel for 3 minutes. Add the red pepper and sauté for another 3 to 5 minutes or until tender yet still crisp. Add the orange zest, orange juice, and lemon juice, bring to a boil, and reduce the juice until it coats the vegetables. Correct the seasoning and serve.

--- **VARIATION** ---

Other vegetables, such as carrots, asparagus, squashes, onions, leeks, or greens, may be cooked the same way.

Chapter 4

GRAINS,
PASTAS,
and
POTATOES

*T*HE MATERIAL COMMON TO NOODLES, GRAIN, POTATOES, and rice is starch. Starches are wonderfully compliant and the qualities of each are different. Their flavors are quiet enough to take both strong and mild sauces, yet they are best when not smothered with an abundance of sauce. Most starches blend well with butter, cream, tomato, or vinaigrette sauces, but here I have also included a few new ideas.

When it comes to pasta, anything goes, although I prefer the classic dishes like *Rigatoni all'Amatriciana* (page 135). If the pasta is made with eggs, I like a delicate, more refined sauce; if it is an eggless, macaroni type, I like a heartier sauce.

Grains have distinct nutty tastes and textures that blend well with fruit, nut, and cheese sauces. Cracked Wheat with Grape Sauce (pages 132–133) is a unique example, blending homemade grape juice with nuts and dried fruit and used to sauce the grain.

Potatoes take kindly to all sorts of sauces: tomato, wine or stock reductions, salsas, vegetable or fruit purées, or thin oriental-style sauces. For a change from gravy, try the Mashed Potatoes with Garlic Sauce (pages 154–155). The cooked garlic adds sweetness and the stock adds a savory balance to the dish.

Rice is another starch that is seldom served with unusual sauces. I have included a recipe for braised rice, known as pilaf, but all of the sauces in this chapter may be served on rice.

Baked Polenta with Sage Cream

Polenta is cornmeal pudding—comfort food at its best. After it has cooked and set, it can be cut into slices and served as is with sauce, or fried or baked and topped with a sauce.

You can make the polenta with cornmeal, or for a smoother, finer texture, make it with half cornmeal and half corn flour (finely ground cornmeal, not cornstarch). For crispness, top this dish with cooked, crumbled *pancetta* or bacon. Serve with grilled quail or braised meats and sautéed greens with garlic.

▪ *BAKED POLENTA*

SERVES 6

1 cup cornmeal or ½ cup cornmeal and ½ cup corn flour
3 cups chicken stock (page 7); 1 cold, 2 boiling
½ teaspoon salt
Freshly ground black pepper
½ teaspoon ground nutmeg
4 tablespoons unsalted butter
½ tablespoon olive oil
2 large eggs, beaten
½ cup grated Parmesan cheese

▪ *SAGE CREAM*

MAKES ABOUT 1 CUP

1½ recipes reduced cream (pages 13–14) cooked with ⅓ cup coarsely
   torn fresh sage leaves; about 1 cup finished cream
Salt
Freshly ground black pepper
Nutmeg
2 tablespoons chopped fresh sage

Make the polenta. Preheat the oven to 400 degrees F. Place the cornmeal in a large bowl, add the cold stock, and mix well. Pour the boiling chicken stock over the mixture, whisking until it is smooth. (This technique prevents lumps from forming.) Transfer the mixture to a heavy pan. Add salt, pepper, and nutmeg. Over medium heat slowly bring the polenta to a boil, whisking it. When it is boiling, lower the heat and cook it, stirring all the while, until it is thick enough so that your spoon will stand up in the mixture without falling over. (To make the polenta deep enough, tilt the pan and scrape all the polenta into the corner. Then stand the spoon up in the middle of the mixture.) When it is thickened, transfer the polenta to a bowl.

Add the butter and stir it in as it melts. Set the mixture aside to cool slightly. Oil an oblong or round baking dish that will hold between 4 and 6 cups. Add the beaten eggs to the polenta, mixing constantly until they are incorporated. Correct the seasoning and pour half of the polenta into the dish. Sprinkle with half of the cheese. Spread the remaining polenta in the dish and top with the remaining cheese. Bake the polenta until it is bubbly and the top is golden brown; about 20 to 30 minutes.

While the polenta bakes, make the sauce. Reduce the cream with the torn sage leaves and strain it. Season with salt, pepper, and nutmeg. Add the fresh chopped sage and set the sauce aside.

When the polenta is cooked, remove it from the oven and let it settle for between 10 and 15 minutes before serving. Reheat the sauce. Spoon the polenta or cut it into pieces, place it on plates, and top with the sauce.

VARIATIONS

Add a layer of sautéed garlic and parsley with the cheese in the middle of the polenta before baking it.

Baked polenta may be served with a plain tomato sauce or one that has been flavored with sage, a meat *ragù* (pages 146–147), *Amatriciana* sauce (page 135). Also good are cream sauces with *pesto,* melted cheese (Italian Fontina or Gorgonzola) or tomato sauce (pages 18–22). See also Mushrooms with *Ravigote* Cream Sauce (page 100), Dark Mushroom Sauce (pages 285–286), Mushroom Cardamom Cream Sauce (pages 177–178), and gravy from roasted or braised meats (pages 10–11).

Replace the sage in the sauce with ½ cup Parmesan cheese and serve it over lima, fava, broad, or pole beans. Serve over Brussels sprouts, winter squash purée, artichokes, asparagus, mushrooms, zucchini, spinach, pasta, potatoes, rice, potato or semolina *gnocchi*, or polenta. Spoon it over a purée of beans, such as lima, *cannellini*, or navy.

Change the herb in this sauce, using basil, oregano, rosemary or flat-leaf (Italian) parsley.

Semolina Gnocchi (Gnocchi alla Romana) Substitute 1 cup semolina (which is made from wheat) for the cornmeal. Cook it, according to the directions given on pages 128–129 for preparing polenta, until it is thick enough to support a spoon standing upright. Spread the semolina in a ½-inch layer in an oiled pan with sides. Let it cool and set. Butter a baking dish. Using a 2-inch biscuit cutter, cut out circles to make *gnocchi* and overlap them in the dish. Dot with a little butter and sprinkle with cheese. Bake at 400 degrees F. until a golden brown crust has formed and it's bubbly, between 15 and 20 minutes. Serve with sage cream or any of the sauces mentioned under the variations for baked polenta.

∎

SAGE CREAM may be

Served over chicken, turkey, veal, or seafood

Used over potatoes, egg pasta, lentils, rice, or other grains

Tossed with cooked artichoke hearts and fresh peas

Used for making creamed mushrooms to be served on a crouton, on pasta (particularly buckwheat), or in pastry

❦ *Brown Rice Pilaf with Spice Butter*

Because brown rice has a strong nutty flavor, it blends nicely with a variety of spices. However, you can make this dish with white rice, if you prefer. (Adjust the cooking time accordingly.)

Make the compound butter several hours in advance to allow the flavors to blend. If you are using canned chicken stock, omit the salt from the compound butter and taste the final dish for seasoning before serving.

This dish goes well with all meats, poultry, and salmon.

▮ *SPICE BUTTER*

MAKES ABOUT ³/₄ CUP

3 large shallots
10 tablespoons unsalted butter, softened
1 teaspoon ground cinnamon
Pinch ground cloves
¼ teaspoon salt
Freshly ground black pepper

▮ *RICE PILAF*

SERVES 6 TO 8

1½ cups brown rice
2¾ cups chicken stock, preferably homemade (page 7), or half stock and
    half water
1 small piece stick cinnamon about 1-inch long

Peel and chop the shallots very fine and squeeze them in a dish towel to remove the bitter juices. In a small bowl, combine the shallots, 8 tablespoons of the butter, cinnamon, cloves, salt, and pepper. Mix well to blend completely and set aside, covered.

Melt the remaining 2 tablespoons of butter in a heavy saucepan and add the rice, tossing it well to coat it with butter. Cook the grains for a few minutes, tossing, until the rice is hot to the touch. Add the stock, or mixture of stock and water, and the cinnamon stick and bring the liquid to a boil. Lower the heat to simmer and cover the pan. Cook until all the liquid has been absorbed and the rice is tender; between 35 and 45 minutes. Discard the cinnamon stick and add the spice butter to taste; store any extra butter. Toss the rice well with a fork to coat it with butter. Correct the seasoning and serve hot.

▮

SPICE BUTTER may be
    Served on poultry, lamb, veal, pasta, and other grains

Cracked Wheat with Grape Sauce

In the Middle Ages—since antiquity for that matter—juice made from unripened grapes, called *verjus*, was as common a condiment as vinegar is today. Acid flavors were an integral part of early cooking. The inspiration for this dish began with *verjus*. I wanted to make a sauce for cracked wheat that was not a vinaigrette. So I used grape juice, particularly because grapes and apricots (or peaches)—the garnish in this dish—are a complementary pair.

This dish is simple to make, practically fat-free, and goes well with all meats, poultry, or seafood. Serve at room temperature or chilled.

▌ CRACKED WHEAT

SERVES 4

1 cup cracked wheat
1 tablespoon olive oil or Fennel Oil (page 36)
12 dried apricots or their equivalent in dried peaches, cut in strips
1 teaspoon anise seed
1 cup hot water

▌ GRAPE SAUCE AND GARNISH

MAKES ABOUT ¹/₂ TO ³/₄ CUP

1 cup seedless green grapes, as unripe as possible
1 tablespoon lemon juice
1 large clove garlic, sliced
¹/₄ teaspoon salt
Freshly ground black pepper
¹/₂ cup toasted pistachio nuts (page 54), chopped

Place the cracked wheat in a bowl and add the oil, tossing well to coat the grains. Add the apricots, ¹/₂ teaspoon of the anise seed, and the hot water. Stir the mixture and soak the grains, covered, for 1 hour.

Make the sauce while the wheat soaks. Place the grapes, lemon juice, garlic, the remaining 1/2 teaspoon of anise seed, salt, and pepper in a blender or food processor and blend until the mixture is completely smooth. Transfer it to a bowl.

When the cracked wheat has absorbed all the water and is tender, add the sauce and the pistachios and toss well with a fork. Serve at room temperature or chilled.

■

GRAPE SAUCE may be
> Served over sliced tomatoes
> Tossed with a chicken salad
> Served on grilled seafood or chicken breasts
> Used as a marinade for cooked seafood or chicken
> Served on other grains, rice, or lentils

 ## Lentils with Feta Cream Sauce

Serve this hot dish with whole wheat pita bread and sliced apples.

■ LENTILS

SERVES 4

1/2 pound lentils
1 bay leaf
1 teaspoon fresh thyme leaves or 1/2 teaspoon dried thyme
1/2 teaspoon black peppercorns

■ FETA CREAM SAUCE AND GARNISH

MAKES 1 CUP

3/4 cup heavy cream
1 teaspoon dried oregano
4 ounces feta cheese, crumbled

2 tablespoons chopped fresh dill
Freshly ground black pepper
Salt
¾ cup toasted walnuts (page 54), chopped

Wash and pick over the lentils, place them in a saucepan, and cover them with water. Add the bay leaf and thyme. Place the peppercorns in a cheesecloth bag or a tea strainer with a lid and add that to the pot. Bring the water to a boil, lower the heat, and boil gently for 20 minutes or until the lentils are tender but not mushy.

While the lentils cook, make the sauce. Heat the cream and oregano in a small saucepan. Add the feta and melt it, whisking until the mixture is smooth. Stir in the dill, season with pepper, and remove from the heat.

When the lentils are cooked, remove the peppercorns and drain off the liquid. Discard the bay leaf and place the lentils in a bowl. Add the warm sauce and stir the lentils well to coat them. Correct the seasoning, top with nuts, and serve.

VARIATIONS

This is a versatile technique for making sauce. For other grains, pastas, vegetables, meats, or poultry, vary the cheese and herbs:

Use Camembert and cardamom in place of the feta, oregano, and dill and toss with cooked cracked wheat.

Use goat cheese for lentils, *soba* (buckwheat) noodles, cracked wheat, or rices.

Melt Italian Fontina and use the sauce for pasta (this makes a very rich macaroni and cheese), polenta, fresh corn pancakes, veal *scaloppine*, chicken breasts, cauliflower, or broccoli. Toasted walnuts would go well with any of the cheeses, but you might like to use different nuts.

Replace half of the cream with Fresh Tomato Sauce (pages 19–20).

FETA CREAM SAUCE may be

Tossed with grilled shrimp to be eaten alone or as a topping for pasta

Spooned over poultry

Served with a baked potato

Rigatoni all'Amatriciana

This spicy dish comes from the Italian town of Amatrice in the Lazio region (the area surrounding Rome) and is made with red pepper and *pancetta* (Italian unsmoked bacon). Similar dishes appear in other regions of Italy. It is traditionally made with *bucatini*, long hollow tubes resembling fat spaghetti. I've used *rigatoni* because it is more readily available and sturdy enough for this hearty sauce. Try it with any other short, tubular type of pasta such as *penne*, or with *bucatini* (if available). *Pecorino Romano* is made of sheep's milk and is available in Italian markets, gourmet shops, and some supermarkets.

SERVES 4

12 slices pancetta
Salt
½ pound rigatoni
¾ cup Fresh or Winter Tomato Sauce (pages 20–22)
1 dried hot red pepper, preferably Italian, minced, or
     1 teaspoon red pepper flakes
¼ to ½ cup pecorino Romano *cheese*

Cook the *pancetta* in a large skillet over medium heat until it is golden and crisp. Drain it on paper towels, crumble it, and set it aside.

Bring a large pot of water to a boil. Add salt and the *rigatoni* and cook the pasta, stirring often, until it is tender; between 8 and 10 minutes.

While the pasta cooks, heat the tomato sauce and add the hot pepper.

When the *rigatoni* is cooked, drain it and place it in a bowl. Add the hot sauce and the *pancetta*. Toss the mixture together well and serve. Pass the cheese separately.

∎

AMATRICIANA SAUCE may be
     Served over poached fish fillets, grilled shellfish, or steamed mussels or clams
     Spooned over chicken, veal, beef, lamb, or pork
     Used as a topping for baked polenta, semolina, or potato *gnocchi*

Tagliatelle with Tuna Sauce and Garnishes

The flavor of this sauce is similar to that of *vitello tonnato,* the classic Italian veal dish. I've added a mixture of crunchy garnishes to top the pasta. This dish, like *vitello tonnato,* may be served cold as a salad.

▮ TUNA SAUCE

MAKES ABOUT 1 1/4 CUPS

5 tablespoons olive oil
6 to 7 ounces fresh tuna
1/4 cup lemon juice
1/2 teaspoon salt
Freshly ground black pepper

▮ PASTA

SERVES 4

8 ounces tagliatelle *(1/4-inch-wedge egg pasta)*
1 tablespoon olive oil

▮ GARNISHES

1/2 cup diced celery
1/4 cup drained and rinsed capers
1/4 cup pitted black olives, preferably Greek
3 tablespoons chopped fresh basil

To make the sauce, heat 1 tablespoon of the olive oil in a small skillet over medium heat. Add the tuna and cook it for between 5 and 7 minutes on each side, until it is no longer pink. Remove the fish to a plate, skin it, and place it in the food processor or blender. Add the remaining 4 tablespoons of the olive oil, the lemon juice, salt, and pepper, and purée the mixture until it is smooth. Transfer it to a bowl and set it aside.

Bring a large pot of water to a boil. Add salt and the *tagliatelle* and cook the pasta for between 7 and 8 minutes, stirring often, until it is tender.

While the pasta cooks, mix the celery, capers, olives, and basil in a bowl and set aside.

When the pasta is tender, drain it and place it in a bowl. Toss it with the 1 tablespoon of olive oil and some pepper. Add the reserved tuna sauce and toss the pasta well to coat it. Sprinkle the top with the garnishes in an even layer (do not mix them in) and serve.

∎

TUNA SAUCE, and the garnishes, may be

Served on veal *scaloppine* or chicken breasts, hot or cold, or with white beans

Tossed with cooked baby lima beans, fava beans, broad beans, or green snap beans

Egg Noodles with Hazelnut and Tomato Sauce

This recipe uses a compound butter combined with a tomato sauce. If you like, add fresh herbs such as basil, tarragon, chervil, parsley, or chives. Serve as a side dish with chicken, duck, venison, or turkey.

∎ *HAZELNUTS AND TOMATO SAUCE*

MAKES 1 CUP

1/4 cup whole toasted hazelnuts (page 54), finely chopped
1/4 cup unsalted butter, softened
Salt
Freshly ground black pepper
1/2 cup Fresh Tomato Sauce (pages 19–20)

SERVES 4

1/2 pound egg noodles, about 3/4 to 1 inch wide

To make the butter, mix the hazelnuts and butter with a fork in a small bowl. Season with salt and pepper and set aside to allow the flavors to blend.

Bring a large pot of water to a boil. Add salt and the noodles and cook, stirring often, until the pasta is tender, between 6 and 10 minutes.

While the noodles cook, heat the tomato sauce and, when it is hot, add the hazelnut butter and stir until it melts. Keep the sauce warm.

Drain the noodles and place them in a bowl. Add the hot sauce and pepper and toss the noodles to coat them. Correct the seasoning and serve.

———— VARIATION ————

Instead of using a compound butter, make the sauce of ¼ cup Fresh Tomato Sauce (pages 19–20) and ½ cup purée of roasted red pepper (page 46).

HAZELNUT AND TOMATO SAUCE is wonderful
  With wild rice, brown or white rice, cracked wheat, or lentils, or on chicken, turkey, or veal

 ## *Tortellini in Gorgonzola Cream*

This is a very rich, luxurious sauce, a blend of melted Gorgonzola and *mascarpone* cheese with cream. The toasted pine nuts and bread crumbs add a nice crunch.

▪ GARNISHES

1 tablespoon unsalted butter
3 slices French bread or 1 slice Italian bread, 1-inch thick
⅓ cup toasted pine nuts (page 54)
2 tablespoons chopped fresh parsley
2 tablespoons scissored fresh chives

▌ PASTA

Salt
1 pound fresh tortellini

▌ GORGONZOLA CREAM

MAKES ABOUT 2 CUPS

3/4 cup heavy or light cream
4 ounces Gorgonzola cheese
4 ounces mascarpone *cheese*
Freshly ground black pepper

Melt half the butter in a small skillet over medium heat and add the slices of bread. Brown them well, remove them briefly, add remaining butter, and brown other side of the bread. Set them on plates to cool, then cut them into small pieces, between approximately 1/4 and 1/2 inch square (they will crumble), and place in a bowl. Add the pine nuts, parsley, and chives, mix well, and set aside.

Bring a large pot of water to a boil. Add the salt and the *tortellini*. Cook the pasta, stirring often, until it is tender, between 3 and 5 minutes.

While the pasta water boils, heat cream in a small pot. Add the Gorgonzola and *mascarpone* and stir until the cheeses have melted. Add lots of pepper and set the sauce aside, off the heat.

When the *tortellini* are cooked, drain and place them in a bowl. Add the Gorgonzola Cream and mix the pasta well to coat it. Sprinkle the top with the reserved crumbs, toasted nuts, parsley, and chives, but do not mix in the garnishes. Spoon the pasta into bowls.

VARIATIONS

Use toasted walnuts or almonds in place of the pine nuts.
Add prosciutto, cut in strips, to the cream after the cheese.

Substitute Fresh Tomato Sauce (pages 19–20) for half the cream.
Add chopped, pitted green olives.

■

GORGONZOLA CREAM, with or without garnishes, may be
>Served with any type of pasta; try it with *penne* or *linguine*
>Served on veal, chicken, or turkey
>Spooned over polenta, semolina, potato *gnocchi*, rice, or grains
>Spooned into the center of a baked potato

❦ *Braised Pasta with Tapenade*

This pasta dish is made with the technique used for pilaf. It is a
wonderful noodle dish for mixing sauces into because the stock adds a
richness that boiled pasta does not have.

SERVES 4 TO 6

1 tablespoon unsalted butter
1 onion, chopped
Salt
Freshly ground black pepper
2 cups orzo *(rice-shaped pasta)*
2 cups chicken stock (page 7), warmed
1 recipe Tapenade *(page 44)*

>Melt the butter in a heavy saucepan over medium heat. Add the
>chopped onion, sprinkle it with salt and pepper, and sauté it until it
>is soft. Add the *orzo* and toss the ingredients together. Cook until the
>*orzo* is hot to the touch, but not browned, just a few minutes. Stir the
>mixture often while you are searing it. Add the chicken stock and
>bring the liquid to a boil. Lower the heat, cover, and simmer until
>the stock has been absorbed and the pasta cooked. Add the *tapenade*.
>Gently stir the mixture with a fork, correct the seasoning, and serve.

Add cooked, scraped kernels of fresh corn and chopped fresh basil to the finished
pasta, along with the *tapenade.*
In place of the *tapenade,* mix in any type of herb or vegetable purée (pages 43–47).

∎

For other recipes with TAPENADE see the index.

❦ *Linguine with Tomato and Cinnamon Sauce*

While visiting a greenhouse one afternoon, I saw cinnamon basil
growing in pots. I nibbled on a leaf and instantly wanted to try the
flavor on pasta. Here I've created a sauce using cinnamon sticks and
fresh basil.

∎ *TOMATO AND CINNAMON SAUCE*

M A K E S   2   T O   3   C U P S

3 pounds tomatoes, preferably Italian plum, cored
2 tablespoons olive oil
2 large red peppers, chopped
1 onion, chopped
3 large cloves garlic, chopped
Salt
Freshly ground black pepper
2 sticks cinnamon, each 3 inches long
½ cup chicken stock (page 7)
¼ cup chopped fresh basil
Pinch cayenne pepper

▮ *PASTA*

1 pound linguine
Salt
Grated Parmesan cheese

Bring a pot of water to a boil. Add the tomatoes (you may have to do this in batches) and blanch them for 1 minute. Transfer the tomatoes to a bowl of cold water. When they are cool enough to handle, peel off the skins and cut the tomatoes in half lengthwise. Run your thumb around the inner cavities of the tomatoes, dislodging and removing the seeds. Chop the tomatoes and set them aside.

Heat the oil in a sauté pan or a pan with high sides, like a Dutch oven, over medium-high heat. Add the red peppers, onion, garlic, and salt. Stir and sauté the mixture for 5 minutes. Add the pepper and mix. Add the tomatoes, cinnamon sticks, and stock. Bring the liquid to a boil, lower the heat to a simmer, and cook the sauce for 1 hour, stirring occasionally. Towards the end stir the mixture frequently to prevent sticking and burning. Discard the cinnamon sticks. Let the sauce cook a bit, then transfer it to a blender or food processor. Purée the sauce and return it to the heat. Add the basil and cayenne pepper.

Bring a large pot of water to a boil. Add salt and the *linguine.* Cook, stirring often, until the pasta is tender. Drain it and mix it with the sauce. Serve with Parmesan cheese.

▮

Tomato and Cinnamon Sauce may be
> Served on any type of pasta; it is particularly good over ricotta-stuffed *manicotti* or shells
> Served over roast pork
> Spooned on slices of grilled pork tenderloin
> Used to top browned chicken breasts
> Served on lamb
> Mixed with steamed vegetables
> Tossed with cooked chick-peas or other legumes

Lainie's Pasta

My close friend and colleague Linda Marino passed along the idea for this dish, which originally came from her Greek neighbor Lainie. To Lainie's dish I have added garlic, herbs, and yogurt. Use goat's milk yogurt if available.

▮ VEGETABLES

SERVES 6 TO 8

1 large or 2 medium cucumbers
2 tomatoes, medium to large
³/₄ cup black brine-cured olives, pitted
³/₄ cup olive oil
Salt
Freshly ground black pepper

▮ FETA SAUCE

MAKES ABOUT 2 CUPS

1 large clove garlic, minced
¹/₄ cup chopped fresh dill, oregano, or mint
¹/₂ pound feta cheese
1 cup plain yogurt

▮ PASTA

1 pound fusilli *(spiral-shaped pasta)*

Peel and quarter the cucumber lengthwise. Remove the seeds and dice it. Core and dice the tomatoes. Cut the olives into quarters. Pile the cucumber, tomatoes, and olives in a pasta bowl or any large bowl. Pour ¹/₂ cup olive oil over the ingredients and toss to coat them, season with salt and pepper, and gently toss them. Set the mixture aside at room temperature.

Mince the garlic and place it in a food processor or blender along with the chopped herb, feta, yogurt, and remaining ¼ cup olive oil. Blend until the mixture is smooth. Season the sauce with lots of pepper and set it aside at room temperature.

Cook the pasta. Drain it and add it directly to the bowl with the vegetables. Pour sauce over the pasta and toss everything together until it is coated. Serve warm or at room temperature.

■

FETA SAUCE may be

Used as a marinade for grilled chicken, lamb, or seafood; reserve some of the sauce and spoon it on top of the cooked food along with the vegetables as a garnish

Served with potatoes, hot or cold

Tossed with cooked *cannellini* beans

Corn Sauce on Little Pasta Shells

■ *PANCETTA AND CORN SAUCE*

MAKES ABOUT 2 TO 2 ½ CUPS

1 tablespoon olive oil
¼ pound pancetta, *thinly sliced*
1 large red onion, *chopped*
Salt
Freshly ground black pepper
1 tablespoon fresh thyme or summer savory leaves, or 1 teaspoon dried thyme or summer savory
1 cup heavy cream
1½ cups chicken stock (page 7)
4 ears corn, husked, kernels removed with a sharp knife, and cobs reserved (there will be between 2 and 3 cups kernels)

1 pound small- to medium-sized pasta shells

Heat the oil in a small Dutch oven or stew pan. Brown the *pancetta* slices on both sides. Remove, drain them on paper towels, and set them aside. Add the onion to pot, season it with salt and pepper, and cook until it begins to lose its moisture and soften. Add the thyme or savory, cream, stock, and corn cobs. Bring the liquid to a boil, lower the heat, and simmer for 10 minutes. Add the corn kernels and simmer another 5 minutes. Remove the cobs, scrape any corn, herbs, or onions off them and back into the sauce, and discard them. Take the sauce off the heat, correct the seasoning, and set it aside.

Bring a large pot of water to a boil. Add salt and the pasta shells and cook until they are done. Drain and place them in a large bowl. Add the warm sauce and toss it well to coat the pasta. Crumble the slices of *pancetta* over the top. Serve at once.

VARIATION

Fettucine and Walnuts with Leek Sauce Replace the *pancetta* with ¹/₃ cup toasted (page 54) and chopped walnuts and the red onion with 6 leeks, washed and sliced. Sauté the leeks in oil or butter. Add thyme and ³/₄ cup cream. Omit the stock and the corn. Remove the sauce from the heat. Cook ¹/₂ pound *fettuccine* and toss the pasta with the sauce. Top with walnuts and sprinkle with chopped parsley. Add fresh peas and Parmesan cheese if you like.

This sauce is also good on ravioli, polenta or *gnocchi*, mushrooms, and zucchini.

∎

CORN SAUCE may be
Served over boneless chicken breasts that have been either poached in the oven or browned in a skillet
Served on pan-fried *scaloppine* or whole roasted and sliced turkey breast
Served on oven-poached salmon, halibut, or other thick cuts of white-fleshed fish

Potato Gnocchi with Ragù

This is a variation of *ragù Bolognese,* a classic meat sauce from Bologna, Italy. Purists believe that, as an authentic Bouillabaisse can only be made in France, a genuine *ragù* can only be made in Italy. While that may be true, I urge you to try this wonderful sauce. The *gnocchi* are shaped in a somewhat unconventional manner, but they are easier to make.

▪ *RAGÙ*

MAKES ABOUT 3 CUPS

1 tablespoon olive oil
½ pound ground veal
½ pound ground pork
¼ cup dry white wine
¼ cup heavy cream
¼ cup chopped fresh basil or sage
Salt
Freshly ground black pepper
⅛ teaspoon nutmeg
½ recipe Winter Tomato Sauce, about 2 or 3 cups (pages 20–22)

▪ *POTATO GNOCCHI*

SERVES 6

1 pound boiling potatoes (not baking or new potatoes), about 2 or 3
Approximately 1 cup flour
1 teaspoon salt
Freshly ground black pepper
Nutmeg
2 tablespoons chopped fresh herbs (optional)
½ cup grated Parmesan cheese

To make the *ragù,* heat the olive oil in a skillet or pot over medium heat. Add the ground meats, crumbling them into the pot with a fork. Stir the meat and cook until it is no longer pink and raw colored, but not yet brown. Add the wine, raise the heat, and cook until the liquid is reduced to a tablespoon or so of juices. Add the cream, herbs, salt, pepper, and nutmeg. Bring the mixture to a boil, lower the heat, and simmer for 5 minutes. Add the tomato sauce and simmer for about 30 minutes to 1 hour. Correct the seasoning and set the *ragù* aside until you are ready to serve.

Make the *gnocchi.* Butter a baking dish or platter and set it aside. Steam the potatoes until they are tender when pierced with a knife. Cool for a minute and peel them. Put them through a ricer or food mill. Add the flour, salt, pepper, a little nutmeg, and herbs if using any. Mix to form a soft, smooth dough.

Using a teaspoon, make 1-inch-oval, football-shaped dumplings. Keep them on a lightly floured board until all the *gnocchi* are shaped. Bring a large pot of water to a boil. Add salt and the *gnocchi,* stirring them gently with a wooden spoon so that they do not stick. When they come floating to the surface of the water, cook them for another minute and then transfer them with a slotted spoon to the baking dish. Do this in batches if necessary.

While the *gnocchi* cook, reheat the *ragù.* Top the *gnocchi* with warmed *ragù,* toss them gently, and serve. Pass the cheese separately.

∎

Ragù may be

> Served on any pasta, such as *tagliatelle, lasagne, ravioli, rigatoni,* or *soba* (buckwheat) pasta
> Used as a sauce over semolina *gnocchi,* polenta, risotto, rice, or potato
> Served over sautéed chicken livers
> Served on any hot vegetable terrine, timbale, or custard
> Spooned over slices of grilled eggplant, potatoes, or red peppers after they have been peeled
> Used to top grilled poultry or sausages

 Baked Potatoes and Vegetables with Pesto

S E R V E S   6   T O   8

1 clove garlic, split in half
2 potatoes, about 1 pound, cut in 1-inch chunks
Salt

Freshly ground black pepper
3 onions, cut in 1-inch chunks
3 zucchini, cut in 1-inch chunks
1½ cups chicken stock (page 7)
½ recipe Pesto (pages 44–45), ½ to ¾ cup, at room temperature

Preheat the oven to 350 degrees F. Rub an oblong baking dish with the split garlic and discard the garlic. Arrange a layer of half the potatoes in the dish and sprinkle them with salt and pepper. Add a layer of half the onions, then half the zucchini, sprinkling each vegetable with salt and pepper. Repeat with the remaining vegetables. Pour the stock into the dish and cover it with foil. Bake for 45 minutes and remove the cover. Bake for another 45 minutes or until the vegetables are very tender and browned slightly on the top. Top each serving with a spoonful of *pesto*.

VARIATIONS

Add 2 sliced tomatoes, layered in the middle of the dish and sprinkled with salt and pepper.

For a very rich sauce, heat about ⅔ cup Reduced Cream (pages 13–14) and add it to the *pesto*.

FOR OTHER RECIPES USING PESTO, SEE THE INDEX.

 # Grilled Potatoes with Green Goddess Dressing

This dressing always sounded so glamorous to me as I was growing up. It was one of my grandmother's favorites. She ordered it at lunch with her Mai Tai cocktail, another exotic concoction.

The sauce was created in the mid-1920s at San Francisco's Palace Hotel. The dressing was originally tossed with a blend of greens and topped with cold chicken or shellfish.

▮ GREEN GODDESS DRESSING

MAKES ABOUT 1 1/2 CUPS

1 recipe Basic Mayonnaise (pages 39–40) made with tarragon vinegar
*   in place of the lemon juice; about 1 1/4 cups*
4 anchovy fillets, minced
2 scallions, green part only, minced
1/4 cup chopped fresh parsley
1/4 cup scissored fresh chives
3 tablespoons chopped fresh tarragon

▮ GRILLED POTATOES

SERVES 4

4 potatoes, sliced 1/2-inch thick
Olive oil
Salt
Freshly ground black pepper

Make the mayonnaise and add the anchovies, scallion, parsley, chives, and tarragon. Mix the dressing well and keep it refrigerated until you are ready to serve.

Light the grill or preheat the broiler. Brush the potato slices with oil and grill them until they are tender and well browned, about 3 to 5 minutes a side. Remove the potato slices to plates and season them with salt and pepper. Serve with a spoonful of Green Goddess Dressing on the side.

▮

GREEN GODDESS DRESSING may be
    Served on steamed or baked potatoes or as a dressing for potato salad
    Served with poached or grilled seafood or chicken
    Served with cold seafood or chicken

Tossed with cooked vegetables, such as carrots or cauliflower, and chilled

♥ *Two Baked Potatoes, Three Butters*

A baked potato is both satisfying and delicious. Mostly we eat them with butter or sour cream, but there is an almost endless stream of garnishes and toppings to experiment with. In this recipe I offer Mustard-Thyme Butter and *Gremolata* Butter for white potatoes, and Apple-Spice Butter for sweet potatoes. *Gremolata* is a traditional garnish—consisting of lemon zest, garlic, and parsley—that is used in the Italian veal dish *Osso Bucco.*

Unsweetened apple butter is a cooked paste of puréed apples with spices. It is available in health food stores.

▮ *MUSTARD-THYME BUTTER*

M A K E S 1/3 C U P

4 tablespoons unsalted butter, softened
2 tablespoons Dijon-style mustard
1 teaspoon fresh thyme leaves
Salt
Freshly ground black pepper to taste

▮ *GREMOLATA BUTTER*

M A K E S 1/4 C U P

4 tablespoons unsalted butter, softened
1 clove garlic, minced
1 tablespoon chopped fresh parsley
1 anchovy fillet, mashed
1 teaspoon grated lemon zest
Salt
Freshly ground black pepper to taste

▮ APPLE-SPICE BUTTER

MAKES ½ CUP

5 tablespoons unsalted butter, softened
2 tablespoons unsweetened apple butter
2 tablespoons minced smoked ham
Pinch ground cloves, or to taste
Salt
Freshly ground black pepper

▮ POTATOES

SERVES 4

4 baking potatoes or 4 sweet potatoes

To make the Mustard-Thyme Butter, combine the softened butter and the mustard in a small bowl and, with a fork, cream them until they are smooth. Add the thyme, salt, and pepper. (The flavor of thyme becomes stronger as the butter sits.) If it is made only a few hours before serving or at the last minute, set the butter aside at room temperature to allow the flavors to blend. Otherwise, chill or freeze the butter and bring it to room temperature before serving.

To make the *Gremolata* Butter, cream together the butter, garlic, parsley, anchovy, lemon zest, salt, and pepper in a small bowl. Set the butter aside for 1 hour to let the flavors blend. The butter can then be refrigerated or frozen. Bring it to room temperature before serving.

To make the Apple-Spice Butter, combine the butter and apple butter in a small bowl and, with a fork, cream them until they are smooth. Add the ham, cloves, salt, and pepper. Set the butter aside at room temperature to allow the flavors to blend. Taste for seasoning just before serving. The butter may be refrigerated or frozen. Bring it to room temperature before serving.

To bake the potatoes, preheat the oven to 400 degrees F. Scrub the potatoes and prick them in a few places. Bake until they are soft when pierced with a knife (between 45 minutes and 1 hour). Split the potatoes, top with a spoonful of butter, and serve.

To make low-fat toppings, substitute Drained Yogurt (page 49) for the butter.
Baked white potatoes may be topped with sautéed or stir-fried vegetables mixed
with a little yogurt or hot sauce, or topped with a mixture of equal
parts of cottage cheese and salsa.
Add a sprinkling of Parmesan cheese if you are topping white potatoes with the
apple-spice butter.
Baked sweet potatoes may be topped with sautéed onions mixed with curry
powder and yogurt, avocado butter, or nut butter (page 42), made
with toasted pecans.

∎

MUSTARD-THYME BUTTER may be
Served with steak, especially a porterhouse steak: sprinkle the grilled
steak with salt and pepper and squeeze lemon juice over it before
topping it with the butter
Served with chicken breasts or veal *scaloppine*
Melted over braised lamb shanks, (remove the meat from the bone)
and served with wide egg noodles
Served with other vegetables such as cauliflower, green beans,
browned mushrooms, sautéed apple slices, Brussels sprouts, baked
onions, carrots, or artichoke hearts
Tossed with any egg pasta, potato *gnocchi,* or rice
Spread on biscuits before they are filled with smoked ham
Used to top oysters on the half shell before they are broiled
Used in cooking eggs

∎

GREMOLATA BUTTER may be
Served on seafood, veal, poultry, lamb, eggs, wilted greens, carrots,
cauliflower, green beans, asparagus, pasta, or rice

∎

APPLE-SPICE BUTTER may be
Served on a hot croissant or on raisin toast
Used on chicken breast, turkey *scaloppine,* or pork
Mixed into rice; it is especially good on brown or wild rice

Potato Pancakes with Leek Topping

This recipe is my favorite way to highlight leeks and potatoes.
The topping will keep for 2 or 3 days.

▪ LEEK TOPPING

MAKES 1 ½ TO 2 CUPS

3 leeks, white and light green parts only
1 tablespoon unsalted butter
½ teaspoon salt
Freshly ground black pepper
1 cup sour cream or Drained Yogurt (page 49)
1 teaspoon caraway seeds
1½ teaspoons paprika

▪ POTATO PANCAKES

SERVES 4 AS A SIDE DISH

1 large Idaho (baking) potato
1 large egg
Oil

To make the topping, cut the leeks in half lengthwise and then cut
them crosswise into ¼-inch slices. Under cold running water, wash
the leeks to remove all dirt and grit and then dry them.

Heat the butter in a small skillet over medium heat and add the
leeks. Sprinkle them with salt and pepper and cook, stirring often,
until they have softened, about 10 minutes. Remove them to a bowl
and allow them to cool. Add the sour cream or yogurt, caraway seeds,
paprika, salt, and pepper. Stir to mix well. Set aside.

To make the pancakes, peel and grate the potato and mix it in a
bowl with the egg. Sprinkle in some salt and pepper. Heat a little oil
in a large skillet over medium-high heat. Stir the potato mixture and
drop it by spoonfuls into the pan. Flatten the pancakes with a spatula
and cook until they are well browned. Flip them over and brown the
other side. Remove the pancakes to plates. Repeat with more oil if

necessary and the rest of the mixture. Serve with a spoonful of topping on each pancake.

VARIATION

Instead of using this leek topping, serve pancakes with the Apple and Garlic Compote (pages 234, 235).

■

Leek Topping may be
>   Used for boneless chicken breasts, veal, or pork
>   Mixed with egg noodles for a side dish
>   Used on baked potatoes

 Mashed Potatoes with Garlic Sauce

This dish makes a wonderful meal when it is accompanied by a salad or crisply steamed vegetables. The sauce is creamy in texture, sweet, and mild.

■ MASHED POTATOES

S E R V E S   4   T O   6

2 pounds potatoes, scrubbed and pricked
1 cup light cream or milk
2 tablespoons unsalted butter
Salt
Freshly ground black pepper

■ GARLIC SAUCE

M A K E S   A L M O S T   1   C U P

2 whole heads garlic, cloves peeled

2 cups stock, chicken (page 7) or chicken and veal (pages 5–6)
2 tablespoons unsalted butter
Salt
Freshly ground black pepper
2 tablespoons chopped fresh parsley or scissored fresh chives

Preheat the oven to 400 degrees F. Scrub and prick the potatoes and bake them until they are tender, about 45 minutes or 1 hour, depending on their size.

While the potatoes bake, make the sauce. Place the garlic in a saucepan with the stock. Bring the liquid to a boil, lower the heat, and simmer gently until only 1 cup of stock is left and the garlic is falling apart, between 20 and 30 minutes. Purée the mixture until it is smooth and return it to the pan. Place the pan back on the heat and bring the mixture to a boil. Lower the heat and simmer until the liquid is reduced to 3/4 cup. Bring the mixture back to a boil and add 2 tablespoons butter. Whisk the ingredients to combine them, season with salt and pepper, and set aside.

Place the cream or milk in a pan and warm it over medium-low heat. When the potatoes are done, cut them in half and scoop or squeeze out the flesh directly into the cream. Add 2 tablespoons butter and mash the potato. Add salt and pepper.

Reheat the sauce and add the parsley or chives. Serve scoops of potatoes with the sauce spooned over the top.

∎

GARLIC SAUCE may be
> Served on any pasta, grain, or rice
> Tossed with potato *gnocchi*
> Used with eggs, cooked any style
> Served on roasted chicken or turkey
> Served with deeply cooked lamb, such as braised lamb shanks or a stew
> Served with braised short ribs of beef
> Served on grilled vegetables, particularly eggplant or potatoes

Chapter 5

FISH,
SHELLFISH
and
SAUCES

*I*N THIS CHAPTER YOU WILL FIND A NUMBER OF DIFFERENT sauces for fish and shellfish. I have included *beurre blanc,* the classic French white butter sauce which is delicious. Although it has a high fat content, *beurre blanc* is still used extensively today and has replaced the classic fish *velouté* or hollandaise style of sauces.

When I first started cooking, French sauces were all I prepared. Since then, I have realized that there are many other techniques and cultures to draw upon when considering a topping for seafood. I think we tend to forget about the abundance of choices we have, especially when single ideas such as grilling or the use of salsa are so strongly promoted. Marinades, relishes, mayonnaises, vinaigrettes, fruit-based and tomato sauces, yogurt, and sour cream can all be made into sauces for seafood. The fish itself may be baked, poached, broiled, grilled, fried, steamed, cooked in parchment or leaves, or stir-fried. There are many exciting ingredients and techniques to be tried when preparing seafood.

The recipe for Chili Scallops (pages 160–161) is a good example. The shellfish is lightly poached and then marinated for a day. Basil and hot chilies are added at the end of marination to provide a sweet and spicy garnish. For further contrast, the scallops are served cold over crisp lettuce.

Another favorite technique is used in the recipe for Mushroom and Cardamom Cream Sauce for Halibut (pages 177–178). The fish is simply covered and baked in a hot oven, which keeps it moist and succulent. A luxurious sauce of reduced cream and cardamom-scented mushroom liquid is then poured over the baked fish.

Feel free to substitute the best fish available in your area for the fish used in these recipes.

 # Chili Scallops

The scallops for this dish marinate for twenty-four hours in the broth before the chilies and basil are added. Plan to prepare the garnishes on the second day. Serve the scallops in lettuce leaves or, as an hors d'oeuvre, on cucumber slices that have been seasoned with salt, pepper, and cayenne pepper.

SERVES 4

½ cup rice vinegar
½ cup dry white wine
2 tablespoons lemon juice
4 cloves garlic, crushed
Salt
1 pound sea scallops, tough membrane removed, sliced ¼-inch thick
6 thin slices lemon
½ cup chopped fresh basil leaves
2 hot serrano *or* jalapeño *chiles, seeded and minced*
Lettuce leaves

To make the marinade, combine the vinegar, wine, lemon juice, and garlic in a small saucepan. Bring the mixture to a boil and boil it for 1 minute. Transfer the marinade to a bowl and allow it to cool to room temperature.

Bring a pot of water to a boil. Add salt and the scallops, stir, and cook them for 30 seconds. Drain and transfer the scallops to a small, nonaluminum baking dish. Pour the marinade over the scallops and gently toss them until they are coated. Arrange the lemon slices over the scallops, cover the dish, and marinate the scallops in the refrigerator for 24 hours.

Before serving the scallops, remove the lemon slices and discard them. Drain off and discard all but ¼ cup of the marinade and add the basil and chilies to the scallops. Gently toss to mix in the garnishes. Arrange the lettuce on 4 plates and divide the scallops and marinade among them.

VARIATION

Make this dish with shrimp, mussels, clams, or a white-fleshed fish such as ocean perch, haddock, or halibut.

 # Grilled Fish with Rhubarb-Mustard Sauce

This dish is dedicated to my friend and colleague, Beth Gurney-Piskula, who loved the sauce so much she requested it for her birthday with the rest of her all-rhubarb meal. The idea for the sauce came from the Italian technique of cooking fruit in sugar syrup with mustard oil for a condiment called *mostarda*.

Buy the reddest rhubarb you can find. The color enhances the dish.

▮ *RHUBARB-MUSTARD SAUCE*

MAKES 1 ½ TO 2 CUPS

½ pound rhubarb, cut in ¼-inch slices
2 tablespoons sugar
2 tablespoons Dijon-style mustard
¼ cup Fish Fumet (pages 9–10) or bottled clam juice
Freshly ground black pepper
Pinch salt

▪ GRILLED FISH

S E R V E S   4

1½ pounds halibut, swordfish, tuna, bluefish, or salmon
Olive oil for grilling

To make the sauce, combine the rhubarb and sugar in a pan. Toss them, and let the mixture sit for 15 minutes to draw out the juices. Then place the pan over medium heat and bring the mixture to a boil. Cook for about 3 to 5 minutes, stirring often, until the rhubarb is softened and tender. Remove from the heat and add the mustard, mixing until the sauce is smooth. Add the fish *fumet* or clam juice, pepper, and salt, mix to blend all the ingredients, and set aside.

Preheat the grill or broiler and brush the fish lightly with oil. If the fish is to be grilled, cook it, searing it well on both sides, until it is just cooked through and is still moist. The cooking time depends on the type and thickness of the fish. If the fish is to be broiled, place it on a rack in a pan close to the source of heat (about 4 inches) and broil it for between 3 and 7 minutes per side, depending on the thickness and the type of fish you are using. If the sauce has cooled, reheat it over low heat until it is just warm. Transfer the fish to plates, season with salt and pepper, and serve with the warm sauce spooned over the top.

VARIATION

When rhubarb is out of season, the sauce may be made with apples, pears, apricots, grapes, figs, or plums.

▪

RHUBARB-MUSTARD SAUCE may be
>	Served with chicken, turkey, duck, quail, squab, game hen, rabbit, baked ham, or roast pork (use chicken stock in place of the fish *fumet*)
>	Served with other seafood, such as shrimp or lobster, or other nonoily white fish, such as haddock or ocean perch

A Mignonette Dipping Sauce for Steamed Mussels

Mignonette is a French word referring to coarsely ground black pepper-corns. Traditionally it is mixed with vinegar and used with raw shell-fish, particularly oysters. Here I'm serving it with steamed mussels and have added the steaming juices for extra flavor. This dish is good served either warm or cold.

SERVES 2

2 tablespoons sherry vinegar
1½ teaspoons coarsely cracked black peppercorns
1½ pounds mussels, scrubbed
½ cup dry white wine

Combine the vinegar and pepper in a small bowl and set it aside.

To cook the mussels, remove the beard (the hairy growth on the side of the mussel) from each mussel. Combine the mussels and wine in a large saucepan with a lid. Cover and steam on high heat, tossing the mussels once or twice while holding the lid on, until they open, about 3 to 5 minutes. Discard those that do not. Remove the pan from the heat, divide the mussels between two bowls and place them near the stove to keep warm.

Strain the steaming juices through cheesecloth or a fine strainer into a saucepan. Bring the juices to a boil and reduce them over high heat to 2 tablespoons. Add the reduction to the vinegar and pepper and mix well. Divide the sauce between 2 small dishes and use as a dipping sauce for the warm mussels.

VARIATION

The flavor of the sauce may be varied by the addition of other spices, such as cayenne pepper, ground cloves, coriander, or ginger.

MIGNONETTE DIPPING SAUCE may be
Served with raw shellfish. Simply combine the vinegar and pepper-
corns
Served with clams cooked in the same way
Served with cooked fish, such as tuna, salmon, swordfish, or bluefish

❧ *Pan-Fried Trout with Bacon and Wine Sauce*

This sauce is a simple reduction blending several ingredients. I have
kept it unenriched because the fish is pan-fried. Serve this delicate dish
with sautéed mushrooms.

S E R V E S   4

1 cup Riesling or other white wine
½ cup Fish Fumet (pages 9–10) or bottled clam juice
½ cup water
1 tablespoon lemon juice
8 slices bacon
4 tablespoons chopped fresh parsley
1 clove garlic, minced
Flour

4 small whole trout, boned and trimmed
Salt
Freshly ground black pepper

Combine the wine, fish *fumet* or clam juice, water, and lemon juice in
a saucepan. Bring the mixture to a boil, lower the heat, and simmer
until it is reduced to ½ cup. Set the reduction aside.
To make the garnish, in a large skillet over medium heat cook the
bacon until it is crisp and drain it on paper towels. Pour off all but ½
tablespoon fat into a bowl and reserve. Add the parsley and garlic to

the skillet and cook for 1 minute, stirring constantly. Transfer the mixture to a bowl scraping the pan well. Crumble the bacon, add it to the bowl, and keep it warm in a low oven.

Place the flour on a plate and flour the trout, shaking off any excess. When the garlic and parsley are cooked, return 2 tablespoons of the reserved bacon fat to the skillet and turn the heat to high. Add the trout and cook them for between 2 and 3 minutes on each side, until they are browned and cooked through. Transfer the fish to plates, season with salt and pepper, and keep them warm in the oven. Add the reserved reduction to the pan and deglaze it over high heat, scraping the pan. Bring the liquid to a boil, remove it from the heat. Scatter the garnish over the fish and spoon the sauce over the whole dish.

♥ Skewers of Swordfish with Lemon and Herb Dressing

This dish relies on the use of a lemon- and black pepper-flavored oil that makes a tremendous difference in the sauce. Try it once and you will want to make the oil for many dishes. The oil steeps in the refrigerator for one day, but once you have made it, the dish is quick and simple to assemble. Serve the fish skewers on a bed of cooked rice.

▮ *LEMON, DILL, AND MINT DRESSING*

MAKES ABOUT 1 ¼ CUPS

⅓ cup white wine vinegar
⅓ cup chopped fresh dill
⅓ cup chopped fresh mint
⅔ cup Black Peppercorn and Lemon Oil (pages 34–35)
Salt
Freshly ground black pepper to taste

SERVES 4

1½ pounds swordfish, skinned

Make the sauce by combining the vinegar, dill, and mint in a small bowl. Slowly whisk in the oil. Add salt and pepper to taste (you may not need any more pepper because of the oil). Set the sauce aside.

Cut the swordfish across the grain into between $1/4$- and $1/2$-inch slices. Place the fish in a shallow, nonaluminum pan and pour over it half of the dressing. Gently turn all the slices to coat them completely with the sauce. Marinate for between 1 and 4 hours.

Preheat the grill or broiler and skewer the slices of swordfish gently so that they do not fall apart. Pat them dry and discard the marinade. Grill or broil the fish close to the heat for 1 or 2 minutes on each side depending on its thickness. Gently transfer the skewers to plates and season with salt and pepper. Whisk the remaining dressing and spoon it over the swordfish.

∎

LEMON, DILL, AND MINT DRESSING may be

Used with tuna, bluefish, or other seafood

Spooned over cooked cauliflower, asparagus, fiddleheads, potatoes, or carrots

Served with fresh peas, sugar snap peas, snow peas, or a combination

Tossed with hot or cold cooked rice, barley, cracked wheat, or lentils

❦ *A Yellow Raisin and Green Peppercorn Sauce for Smoked Salmon*

The inspiration for the combination of raisins and pepper comes from a recipe in Paula Wolfert's book *Paula Wolfert's World of Food* (New York: Harper & Row, 1988). When used together, yellow raisins and green peppercorns produce a delicious hot and sweet blend and make an unusual topping for smoked salmon.

Slices of smoked salmon vary tremendously in size. Buy enough for between two and four slices per person. Serve this with your favorite dark bread or with toasted bagels.

▮ *YELLOW RAISIN AND GREEN PEPPERCORN SAUCE*

MAKES ABOUT 1 ½ CUPS

¼ cup yellow raisins
1 tablespoon cognac
¼ cup cream cheese at room temperature
1 cup sour cream or Drained Yogurt (page 49)
¼ cup drained green peppercorns, rinsed and chopped
Salt

SERVES 4

4 leaves lettuce, washed and dried
Approximately 6 ounces smoked salmon

Soak the raisins in cognac for 30 minutes, stirring occasionally.

Beat the cream cheese, add the sour cream, or drained yogurt, a little at a time, and mix until smooth. Drain the cognac off the raisins and stir it into the sour cream. Chop the raisins, add them to the sauce with the green peppercorns, and stir to combine. Season with salt if desired. Keep the sauce refrigerated until you are ready to serve.

Arrange the lettuce on 4 plates and lay the salmon slices over the lettuce. Spoon the sauce over the salmon and serve with bread.

VARIATIONS

For a more traditional topping, use diced red onion and capers in place of the raisins and peppercorns.

Try the smoked salmon with the Cream Cheese with Horseradish sauce (page 271).

▮

YELLOW RAISIN AND GREEN PEPPERCORN SAUCE may be
Served with other smoked fish such as whitefish, trout, or bluefish
Served with smoked turkey, chicken, pheasant, or ham
Served on cold poultry, beef, or lamb

Scallops with Lime and Mint Butter

This sauce is a variation of the classic *Beurre Blanc* (white butter sauce) (pages 17–18). The dish makes a perfect first course or main course for a formal dinner party. Serve with rice.

▮ LIME AND MINT BUTTER

MAKES ABOUT 1 CUP

4 large shallots, coarsely chopped
⅓ cup lime juice
⅓ cup white wine
2 strips lime zest, measuring about ½ inch by 2 inches
2 tablespoons coarsely chopped fresh mint sprigs (leaves and stems)
1 cup unsalted butter, softened
Salt
Freshly ground black pepper
2 teaspoons grated lime zest
2 tablespoons chopped fresh mint leaves

▮ SAUTÉED SCALLOPS

SERVES 6

1½ pounds scallops, tough membrane removed
2 tablespoons olive oil
Mint sprigs

Make a white butter sauce (pages 17–18), using the shallots, lime juice, wine, strips of lime zest, and chopped sprigs of mint for the reduction and then add the butter, salt, and pepper. When the sauce is done, strain it and add the grated lime zest and chopped mint leaves. Set the sauce aside, off the heat.

Cut the scallops crosswise into ¼-inch slices or cut them into quarters or sixths. Heat the olive oil in a skillet over high heat and toss in the scallops. Cook them, tossing frequently, until they are opaque and cooked through, about 2 to 3 minutes. Remove from the heat, season with salt and pepper, and spoon them onto plates, using a slotted spoon. Pour the sauce over the scallops and serve them garnished with mint sprigs.

■

LIME AND MINT BUTTER may also be
Served on broiled or grilled split jumbo shrimp, or poached halibut, monkfish, ocean perch, trout, or salmon

▼ *Crab Cakes with Confetti Sauce*

I spent every summer of my childhood in Maryland on my grandparents' tobacco farm. I can still smell the fried chicken and cream gravy and the sizzling chipped beef served on warm fluffy biscuits. At my grandmother's insistence, we would frequently travel to a special restaurant on the shore to sample crab and fish cakes. Years later, my great aunt, Frances Kelly, compiled a cookbook called *Maryland's Way* (Annapolis: The Hammond-Harwood House Association, 1963) full of exciting, historical Southern recipes. These crab cakes are a variation of one of the recipes in that book.

This recipe is dedicated to the late Beverly Stobaugh and her husband, Robert. They both loved these crab cakes very much, and they also inspired much of my sauce cooking.

■ *CONFETTI SAUCE*

MAKES ABOUT 1 ¼ CUPS

½ cup olive oil
¼ cup lemon juice
1 large clove garlic
Salt
Freshly ground black pepper
Tabasco sauce to taste
2 tablespoons finely chopped cucumber

2 tablespoons finely chopped fennel
2 tablespoons finely chopped red pepper
2 tablespoons sliced scallion greens
1 tablespoon chopped fresh parsley or dill

▪ *CRAB CAKES*

SERVES 6 *as a first course and 4 as a luncheon dish*

1 pound fresh, cooked, and shelled crabmeat
1 tablespoon flour
1 large egg
1/3 cup heavy cream
Salt
Freshly ground black pepper
Cayenne pepper to taste
Tabasco to taste
1/4 cup fresh bread crumbs
Unsalted butter
Lemon wedges
Parsley sprigs

To make the sauce, combine the olive oil, lemon juice, garlic, salt, pepper, and Tabasco in a blender and blend until smooth. If you like it spicy, add more Tabasco. Place the cucumber, fennel, red pepper, scallion, and chopped parsley in a small bowl and pour the dressing over them. Stir to combine and set aside.

To make the crab cakes, place the crabmeat in a bowl and toss it with the flour. Beat the egg with the cream and add the mixture to the crabmeat with the salt, pepper, cayenne, Tabasco, and bread crumbs. Toss to combine.

Melt 1 tablespoon butter in a heavy skillet over medium-high heat and spoon cakes, using about 2 tablespoons of the crab mixture, into the butter. Flatten the cakes and cook until the outside is dark golden brown, about 1 or 2 minutes. Turn and brown the second side, also 1 or 2 minutes. Remove the cakes to a plate and repeat with the remaining crab mixture.

Arrange 3 crab cakes per person on plates and spoon the dressing over the cakes, stirring the sauce from the bottom of the bowl to combine all the ingredients. Garnish the dish with lemon wedges and parsley sprigs and serve.

CONFETTI SAUCE may be
Spooned over any cold sliced meat or poultry
Served with smoked poultry
Tossed with vegetables, cooked or uncooked

 Linguine with Shrimp

This is a sumptuous, rich dish that is well worth the calories. To make the preparation easier, the shrimp and sauce can be cooked one day ahead or early in the morning. Serve it to guests, on a holiday, or on a special occasion. It is delicious with a plain green salad and crisply sautéed slices of red pepper and fennel. The recipe can be easily cut in half.

SHRIMP SAUCE

MAKES ABOUT 5 CUPS

Olive oil
3 pounds large shrimp in their shells
4 cups heavy cream
2 cups Fish Fumet (pages 9–10) or bottled clam juice
1 cup Fresh or Winter Tomato Sauce (pages 20–22)
Salt
Freshly ground black pepper
4 large cloves garlic, minced
¼ cup chopped fresh parsley

SERVES 8

1½ pounds linguine

Heat some olive oil in a skillet over high heat. Add enough shrimp to cover the pan in one layer. Cook the shrimp for about 1 minute on each side and remove them to a plate. Repeat with the remaining shrimp, using more olive oil as necessary. Cool the shrimp and then remove the shells. Place all the shells in a 2- or 3-quart saucepan. Cut the shrimp in half lengthwise through the back and devein them. Place the shrimp in a bowl, cover, and refrigerate.

Add the cream and fish *fumet* or clam juice to the pan containing the shrimp shells and bring the liquid to a boil. Lower the heat and simmer until it is reduced to 4 cups. Strain out the shells, return the reduction to the pan, and add the tomato sauce. Cook for another 5 to 10 minutes. Season the sauce with salt and pepper and remove it from the heat.

Bring a large pot of water to a boil and add salt. Add the *linguine* and cook until it is tender. Just before the *linguine* is done, place the sauce back on the heat and add the shrimp, garlic, and parsley. Heat through and correct the seasoning. Drain the *linguine* and place it in a large bowl. Pour the sauce over the pasta, toss well, and serve.

■

SHRIMP SAUCE may be

Served on rice, potatoes, in pastry shells, or over slices of toasted French bread

 Salmon Fillets with Saffron and Lemon

The inspiration for this dish comes from a recipe for sole and salmon with saffron in Fredy Girardet's book, *La Cuisine Spontanée* (Paris: Robert Laffont, 1982).

■ *SAFFRON AND LEMON SAUCE*

MAKES ABOUT 2 CUPS

¹/₃ cup dry white wine
¹/₃ cup bottled clam juice

⅓ cup Fish Fumet *(pages 9–10); if it is not available, substitute ½ white wine and ½ bottled clam juice*
18 shallots, thinly sliced
6 cloves garlic, crushed
2 lemons
1 cup fresh parsley stems, about 1 bunch
10 tablespoons unsalted butter
Salt
Freshly ground black pepper
1 package saffron threads, .25 grams, about 1 teaspoon threads, crushed
1 cup fresh parsley leaves, chopped
¼ cup heavy cream

S E R V E S   6   T O   8

Unsalted butter
3 pounds boneless salmon fillet, skinned

Place the wine, clam juice, fish *fumet*, 6 of the shallots, and the garlic in a pot. Grate the zest of the lemons and reserve it in a covered bowl. Squeeze the lemons and add the juice to the pot along with the parsley stems. Bring the mixture to a boil, lower the heat, and simmer to reduce it to ¼ cup. Strain the reduction into a clean pot and set it aside.

Melt 2 tablespoons of the butter over medium heat in a small skillet or saucepan and cook the remaining shallots until they are soft and golden, about 8 minutes, stirring frequently to prevent burning. Season with salt and pepper. Remove the pan from the heat. Add the grated lemon zest and set aside, keeping the mixture in the pan.

Preheat the oven to 400 degrees F. Using extra butter, lightly butter a jelly-roll pan. Place the salmon in the pan and cover it with foil. Bake the salmon for between 15 and 20 minutes, depending on the thickness of the fish, until it is just cooked through.

While the salmon cooks, finish making the sauce. Place the wine reduction over low heat and whisk in the remaining 8 tablespoons butter, 2 tablespoons at a time. Add the cream, saffron threads, season with salt and pepper, and pour the sauce over the cooked shallots. Set the sauce aside for between 5 and 10 minutes to bring out the full flavor of the saffron. Just before serving, rewarm the sauce over very low heat, correct the seasoning, and add the chopped parsley.

Cut salmon fillets and place them on plates, season with salt and pepper, and spoon the sauce over them. Serve immediately.

<hr>

VARIATION

Omit the garnish of shallots and the saffron. Use orange juice and zest in the reduction in place of lemon juice and zest and finish the sauce with a small spoonful of honey and heavy cream instead of butter. Garnish the dish with crisp bacon and lots of sliced scallions.

■

SAFFRON AND LEMON SAUCE may be
Used over any seafood

 ## Chilled Salmon with Creamy Shallot and Balsamic Vinegar Sauce

The blend of caramelized shallots and balsamic vinegar used in this recipe is one that goes well with fatty meats or fish because the vinegar balances the richness. See also the recipe for Pork Medallions *Agrodolce*, pages 218–219.

∎ SALMON

SERVES 4

1 teaspoon unsalted butter
2 pounds boneless salmon fillet, skinned

∎ SHALLOT AND BALSAMIC VINEGAR MAYONNAISE

MAKES ABOUT 1 ½ TO 2 CUPS

1 tablespoon olive oil
½ pound shallots, thinly sliced
Salt

¼ cup balsamic vinegar
½ cup Basic Mayonnaise (pages 39–40)
½ cup plain yogurt
Freshly ground black pepper
1 tablespoon chopped fresh parsley

Preheat the oven to 400 degrees F. Butter a baking sheet and place the salmon on it. Cover it with foil and bake for between 15 and 20 minutes, depending on the thickness of the fish. Cool the fish and then chill it until you are ready to serve.

To make the sauce, heat the oil over low heat. Add the shallots and sprinkle them with salt. Toss and cook the shallots, stirring often, until they caramelize, about 30 minutes. Add the vinegar and scrape the pan to remove all the glazed bits of shallot. Cook for 1 minute to reduce the liquid slightly. Remove the mixture to a bowl to cool. Add the mayonnaise, yogurt, and salt and pepper to taste, and stir. Chill the sauce until you are ready to serve.

Arrange the fish on 4 plates and spoon the sauce over the top of each piece. Garnish with parsley.

VARIATION

You can serve this as a hot sauce for salmon by omitting the mayonnaise and yogurt, substituting equal parts of heavy cream and clam juice, and reducing the liquid by half. Add the caramelized and vinegared shallots and season. Cut the hot salmon fillet into servings, spoon the sauce over them, and top with the parsley.

∎

SHALLOT AND BALSAMIC VINEGAR SAUCE may be
Used with hot or cold chicken breasts or sliced turkey
Used with pan-fried beef steak or leg of lamb
Used as an accompaniment to baked, steamed, or boiled sweet or white potatoes
Poured on cooked carrots, mushrooms, green beans, broccoli, cauliflower, or zucchini

Used as a dipping sauce for poached oysters, grilled shrimp, or fried clams

▼ *Cherry Tomato Salsa on Swordfish*

Substitute yellow tomatoes—cherry or regular—for half of the total amount in the salsa when available.

▌ SALSA

MAKES ABOUT 2 CUPS

¾ pound cherry tomatoes or 2 regular-sized tomatoes
2 jalapeño *chiles, cored, seeded, and minced*
1 scallion, trimmed and sliced
1 large clove garlic, minced
1 or 2 limes
1 tablespoon chopped fresh cilantro
Salt

SERVES 4 TO 6

2 pounds swordfish, 1-inch thick
Vegetable oil
Freshly ground black pepper

If using regular tomatoes, core and seed them; if using cherry tomatoes, there is no need to core and seed them. Chop the tomatoes finely and place them in a bowl. Add the chiles, scallion, garlic, juice of 1 lime, cilantro, and salt to taste. Depending on the sweetness of the tomatoes or, if you like lots of lime, use the second lime. Set the salsa aside until the fish is ready.

Preheat the grill or broiler and brush the fish lightly with oil. Grill or broil it for about 5 minutes on each side, or until no longer pink in the middle. Season with salt and pepper and serve with salsa.

Replace the tomatoes in this basic salsa with other ingredients such as mango, papaya, pineapple, or cucumber

∎

SALSA may be

    Served alongside cold roasted beef, pork, lamb, or poultry

    Used as a dipping sauce with grilled shrimp

    Served with steamed fish, such as sole, halibut, ocean perch, or flounder

    Served with cooked vegetables or potatoes

    Served with eggs in the morning

    Served with tacos or tortillas

    Used to top cooked navy, cranberry, pinto, kidney, or *cannellini* beans

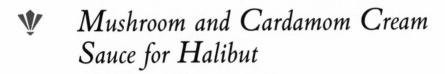

Mushroom and Cardamom Cream Sauce for Halibut

One day, my friend Carol Williams was describing a mushroom and cardamom soup prepared by a mutual friend, Olga Meyer, and wondering if it would be good on fish. I was inspired by the idea and this dish is the result. The overtones of lemon in cardamom are wonderful with the mushrooms and fish. Serve the dish with a brightly colored vegetable stir-fry and rice flavored with lemon zest.

∎ *MUSHROOM AND CARDAMOM CREAM SAUCE*

M A K E S   A B O U T   3   C U P S

2 tablespoons unsalted butter
1½ pounds cultivated mushrooms, sliced
¼ teaspoon salt
Freshly ground black pepper

1 tablespoon ground cardamom
2 cups heavy cream
1 cup Fish Fumet (pages 9–10) or bottled clam juice

SERVES 6

6 halibut steaks or 3 pounds halibut fillet
Ground cardamom

Melt the butter in a large skillet over medium heat and add the mushrooms. Season with salt and pepper and toss well. Cover the pan to collect as much juice as possible from the mushrooms. When the juices have been released, pour them off into a saucepan and return the skillet to the heat. Raise the heat and brown the mushrooms well. Towards the end of the browning, add half of the cardamom and toss well for 1 to 2 minutes. Remove the mushrooms to a bowl and set aside.

Add the remaining cardamom to the saucepan with the mushroom juices. Add the cream and fish *fumet* or clam juice. Bring the liquid to a boil, lower the heat, and simmer to reduce it to 1½ cups. Whisk every once in a while to keep the mixture smooth. When it is done, add the mushrooms and set the pan aside, off the heat.

While the sauce is reducing, cook the fish. Preheat the oven to 400 degrees F. Butter a baking dish large enough to hold the fish in one layer without touching. Sprinkle the fish liberally with pepper and cardamom. Cover with foil and bake the steaks for between 15 and 25 minutes, depending on their thickness. If you are using fillets, check at 15 minutes.

Reheat the sauce just before serving and correct the seasoning. Season the cooked fish with salt and serve it topped with the hot sauce.

∎

Mushroom and Cardamom Cream Sauce may be
   Served with salmon, trout, haddock, scrod, flounder, sole, cod, or
      other white fish
   Served with chicken or turkey, if the fish *fumet* or clam juice is re-
      placed with chicken stock
   Served on egg pasta; make the sauce with either chicken stock or fish
      fumet or clam juice and top the pasta with crumbled, cooked bacon
      and chopped parsley

Shrimp Cocktail

The original cocktail sauce calls for ketchup. Here sweet spices and sugar are added to a fresh tomato sauce to evoke the taste of cocktail sauce and grated lemon zest and saffron are added. Serve this dish as an hors d'oeuvre, a first course, or a luncheon dish with other cold salads.

▮ COCKTAIL SAUCE

MAKES 1 CUP

1 teaspoon oil
1 small onion, finely chopped
1 small clove garlic, finely minced
1 cup Fresh Tomato Sauce (pages 19–20)
1/4 cup lemon juice
1 tablespoon sugar
1 large pinch each ground cinnamon, allspice, and nutmeg
1 small pinch ground cloves
1/4 teaspoon salt
Freshly ground black pepper
1 teaspoon grated lemon zest
1/4 teaspoon saffron threads (optional)
Tabasco sauce

▮ SHRIMP

SERVES 4 TO 6

4 quarts water
1/4 cup cider vinegar
1 tablespoon salt
24 medium or large shrimp, shelled and deveined
Parsley sprigs
Lemon wedges

To make the sauce, heat the oil in a small saucepan over medium heat. Add the onion and garlic and cook until the vegetables have softened, between 5 and 10 minutes. Add the tomato sauce, lemon juice, sugar, spices, salt, and pepper and bring the mixture to a boil. Lower the heat and simmer until the sauce is reduced to 1 cup, between 20 and 30 minutes. Add the lemon zest. If you are using saffron, break the threads with your fingers and add them to the sauce. Cook for 3 minutes more. Remove the sauce from the heat and place it in a bowl and leave it to cool to room temperature. Cover the bowl and refrigerate it until you are ready to serve. Add Tabasco sauce to taste just before serving.

To cook the shrimp, combine the water, vinegar, and salt in a large pan and bring the mixture to a boil. Lower the heat to simmer, add the shrimp, and simmer them for between 2 and 5 minutes or until they are cooked through. Drain and rinse the shrimp and dry them. Place them in a bowl, cover the bowl, and chill the shrimp until you are ready to serve them.

To serve, arrange the chilled shrimp on plates around small bowls of sauce. Garnish the plates with parsley sprigs and thin wedges of lemon.

■

COCKTAIL SAUCE may be
Served with all cold, cooked shellfish
Used as a dipping sauce for cooked fish, chicken, lamb, or veal

▼ *Fish and Chips with Tartar Sauce*

There are many variations of tartar sauce. This version has lots of crunch and tartness.

It is best to use one pan for the chips and one for the fish and cook both at the same time. If that is not possible, cook the potatoes first, keep them warm in a low oven, and then cook the fish. I prefer to use a small amount of oil when cooking the fish instead of deep frying.

■ *TARTAR SAUCE*

M A K E S   A B O U T   1 ½   T O   2   C U P S

1 cup Basic Mayonnaise (pages 39–40)
2 tablespoons lemon juice

1 tablespoon grainy mustard
1/4 cup chopped red pepper
1/4 cup chopped red onion
1/4 cup chopped dill pickle
2 tablespoons drained capers, rinsed and drained again
2 tablespoon chopped fresh parsley
1 tablespoon scissored fresh chives
Salt
Freshly ground black pepper
Cayenne pepper to taste (optional)

■ FISH AND CHIPS

S E R V E S   4

1/2 cup flour
1 large egg
1/2 cup milk
1/4 teaspoon salt
Freshly ground black pepper
Pinch cayenne pepper
4 Idaho potatoes, weighing between about 1 1/2 and 2 pounds total
2 pounds scrod, haddock, or other firm fish fillets
Oil for frying

For the tartar sauce, combine the mayonnaise, lemon juice, and mustard in a bowl and mix well. Add remaining ingredients and stir. Set the sauce aside in the refrigerator until about half an hour before you are ready to serve.

Make a batter for the fish by placing the flour in a bowl, making a well in the flour, and adding the egg and milk. Whisk the egg and milk together and gradually incorporate the flour. Add the salt, pepper, and cayenne and stir to combine. Set the batter aside to rest for 20 minutes.

Preheat the oven to its lowest setting. Peel and rinse the potatoes and cut them into 3/8-inch-wide sticks. Keep the chips in cold water to cover until you are ready to fry them. Cut the fish into serving-size pieces.

Arrange the potatoes on towels to dry while you heat the oil. For the chips, heat 3 inches of oil to 350 degrees F. in a deep-fryer or large saucepan over medium-high heat. For the fish, place about 1/2 an inch of oil in a large skillet, but do not heat it yet.

When the chip oil is hot, place half the potatoes in a fryer basket. If you do not have a fryer basket, use a slotted spoon or skimmer to lower the potatoes into the hot oil. Fry the chips in two batches for about 2 or 3 minutes, until they are lightly golden. Remove and drain them on paper towels. Cool the potatoes.

Reheat the chip oil to 375 degrees F. Return half of the potatoes to the chip oil and fry them again until they are crisp and nicely browned; between 3 and 5 minutes. Drain them on paper and repeat with remaining potatoes. Keep warm in the oven if cooking before the fish.

At the same time or after the potatoes are done, heat the fish oil over medium-high heat. Dip the fish into the batter and transfer it to the hot shallow oil. Leave enough room in the pan so that you can turn the fish easily and so that it crisps and browns and does not steam. Cook until it is a deep, golden brown on both sides.

Remove the fish to paper to drain, sprinkle both fish and chips with salt and pepper, and serve with tartar sauce.

VARIATIONS

Tartar Sauce may be flavored with chopped celery, chopped green or black olives, chopped hard-cooked egg, chopped pickled onions, chopped sweet pickle, or sliced *cornichons*.

∎

Tartar Sauce may be
    Used to make potato, egg, or chicken salad
    Served with grilled, baked, or poached fish or poultry
    Served with cold lamb or beef

 Grapefruit and Tomato Compote for Perch

For a long time I have wanted to make a sauce with fennel and grapefruit. There was no fresh fennel available when I was testing this recipe, so I settled on fennel seed. This sauce is light and delicious and keeps well for about one week.

▮ GRAPEFRUIT AND TOMATO COMPOTE

MAKES ABOUT 3 CUPS

2 pink grapefruit
6 plum tomatoes, cored
2 tablespoons Fennel Oil (page 36) or olive oil
Salt
Freshly ground black pepper
2 cloves garlic, minced
¼ cup chopped fresh parsley
1 teaspoon fennel seeds

SERVES 4

1 tablespoon Fennel Oil or olive oil
4 perch fillets, skinned

With a sharp knife, remove all the peel and white pith from the grapefruit. Working over a bowl to catch the juices, cut out the sections of the grapefruit between the membranes that separate each section and place in the bowl with the juices. When all the sections have been removed, squeeze the pulp to extract all the juice. Set the bowl aside.

Cut the tomatoes into eight wedges each and set aside.

Heat the oil in a skillet over high heat. Add the tomatoes, salt, and pepper and cook, stirring often, for 3 minutes. Add the garlic, parsley, and fennel seeds and continue cooking for 2 minutes, stirring often. Pour in the grapefruit juice, but not the sections, and reduce the liquid; about 2 minutes. Transfer the mixture to a bowl and cool it to room temperature. Gently fold in the grapefruit sections. Keep the compote at room temperature or chill it until the next day.

To cook the fish, heat the oil over high heat in a skillet large enough to hold the fish in one layer. Add the fish and brown it well, cooking it for about 2 or 3 minutes on each side. Transfer the fish to plates, sprinkle it with salt and pepper, and spoon compote on the side.

▮

GRAPEFRUIT AND TOMATO COMPOTE may be

> Served over other pan-fried or grilled seafood, such as shrimp, sword-fish, salmon, flounder, or halibut
>
> Served with chicken, turkey, duck, goose, ham, pork, or game
>
> Served over beef steaks, lamb, or veal; for these foods, replace the grapefruit with orange

Chapter 6

■ ■ ■ ■

POULTRY

and

ACCOMPANYING

SAUCES

*F*IVE YEARS AGO I HAD A BABY AND IN THOSE DAYS WAS lucky if I had time enough to boil a pot of spaghetti. More often than not, we did not eat a square meal. As the years rolled on I could manage to throw a chicken in the oven and maybe some potatoes with it. Now, life is somewhat easier and I am more organized, but I still rely heavily on roast chicken. I do, however, manage to make a sauce. The first six recipes in this chapter are for that basic bird, simply because it is affordable and easy to prepare. Four of the sauces can be made quickly; two, Woodsy Red Wine Sauce (pages 190–191) and Essence of Chicken and Citrus (pages 192–193), make use of your time while the chicken roasts. The six sauce recipes following the recipe for roast chicken are as distinctive on other cuts of poultry.

The recipes included here illustrate a variety of sauce techniques. The Corn Relish (pages 198–199) makes use of vegetables at their peak in late summer, in a painlessly easy sauce. The recipe for Broiled Chicken with Herb Butter (pages 196–198) demonstrates the useful and basic technique of sliding a compound (flavored) butter under the skin of the bird. The meat is then broiled (or baked or grilled) to make a juicy yet crispy dish basted by the melting butter.

Many sauces in this chapter are interchangeable. For instance, the fresh mint sauce for chicken breasts (pages 200–201) is also delicious on other cuts of poultry such as roast duck, and the corn relish served with the Parmesan-baked chicken (pages 198–200) makes an unusual condiment for stir-fried chicken breast strips. Experiment and enjoy pairing various sauces with different types of poultry.

Roast Chicken with Six Sauces

Everyone has his or her own method for roasting chicken. I prefer to roast it in a high oven for the entire cooking time. The finished bird is appetizingly golden and particularly juicy.

Choose a sauce from any one of the following six recipes.

SERVES 4

1 chicken, weighing about 4 pounds
1 cup stock, chicken (page 7) or chicken and veal (pages 5–6)
Salt
Freshly ground pepper to taste

Preheat the oven to 400 degrees F. Fold the wing tips under the chicken. Tie the drumsticks together and place the chicken, breast-side down, on a rack in a roasting pan. Place in the oven and roast for 30 minutes. Turn the chicken breast-side up and continue roasting for another 30 or 50 minutes or until the juices run clear from the thickest part of the thigh when pierced with the tip of a knife. Remove the roast from the oven and place the chicken on a cutting board; let it rest for between 5 and 10 minutes.

Pour off all the fat from the roasting pan and deglaze it with stock, scraping the pan. Bring the mixture to a boil and reduce it until the juices coat the back of a spoon and the flavors are concentrated. Strain the pan juices into a small saucepan and keep them warm. Carve the chicken into pieces and arrange on plates. Season with salt and pepper and drizzle with the warm pan juices.

 # Terry's Curry and Cranberry Sauce

The inspiration for this dish came from my friend Terry Bartow one night over dinner as he pondered the idea of serving curry and cranberries with fish pie. Because the flavors of cranberry and curry are so distinctive, buttered brown or white rice would be a good choice for a side dish.

MAKES ABOUT 2 CUPS

2 tablespoons unsalted butter
1 onion, thinly sliced
2 tablespoons curry powder
12 ounces (1 package) fresh cranberries
2 tablespoons toasted sliced almonds (page 54) (optional)

Melt the butter in a skillet and add the onion. Cook over medium heat until the onions are very soft and lose their moisture. Add the curry powder and continue cooking for 1 minute. Add the cranberries and cook, stirring occasionally, for about 10 minutes. Remove the sauce from the heat and allow it to cool to room temperature. Place the sauce in a bowl and top it with toasted almonds.

▪

TERRY'S CURRY AND CRANBERRY SAUCE is also delicious with
Roasted lamb, pork, duck, or turkey
On baked, broiled, or grilled fish
With a wedge of fish pie—Terry was right!

❦ *Raita Yogurt Sauce*

Raita is a refreshing sauce made with a yogurt base to which different seasonings, fruits, or vegetables are added. In India, it is served with spicy food to contrast with and cool the heat. For variations on the *raita*, see the index.

MAKES ABOUT 2 CUPS

1 recipe Drained Yogurt (page 49)
¼ cup finely diced European, seedless cucumber; about a 2-inch piece
¼ cup thinly sliced snow peas, trimmed; about 6 or 8
¼ cup finely diced red onion

3 tablespoons chopped fresh mint or 2 tablespoons chopped fresh parsley
    mixed with 1 teaspoon dried mint
1/4 teaspoon salt
Freshly ground black pepper to taste
Cayenne pepper to taste (optional)

Place the drained yogurt in a small bowl. Add the remaining ingredients and stir well to combine. This sauce can be served immediately or refrigerated. If it is refrigerated, let it sit at room temperature for 30 minutes before serving.

RAITA YOGURT SAUCE is also delicious with
    Grilled lamb or fish, or grilled chicken
    As a dip for carrot sticks, apple slices, endive leaves, or other vegetables

Woodsy Red Wine Sauce

This is a very quick reduction sauce thickened with a *Beurre Manié* (page 357). The packages of dried *porcini* mushrooms that weigh .35 of an ounce are the approximate equivalent of one-third of a cup. If fresh peas are available, blanch them in boiling water for 1 or 2 minutes before adding them to the sauce.

MAKES ABOUT 2 CUPS

About 1/3 cup dried porcini mushrooms
1 cup dry red wine
1 cup chicken stock (page 7)
2 tablespoons unsalted butter, softened
6 medium cultivated mushrooms, thinly sliced
Salt
Freshly ground black pepper to taste
4 slices prosciutto, fat removed and cut crosswise in 1/4-inch slices
1/2 cup tiny frozen peas, thawed
1 tablespoon flour

Cover the dried mushrooms with boiling water, stir, and let them sit for 20 minutes. Strain the mushrooms, reserving the liquid. Rinse the mushrooms, pat them dry, and slice them. Pour the reserved liquid through a fine strainer and let it sit for 10 minutes. Place the mushroom liquid into a small saucepan, leaving behind any sediment that has accumulated at the bottom of the bowl. Add the wine and stock to the saucepan. Bring the mixture to a boil, lower the heat to a simmer, and reduce to 1 cup. Remove the reduction from the heat and set it aside.

Melt 1 tablespoon of the butter in a small skillet over medium-high heat. Add both types of mushrooms, season with salt and pepper, and toss well. Cook the mushrooms until they are well browned. Add the prosciutto and again toss well. Cook for 1 minute and remove the pan from the heat. Add the peas, toss, and set the pan aside.

Cream the remaining tablespoon of butter on a small plate with the flour. Place the wine mixture back on medium heat and bring it to a boil. Whisk the *beurre manié* into the boiling sauce. Add the mushroom mixture, heat through briefly, and remove from the heat. Correct the seasoning and serve.

∎

WOODSY RED WINE SAUCE is good on
Egg noodles, a baked potato, or mashed potatoes; serve with a green salad for a quick meal
With duck, rabbit, veal, beef, calves' liver, or quail

 *Spicy Lemon Aïoli*

In Provence, they sometimes make aïoli with two cloves of garlic per person. Temper the number of cloves to your palate, keeping in mind that there is no such thing as subtle aïoli. I have added hot pepper and lemon zest to an already stimulating sauce. You can make the aïoli up to two days in advance.

4 to 8 large cloves garlic, minced
1 recipe Basic Mayonnaise (pages 39–40), made with lemon juice and
    olive oil
2 teaspoons grated lemon zest
½ teaspoon red pepper flakes
2 tablespoons chopped fresh parsley

Mash the garlic with the side of a knife blade until it is almost a purée and place in a small bowl. Add the mayonnaise, lemon zest, hot pepper flakes, and parsley. Stir to combine and correct the seasoning. Let the sauce sit in the refrigerator for an hour to blend the flavors.

VARIATION

To make a *rouille*, the classic garnish for *bouillabaisse*, omit the lemon zest and replace the hot pepper flakes with ½ to 1 teaspoon cayenne pepper and some paprika if you like. Decrease the garlic to 2 or 3 cloves. Serve with steamed mussels or clams; cold lobster or shrimp; grilled eggplant, tomatoes, leeks, or zucchini; beef, lamb, rabbit, or poultry; potato salad; on sandwiches; as a dipping sauce for raw vegetables; or with deviled or hard-cooked eggs.

■

AïOLI is delicious with
    Seafood, turkey, lamb, or chicken breasts
    On sandwiches or as a dip for cold shellfish, vegetables (artichokes,
       broccoli, cauliflower, asparagus), or fruit such as apples

 ## *Essence of Chicken and Citrus*

This sauce starts with an essence made of chicken pieces and stock. It needs to be made with homemade stock, because the canned varieties do not have the natural gelatin needed to give the sauce its texture and most are too salty. Served with roast chicken, this tart sauce provides a good contrast. Accompany with colorful vegetables, either steamed or stir-fried, and any pasta, grain, potato, or rice.

MAKES ABOUT 2 CUPS

1 teaspoon oil
8 chicken wings, cut in 1-inch pieces
1 quart stock, chicken (page 7) or chicken and veal (pages 5–6)
1 orange
1 lemon
1 lime
2 tablespoons unsalted butter
2 tablespoons Grand Marnier liqueur
1 tablespoon chopped fresh parsley
Salt
Freshly ground black pepper

Following the recipe on pages 16–17, start the essence using the oil, chicken wings, and stock. Strain and set it aside. (You will add the butter before serving.)

While the essence cooks, prepare the citrus. Peel the orange, lemon, and lime, removing all the white pith, and cut each into 1/4-inch slices. Cut the slices into half moons, remove any seeds, and set aside. The citrus may be sliced several hours ahead.

When you are ready to serve, bring the essence to a boil in a saucepan. Add the butter and whisk until it has emulsified. Add the liqueur and turn off the heat. Add all the citrus slices. Carefully stir in the parsley and season to taste with salt and pepper. The citrus slices should just warm in the sauce, not cook, or they will fall apart.

∎

ESSENCE OF CHICKEN AND CITRUS is delicious
    On veal, pork, turkey, duck, quail, game birds, and rabbit
    Spooned over egg pasta, potatoes, rice, or grains (try it with a mixture
      of cracked wheat and wild rice)

Cider and Apple Sauce with Ginger Threads

Apple cider is a wonderful liquid for sauces. When reduced, it has a delicious, cream-like texture, and it teams well with many foods including pork, veal, chicken, cabbage, potatoes, carrots, onions, apples, pears, bananas, and herbs (marjoram, thyme, basil, and rosemary).

MAKES ABOUT 1 ½ TO 2 CUPS

1 tablespoon unsalted butter
2 tablespoons fine julienne of fresh ginger
1 apple, quartered, peeled, cored, and sliced crosswise into ⅛-inch pieces
3 tablespoons cider vinegar
¾ cup reduced apple cider (page 15)
2 scallions, green part only, thinly sliced on the diagonal
Salt
Freshly ground black pepper

Melt the butter in a skillet over medium-high heat. Add the ginger and sauté for 1 minute. Add the apple slices and cook for 3 minutes. Add the vinegar and let it cook until almost evaporated. Add the cider and bring just to a boil to heat it through. Add the scallions, correct the seasoning, and serve.

--- **VARIATION** ---

This sauce may be made with slices of pear instead of apple.

CIDER AND APPLE SAUCE WITH GINGER THREADS may be
    Poured over boneless, baked chicken breasts
    Served over grilled or pan-fried veal chops
    Served with roast turkey or pork
    Spooned into a baked sweet potato or over a mixture of blanched carrots and cooked sweet peas
    Omitting the scallion, served with pancakes or French toast

Chicken on the Grill with Ginger Barbecue Sauce

Of the many barbecue sauce recipes around, this is one of my favorites. The candied ginger adds a welcome chewiness. You may marinate the chicken in some of the cooled sauce for between six and forty-eight hours.

▌ *GINGER BARBECUE SAUCE*

MAKES ABOUT 3 CUPS

2 tablespoons safflower oil
4 cloves garlic, minced
1 green or red pepper, chopped into ⅓-inch dice
1 large red onion, chopped into ⅓-inch dice
4 cups tomatoes, fresh or canned, peeled and seeded
¼ cup dark brown sugar
2 teaspoons Tabasco sauce
2 tablespoons Dijon-style mustard
2 tablespoons drained prepared horseradish
1 teaspoon Worcestershire sauce
1 tablespoon ground ginger
2 tablespoons lemon juice
Salt
Freshly ground pepper to taste
¼ cup minced candied ginger, first scraped of excess sugar

SERVES 4

1 chicken weighing between 3 and 4 pounds, cut in pieces

To make the sauce, heat the oil and sauté the garlic, pepper, and onion until they are soft and the onion starts to lose moisture. Crush the tomatoes and add them to the pot along with the sugar, Tabasco sauce, mustard, horseradish, Worcestershire sauce, and ground ginger. Bring the mixture to a boil, lower the heat, and simmer it for about an hour, stirring often. The sauce should be thick and taste powerful. Add more of the seasonings if you prefer a hotter or sweeter sauce. Add the lemon juice, salt, and pepper to taste. Add the candied ginger and heat through, about 10 minutes. At this point the sauce is ready to be used or stored. If you plan to marinate the bird in the sauce, use between 1 and 1½ cups cooled sauce. Discard this sauce after marinating.

If you aren't marinating, set aside 1½ cups sauce for basting the chicken and store the rest. Prepare the grill and place the chicken on the rack. Grill the chicken for 10 minutes on each side. Then start basting, turning the chicken every 5 minutes for another 25 minutes or until the juices run clear. To build up a nice crusty layer of sauce, baste the chicken every time it is turned. If you need more sauce for basting, pour some into the basting bowl from the stored batch to avoid contamination. Note that it would be unwise to store leftover basting sauce to be used again. (See page 23 for further comments on contamination.) Serve the chicken hot or at room temperature.

◻ NOTE

This dish may be prepared in the oven at 400 degrees F. Baste the chicken every 15 minutes after it has gone into the oven. It may also be broiled: Cook the chicken without sauce for the first 20 minutes, 10 minutes on each side, then baste it every 5 minutes until done. Keep the chicken between 8 and 10 inches from the source of heat.

∎

GINGER BARBECUE SAUCE may be
> Used with rabbit, lamb, goat, beef short ribs, slices of veal shank, or any cut of pork

▼ *Broiled Chicken with Herb Butter*

In this recipe, the chicken is first cut open along one side of the backbone, spread open, and flattened. A butcher will do this for you and the technique may be used for whole poussins and game hens. Served with biscuits and coleslaw, the cooked bird makes an ideal picnic dish.

▌HERB BUTTER

MAKES ABOUT ¼ CUP

3 tablespoons unsalted butter, at room temperature
2 tablespoons scissored fresh chives
1 tablespoon chopped fresh tarragon, or 1 teaspoon
*   crumbled dried tarragon*
1 tablespoon chopped fresh chervil
1 tablespoon chopped fresh parsley
1 small clove garlic, minced
⅛ teaspoon salt
Freshly ground black pepper

SERVES 4

1 chicken, weighing between 3 and 4 pounds

Place the butter in a small bowl, add the herbs, garlic, salt, and pepper, mix thoroughly, and set aside.

To prepare the chicken, place it on a cutting board, backbone up. Using a small paring knife, make one long cut from the neck end to the tail end along one side of the backbone, cutting through the chicken into the cavity. Place the chicken, breast up, on the board and reach underneath to pull open the cut edges. Flatten the chicken at the breast bone by pushing it down with the heel of your hand. You will hear a crack. Fold the wing tips under the bird. This procedure will give you a neat, compact chicken that will cook evenly and look attractive when done.

To flavor the bird, gently separate the skin from the meat, using your fingertips. Slide the butter under the skin and spread it over the leg and breast meat. Cut two slits through the skin at the tip of the breast near the drumsticks and put the ends of the drumsticks through the slits. Place the chicken on a rack in a roasting pan, cover with plastic wrap, and let it marinate for between 4 and 24 hours in the refrigerator.

Preheat the broiler.

Place the chicken, skin-side down, on a rack in a pan. Place the pan between 8 and 10 inches from the heat. Broil for 25 minutes. Gently turn the chicken skin-side up using spatulas and continue broiling it, basting once or twice, until the juices run clear when it's pierced with the tip of a knife and the chicken browns and crisps, between 10 and 15 minutes, depending on the size of the bird.

⬚ **NOTE**

The chicken can be roasted at 400 degrees F. for between 1 and 1½ hours, skin-side up. It may also be grilled, but the butter will drip on the coals and cause flames. Substitute 3 tablespoons yogurt or mustard for the butter; allow time to have the bird marinate for at least 4 hours in the refrigerator.

—————————————— **VARIATIONS** ——————————————

Using this same technique, flavor the bird with other compound butters (pages 41–43). As in the note about roasted or grilled chicken above, the butter in the recipe may be replaced by 3 tablespoons yogurt or 3 tablespoons of any type of mustard if desired.

■

HERB BUTTER is particularly good
    With freshly shucked peas, baby carrots, spring onions, potatoes, or rice

▼ *Parmesan-Baked Chicken with Corn Relish*

Here the chicken is baked with a crisp coating of cheese and bread crumbs. The relish is a very fresh, colorful mixture of end-of-the-season vegetables. The corn can be cooked by boiling, steaming, or roasting. It may also be grilled, which will give a smoky flavor to the relish.

■ *CORN RELISH*

MAKES ABOUT 3 TO 4 CUPS

1 large tomato, cored

2 cups cooked fresh corn kernels
2 roasted red peppers, peeled and diced (page 46), but not puréed
1/3 cup fresh basil leaves torn in small pieces
2 tablespoons red wine vinegar or flavored red wine vinegar
    (pages 37–38)
2 cloves garlic, minced
Salt
Freshly ground black pepper

▪ PARMESAN-BAKED CHICKEN

S E R V E S   6

Oil
12 chicken thighs
1/2 cup fresh bread crumbs
1/2 cup grated Parmesan cheese
2 tablespoons unsalted butter, melted

To make the relish, preheat the broiler. Place the tomato in a pan and broil it, turning once, until the skin splits, about 1 or 2 minutes. Peel, seed, and cut the tomato into irregular pieces. Place the chopped tomato in a bowl and add remaining ingredients for the relish. Stir to combine and set aside at room temperature until ready to use.

To prepare the chicken, preheat the oven to 350 degrees F. Oil a baking dish or jelly-roll pan. Remove and discard the skin from the chicken. Roll the chicken pieces in the oil on the pan and place them skinned side up. Combine the crumbs, cheese, and butter in a bowl and mix thoroughly, using a fork. Lightly press the crumbs over the chicken pieces. Bake the chicken for between 35 and 45 minutes, depending on size. Serve with a spoonful of relish on the side.

VARIATIONS

The cheese-flavored coating may be embellished with the addition of crushed fennel seeds, garlic, rosemary, ground nuts, basil, oregano, or other herbs.

▪

CORN RELISH may accompany
  All meats, game, and poultry, either hot or cold
  Cooked fish
  Sandwiches, on the side or in bread, such as pita

 # Chicken with Fresh Mint Sauce

This is the classic British sauce, which is made of three ingredients: malt vinegar, mint, and sugar. Make the sauce an hour before you are ready to cook because the mint will need time to steep in the vinegar syrup.

■ FRESH MINT SAUCE

MAKES ABOUT ½ CUP

½ cup malt vinegar
¼ cup sugar
3 large sprigs fresh mint, cut in 3 pieces
2 tablespoons chopped fresh mint leaves

■ CHICKEN BREASTS

SERVES 4

Oil
2 whole boneless chicken breasts, trimmed of all fat and connective tissue
Salt
Freshly ground black pepper

To make the sauce, bring the vinegar, sugar, and mint sprigs to a boil in a saucepan over medium-high heat. Boil for 1 minute, remove from the heat, cover, and steep for an hour until cool. Remove the sprigs and add the chopped mint.

To cook the chicken, preheat the oven to 400 degrees F. Lightly oil a baking pan or jelly-roll pan. Arrange the chicken in the pan, cover with foil, and bake for between 15 and 20 minutes, until it is just slightly resistant when pushed with your finger. (The meat will not be soft, as it is when uncooked, and the center should not be pink.) During the last few minutes of cooking, reheat the sauce over low heat.

Remove the chicken to a cutting board and cut it in thick slices on the diagonal. Arrange the slices on 4 plates, season with salt and pepper, and spoon the sauce over the chicken.

▪

FRESH MINT SAUCE may be

Mixed with leftover chicken and allowed to marinate overnight; this makes wonderful picnic food when served as a salad the next day

Used on grilled lamb chops or shish kebabs or to marinate slices of leftover cooked lamb

Spooned over sautéed liver and onions

Served with any seafood or used as a marinade on cooked seafood

Used as a dip for vegetable tempura

Added to sparkling water to make a bracing summer drink: 2 tablespoons strained sauce to 1 glass of sparkling water

Indian Chicken

The marinade for Indian Chicken is a variation of a typical *tandoori* marinade. Here I use it on boneless chicken breasts. This dish goes well with steamed potatoes or rice and broccoli stir-fried with garlic.

▪ *INDIAN MARINADE*

MAKES ABOUT 1 CUP

1 piece fresh ginger, about 1½ to 2 inches long and weighing about
*   1 ounce, peeled and cut in pieces*
2 cloves garlic
¾ cup plain yogurt
¼ cup olive oil
1 tablespoon lemon juice
1 teaspoon ground cumin

1 teaspoon ground coriander
½ teaspoon ground black pepper
½ teaspoon cayenne pepper
¼ teaspoon ground cardamom
¼ teaspoon ground cinnamon
Pinch ground clove

S E R V E S 6

3 whole chicken breasts, skinned, boned, and split
1 tablespoon vegetable oil

To make the marinade, place the ginger and garlic in a food processor and pulse a few times to break up the pieces (or mince with a knife). Add all the remaining marinade ingredients and process until the ginger and garlic are almost puréed. The marinade will have a grainy consistency.

Pour half the marinade into a dish. Add the chicken and cover it with the remaining marinade. Cover with plastic wrap and refrigerate, turning twice a day, until 1 hour before you are ready to cook. The chicken may be marinated for any length of time between 12 and 48 hours.

When ready to cook, heat the vegetable oil in a skillet over medium-high heat. The pan needs to be large enough to hold the chicken in one layer. Drain and pat the chicken breasts dry. Discard the marinade. Brown the breasts, cooking until they are no longer pink in the center, between 10 and 15 minutes, depending on their size. Lower the heat if they are browning too fast. Serve whole or cut in thick slices on the diagonal.

□ N O T E

The chicken breasts can also be baked. Preheat the oven to 400 degrees F. Place the chicken in an ovenproof dish and, without patting off excess marinade, bake until the meat is no longer pink in the center and a crust has formed, about 20 minutes, depending on size.

--- **VARIATIONS** ---

The marinade can be used on cut-up chicken pieces or whole chicken, poussin, or game hens split down the backbone and flattened (page 197).

INDIAN MARINADE may be
Used for shrimp, lamb, or pork tenderloin, or as a dressing over steamed potatoes

❦ *Chicken Sauté with Cream, Dill, and Asparagus Sauce*

A sauté of chicken uses either a whole, cut-up bird or the legs only. This recipe calls for stock and reduced cream. Have the stock prepared before starting and reduce the cream while the chicken sautés. Serve with grains, noodles, rice, or potatoes.

SERVES 6

1 tablespoon olive oil or vegetable oil
6 chicken legs, skinned and cut into drumstick and thigh portions
Salt
Freshly ground black pepper
1/2 cup chicken stock (page 7)
1 bunch asparagus, about 1 pound
1 recipe Reduced Cream (pages 13–14), about 2/3 cup
1/4 cup chopped fresh dill
1 1/2 teaspoons packed, grated lemon zest
2 teaspoons lemon juice

Heat the oil in a large skillet or sauté pan that has a lid. Brown the chicken well on all sides, in batches if necessary. Season with salt and pepper. When the pieces are brown, pour off the excess fat from the pan, and deglaze it with the stock. Bring the stock to a boil, add the chicken in one layer as best you can, reduce the heat to low, and cover the skillet. Cook for 10 minutes and turn the chicken over. Continue cooking for between 10 and 20 minutes until the juices are no longer pink when the chicken is pierced with the tip of a knife.

While the chicken cooks, steam the asparagus until it is tender yet still crisp. Transfer it to a board and cut into 2-inch pieces. Set aside.

When chicken is cooked, transfer the pieces to a casserole or gratin dish and keep them warm in a low oven. Bring the pan juices to a boil over high heat and reduce to about ¼ cup. Add the reduced cream and reserved asparagus and heat through. Add the dill, zest, and lemon juice. Mix well and correct seasoning. Spoon the gravy over the chicken legs, turning to coat the pieces, and serve them from the casserole.

VARIATION

Use tarragon and fresh peas in place of the dill and asparagus.

■

CREAM, DILL, AND ASPARAGUS SAUCE may be
> Made separately and served over boneless chicken breast, roasted turkey breast, or pan-fried turkey cutlets—deglaze the pan with the chicken stock and continue with the recipe
> Served over fish fillets—replace the chicken stock with fish stock
> Spooned over baked or steamed potatoes or poached eggs on toast

❦ *Cider-Braised Chicken with Marjoram*

Marjoram is a neglected herb, having been overshadowed by its more popular relative, oregano. It has a forceful, aromatic flavor that complements potatoes, poultry, apples, pears, rice, pork, eggs, and carrots. This dish makes its own gravy while it is braising. Then the flavors are concentrated by reduction after the chicken is done. It is not a complex reduction; rather it is a simple finish to a country-style dish. You may spread the work over two days by making the garnish on one day, and then braising and finishing the dish on the second.

Serve this dish with a bowl of cooked baby carrots and rice, with wide egg noodles, or with a buttered baked potato over which some sauce has been poured. A glass of dry Normandy or English cider would be delightful with this dish.

4 tablespoons unsalted butter
1 pound Spanish (mild) onions, cut into ¼-inch slices
¼ pound thinly sliced prosciutto, cut into ¼-inch julienne
4 Golden Delicious apples or 5 Russet apples, quartered, peeled,
    cored, and sliced
Salt
Freshly ground black pepper
1 chicken, weighing between 4 and 5 pounds
1 tablespoon oil
1 small yellow onion, thickly sliced
1 small carrot, thickly sliced
1 stalk celery, thickly sliced
2 large cloves garlic, crushed
1 bay leaf
1 teaspoon dried thyme
2 tablespoons chopped parsley stems
1 tablespoon dried marjoram
2 cups chicken stock (page 7)
2 cups sweet apple cider
1 tablespoon chopped fresh marjoram or 1 teaspoon dried marjoram

To make the garnish, melt 2 tablespoons of the butter in a skillet over moderate heat. Add the spanish onions and sauté until they are soft and browned, about 15 minutes. Add the prosciutto, toss well, and remove the mixture to a bowl. Raise the heat to medium-high and in the same pan, melt the remaining 2 tablespoons butter. Add the apples and toss to coat them with butter. Cook the apple slices, tossing frequently, until they are browned and soft, but not mushy, about 5 minutes. Add the apples to the onion and prosciutto mixture. Season with salt and pepper to taste, toss gently to combine, and set aside. Keep this garnish at room temperature if you are using it on the same day. Otherwise cool and refrigerate it.

To cook the chicken, preheat the oven to 325 degrees F. Truss the chicken. Heat the oil in a heavy pot that has a lid and is large enough to hold the chicken. Brown the chicken on all sides and remove it to a plate. To the same pot, add the yellow onion, carrot, celery, garlic, bay leaf, thyme, parsley stems, and the 1 tablespoon dried marjoram. Toss briefly over high heat. Place the chicken on top of the bed of vegetables and add ½ cup of the chicken stock. Reduce the liquid to a glaze. Add another ½ cup stock, reduce that to a glaze, and then add the remaining stock along with the cider. Bring the liquid to a boil, spread a large piece of foil over the bird and up and over the sides of the pan, and cover the pan with a lid. Braise the chicken until the juices run clear from the thigh when it is pierced with the tip of a knife; between 1 and 1½ hours, depending on size of the chicken.

Remove the chicken to a board and cut it into serving pieces. Arrange the pieces on a platter, season with salt and pepper, and keep warm in a low oven. Strain the braising juices into a pot, let sit for a minute, and defatten. Bring the juices to a boil and reduce until they are tasty, but not sticky. Add the reserved garnish to the pan. Heat through, add the fresh marjoram, and season with salt and pepper. Pour the gravy over the chicken and serve.

▼ *Roast Turkey Breast with Red Onion and Cranberry Compote*

The first time I tasted this sauce it was served as a side dish. My good friend and colleague Richard Kzirian prepared it at my cooking school one night ten years ago. I thought then, as I do now, that it was a spectacular dish, contrasting the sweetness of onion with the sharpness of fresh cranberry.

▮ *TURKEY*

SERVES 6

1 turkey breast, weighing about 6 pounds

▮ *RED ONION AND CRANBERRY COMPOTE*

MAKES ABOUT 4 CUPS

4 tablespoons unsalted butter
6 red onions, about 3 to 4 pounds total, cut into ⅛-inch slices
Salt

Freshly ground black pepper
½ cup stock, chicken (page 7) or chicken and veal (pages 5–6),
    or orange juice
1 bag (12 ounces) fresh cranberries

To roast the turkey breast preheat oven to 400 degrees F. Place the turkey on a rack in a pan and roast it for 1½ hours, basting often with the pan juices.

While the turkey roasts, make the compote. Melt the butter in a large sauté pan over low heat. Add the onions, toss them in the butter, and season with salt and pepper. Sauté the onions until they are soft and sweet, but not browned; about 30 minutes. Set aside until just before serving.

When the turkey is done, remove it from the oven, transfer to a platter, and let it rest for 10 minutes. Pour off all the fat from the roasting pan. Place the pan over high heat and deglaze it with the stock or orange juice. Reduce the liquid to a syrupy glaze (this will take between 1 and 3 minutes) and strain it.

When you are ready to serve, reheat the onions and add the cranberries. Cook for about 2 or 3 minutes to heat through. They should retain their shape and tartness. Correct the seasoning.

To serve, cut slices of hot turkey off the breast and arrange them on plates. Season with salt and pepper. Drizzle the pan juices over the turkey slices and serve with the compote on the side.

VARIATION

Omit the cranberries and replace them with the juice and grated zest of 2 limes. Cook 2 pounds of red onions in 2 tablespoons olive oil. Add the zest and juice, remove from heat, cool, season, and serve. This version is good on baked fish, roast pork, or chicken, baked ham, pan-fried duck breast, or cold slices of beef or veal.

RED ONION AND CRANBERRY COMPOTE may be
    Spooned into cooked acorn or other winter squash, or served with baked sweet potatoes
    Served with chicken, ham, duck, goose, game, pork, or fish

Turkey Scaloppine with Fennel Crumbs and Noisette Butter

Noisette butter is brown butter that is traditionally served with breaded and fried foods. You need only drizzle on a bit of butter to achieve that wonderful taste. The best *noisette* butter is made with whole, not clarified, butter, as most of the flavor comes from the milk solids that are removed in the clarifying. Whole butter requires more attention because the browned milk solids sink to the bottom of the pan and may burn.

Make the bread crumbs ahead of time (one day or up to one week) to let the fennel permeate them. The turkey can be breaded about an hour before cooking and placed on a rack over a pan. Keep it in the refrigerator, uncovered.

▮ FENNEL CRUMBS

MAKES 2 CUPS

4 to 6 slices white bread, enough to make 2 cups fresh bread crumbs
2 teaspoons fennel seeds

▮ NOISETTE BUTTER

MAKES ⅓ CUP

6 tablespoons unsalted butter

▮ TURKEY SCALOPPINE

SERVES 4

Approximately ½ cup flour
1 large egg
1 teaspoon water
8 turkey breast cutlets, weighing about 1¼ to 1½ pounds total
Fennel Oil (page 36) or olive or vegetable oil
Salt
Freshly ground black pepper
4 lemon wedges

To make the crumbs, place 4 slice of bread in food processor or blender and blend until they break down into fine crumbs. Measure out 2 cups and transfer them to a bowl. Use the remaining 2 slices of bread if needed.

Place the fennel seeds in a blender or a mortar and grind them to break them up. Pour them into the bowl with the bread crumbs. Mix the ingredients well and cover. Let the crumbs sit (make them ahead if possible) until you are ready to bread the turkey.

To make the *noisette* butter, melt the butter in a skillet over medium heat and cook it until it turns a deep golden brown and smells of toasted nuts. Whisk it often to prevent its burning. Pour the butter into a small saucepan, using a spatula to scrape all of it out of the skillet and set aside both butter and skillet.

To bread the turkey, place the flour on a plate and the fennel-flavored bread crumbs on another plate. Beat the egg and water together in a small bowl until the mixture is smooth. Flour the turkey cutlets and shake off any excess flour. Brush one side of each cutlet with egg and place it, egg-side down, on the crumbs. Brush the second side with egg and turn the cutlet over to coat that side with crumbs. Place the *scaloppine* on a cake rack over a pan and bread the remaining turkey in the same way.

Heat some oil in reserved skillet over high heat. Cook the turkey for 1 or 2 minutes on each side until it is crisp and golden. Remove the *scaloppine* to plates as they cook, season them with salt and pepper, and keep them warm in a low oven while you cook the rest, using more oil as needed. When all the turkey is done, lower the heat under the pan, wipe out any burned bits of crumbs, and pour the reserved *noisette* butter into the pan. Swirl to reheat it briefly and spoon it over the cutlets. Serve with lemon wedges.

VARIATIONS

Scatter toasted nuts over the turkey or sprinkle it with chopped fresh herbs, such as rosemary or sage.

Instead of turkey, this recipe may be made with slices cut from a butterflied leg of lamb, with chicken breasts, with veal *scaloppine*, or with all types of seafood, especially jumbo shrimp.

Noisette butter may be varied by adding capers, olives, pickles, herbs, or nuts.

∎

NOISETTE BUTTER may be
> Served on vegetables (particularly cauliflower), potatoes, pasta, rice, and grains

Roast Duck with Rhubarb and Leek Sauce

In this recipe, the tartness of rhubarb strikes a nice balance with the richness of duck, and the leek adds a deeper savoriness. The sauce can be made ahead and kept refrigerated. Try to find red rhubarb so that the sauce has a pleasing, rosy hue.

▎ *ROAST DUCK*

SERVES 4

1 duck, weighing between 5 and 6 pounds

▎ *RHUBARB AND LEEK SAUCE*

MAKES ABOUT 2 CUPS

1 pound rhubarb
¼ cup sugar
¼ cup water
2 teaspoons fresh thyme leaves or 1 teaspoon dried thyme
1 small leek, trimmed, halved lengthwise, washed, and drained
1 teaspoon unsalted butter
Salt
Freshly ground black pepper

> Preheat the oven to 375 degrees F. Place the duck on a rack in a roasting pan. Using the tip of a knife, prick the skin all over the duck.

Roast the duck for between 1½ and 2 hours, or until the thigh juices run clear when pierced with the tip of a knife.

While the duck roasts, make the sauce. Trim the rhubarb and cut it into ¼-inch slices. Place them in a saucepan with the sugar, water, and thyme. Bring the mixture to a boil, lower the heat, and simmer it for between 5 and 10 minutes, or until the rhubarb is tender. Stir the sauce occasionally while it cooks. When it is cooked, remove the rhubarb to a bowl and set it aside to cool. Cut the leek into ¼-inch slices. Melt the butter in a small skillet and add the leeks. Season them with salt and pepper and toss them. Cook the leeks over low heat until they are very soft, between 15 and 20 minutes. Add them to the bowl with the rhubarb and stir to combine. Set the bowl aside until you are ready to serve.

When the duck is cooked, tip it up to drain the juices from the cavity into the pan and place the duck on a board. Skim off the fat and strain the juices. Carve the duck into serving pieces and arrange them on plates. Drizzle the juices over the duck and serve it with a spoonful of rhubarb sauce on the side. Any remaining sauce can be served cold, room temperature, or warm.

VARIATIONS

Try making the sauce with only the fresh thyme instead of the leek. It will result in a sweeter sauce that still allows the sharp, pure taste of the rhubarb to come through.

Replace the thyme and leek with 1 to 2 teaspoons ground cinnamon. Serve on ice cream or breakfast dishes such as pancakes, or mix with yogurt and serve on grilled chicken breasts.

∎

RHUBARB AND LEEK SAUCE may be

Served with any pork; it goes particularly well with roast pork or baked ham

Served with pan-fried rabbit, roast chicken or turkey, game hens, poussin, quail, or squab

A Chunky Pear and Ginger Sauce for Duck Legs

I learned this technique for cooking duck legs from Madeleine Kamman. It's a wonderfully simple meal to prepare and duck legs are available at many butcher shops. If you cannot find duck legs, roast two ducks (pages 210–211) that have been brushed prior to cooking with a glaze of warmed honey and lemon juice. Carve the birds and give each person a portion of breast and leg meat.

▮ CHUNKY PEAR AND GINGER SAUCE

M A K E S   A B O U T   2 ½   T O   3   C U P S

3 pounds ripe pears, Comice, Anjou, Bartlett, or Packham quartered,
   peeled, and cored
¼ cup lemon juice
⅔ cup sugar
1 tablespoon finely minced fresh ginger, packed

▮ DUCK LEGS

S E R V E S   6

6 duck legs
2 to 3 tablespoons Dijon-style mustard
½ cup fresh bread crumbs

Cut the pears into chunks and place them in a saucepan with the lemon juice, sugar, and ginger. Bring the mixture to a boil over medium heat. Cook, stirring often, for about 15 minutes or until the pears are tender and the juices reduced. Mash the pears lightly with a potato masher or a fork. Transfer them to a bowl and allow the fruit to cool to room temperature. Serve the sauce at room temperature or refrigerate it until you are ready to serve.

Preheat the oven to 325 degrees F. Place the duck legs on a rack in a roasting pan and brush the skin side with a coating of mustard. Sprinkle the legs with bread crumbs and press the crumbs down lightly so that they cling to the mustard. Bake the legs for 2 hours, basting occasionally with the pan juices. The juices should run clear and the legs will have a crispy brown coating when they are done. Set the legs aside, keeping them warm.

Pour off all the fat from the roasting pan, add a bit of water, and deglaze the pan, scraping off the brown bits. Bring the juices to a boil, taste and reduce them if necessary, and drizzle them over the legs. Serve the duck with a spoonful of the pear and ginger sauce on the side.

∎

CHUNKY PEAR AND GINGER SAUCE may be
Served with baked ham, roast pork or lamb, pork or veal chops, braised lamb shanks, turkey, or chicken

Chapter 7

∎ ∎ ∎ ∎

Pork

and

Accompanying

Sauces

I LOVE PORK, BUT I HAD NEVER REALLY LIKED IT WITH A SAUCE more complex than plain mustard or applesauce. Now that pork is being bred leaner, and since pork tenderloin is readily available, I have changed my thinking.

Traditionally, sauces for pork have been made of fruit in order to balance the fattiness of the meat. Fruit sauces are still popular, and I have included several (see Roast Pork with Cranberry and Dried Cherry Sauce, pages 227–228, and Peach and Basil Chutney for Roast Pork, pages 220–222). However, there are other choices for saucing pork.

Pork tenderloin, because of its mild taste, works well with many different sauces. In this chapter I've included four recipes for pork tenderloin. In one it is marinated and skewered (see Marinated Pork and Citrus Skewers, pages 230–232), and in another it is stir-fried and topped with toasted nuts (Pork Tenderloin Stir-Fry, pages 232–234).

For other cuts of pork I've included sauce recipes using mustard, beets, shallots, and capers. In addition, there are also two sauces for ham: an apple and garlic compote (pages 234–235), and a red wine and citrus zest sauce (Garnet Sauce, pages 236–237).

Feel free to interchange these sauces and serve them with different cuts of pork, ham, and sausage. The Prune and Sekel Pear Sauce for Pork tenderloin (pages 222–224) would be delicious on roast pork or with cubes of braised pork. The apple and garlic compote (pages 234–235) would go well with roast pork, pork chops, or grilled sausages. Experiment and enjoy.

Pork Medallions Agrodolce

Agrodolce means "bittersweet" in Italian. In cooking, it refers to sweet and sour dishes. The deeply caramelized shallots and balsamic vinegar give an Italian flavor to slices of pork loin. The sauce requires reduced stock, so allow a little extra time for that process. Serve with steamed broccoli and sautéed carrots or mushrooms.

▮ *SHALLOT AND VINEGAR SAUCE*

MAKES ABOUT 1 CUP

1 recipe Reduced Stock (page 13), about 1 cup
4 tablespoons unsalted butter
8 large shallots, sliced
Salt
Freshly ground black pepper
2 tablespoons balsamic vinegar
Few drops lemon juice

SERVES 4

8 thin-cut slices boneless pork loin, trimmed of all fat
    and connective tissue
2 tablespoons chopped fresh parsley

Place the stock in a small saucepan and continue reducing it until you have ½ cup. Set it aside.

Melt 1 tablespoon of the butter over medium heat. Add the shallots, season with salt and pepper, and sauté them slowly until they are soft and well caramelized; between 15 and 20 minutes. Add the vinegar and lemon juice, cook for 1 minute more, remove from the heat, and allow the mixture to cool.

Heat ½ tablespoon of the butter over high heat. Cook the pork by browning it quickly on both sides. Remove the chops to plates and sprinkle with salt and pepper. Deglaze the pan with the reserved reduced stock, scraping up the brown bits. Add the shallot mixture and bring the sauce to a boil. Whisk in the remaining 2½ tablespoons butter and correct the seasoning.

Spoon the sauce over the pork and sprinkle it with parsley.

◼

SHALLOT AND VINEGAR SAUCE may be
   Served over chicken, turkey, veal, ham, or beef
   Served on mashed, baked, or sliced cooked sweet potatoes that have
   been sprinkled with salt and pepper

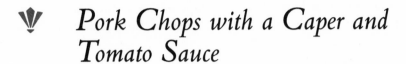

Pork Chops with a Caper and Tomato Sauce

Currants give this tart caper and tomato sauce a wonderful sweet edge.

◼ PORK CHOPS

SERVES 6

1 tablespoon oil
6 center-cut pork chops, about 2½ pounds total, trimmed of all fat
Salt
Freshly ground black pepper
Ground allspice

◼ CAPER AND TOMATO SAUCE

MAKES ABOUT 1 ½ CUPS

2 cloves garlic, minced
1 cup stock, chicken (page 7) or chicken and veal (pages 5–6)
2 tablespoons currants, packed
1 cup Fresh Tomato Sauce (pages 19–20)
¼ cup drained capers, rinsed and drained again

In a skillet large enough to hold the chops in one layer heat the oil
over high heat. Brown the chops well on both sides and season them

with salt, pepper, and allspice. Remove them to a plate, and keep them warm in a low oven with the door ajar.

Add the garlic to the skillet and cook it, stirring constantly, for 30 seconds. Add the stock and the currants and bring the liquid to a boil, scraping any brown bits from the pan. Boil it for 5 minutes to reduce it slightly. Add the tomato sauce and capers and cook everything together a few minutes. Add the chops, reduce the heat to low, cover the pan, and simmer for 5 minutes. Turn the chops over and cook them for another 5 minutes. Arrange the chops on plates and keep in the low oven. Turn the heat back up to high and bring the sauce to a boil. Reduce it until you have about 1½ cups left or until it is tasty; between 3 and 5 minutes. Spoon the sauce over chops and serve them.

■

CAPER AND TOMATO SAUCE may be
Served with beef, lamb, rabbit, chicken, veal, or turkey, particularly *scaloppine*.

❦ A Peach and Basil Chutney for Roast Pork

The combination of peach and basil is as natural and as outstanding a match as tomato and basil. The floral hints in peach and the licorice overtones of basil lend themselves to both sweet and savory dishes.

■ *PEACH AND BASIL CHUTNEY*

MAKES ABOUT 3 TO 4 CUPS

2½ *pounds peaches or nectarines, coarsely chopped*
1 *small red onion, sliced*
1 *large clove garlic, chopped*
1 *cup cider vinegar*
½ *cup honey*
½ *cup brown sugar*

½ cup orange juice
1 teaspoon salt
½ teaspoon ground ginger
½ teaspoon ground cinnamon
¼ teaspoon ground cloves
½ cup chopped fresh basil

■ ROAST PORK

S E R V E S   6   T O   8

1 tablespoon fresh thyme leaves or 1 teaspoon dried thyme
1 teaspoon ground allspice
½ to 1 teaspoon freshly ground black pepper
1 pork loin on the bone, weighing between 4 and 5 pounds, trimmed of
  all fat and connective tissue
½ cup stock (pages 4–10)

To make the chutney, combine all ingredients except the basil in a heavy bottomed pan. Bring the mixture to a boil, lower the heat, and simmer it for between 1 and 1½ hours or until it has thickened. Cool the chutney and refrigerate it. When it is cold, add the basil, stir well, and keep it refrigerated until you are ready to serve.

To roast the pork, preheat the oven to 325 degrees F. Combine the thyme, allspice, and pepper and rub the mixture over the surface of the roast. Roast the pork until a meat thermometer reads 145 to 150 degrees F. or until your preferred degree of doneness; about 1½ to 2 hours, depending on the size. Remove the meat from the oven and let it rest for 15 minutes. Pour off the fat from the roasting pan and deglaze it with stock, scraping up the brown bits. Bring the liquid to a boil and reduce it to a glaze. Carve and arrange the pork on plates. Drizzle it with glaze and serve it with the chutney.

——————— VARIATION ———————

For a cold dish, chill the cooked pork and serve with the cold chutney.

■

PEACH AND BASIL CHUTNEY is so versatile you can serve it

> With yogurt or mayonnaise or a combination of cream cheese and sour cream, as a dipping sauce for vegetables, crackers, or bread
>
> Alongside a grilled cheese sandwich or in a chicken or turkey salad mixture, or on a toasted muffin
>
> Spread in a sliced lamb, roast beef, smoked turkey, ham, chicken, or turkey sandwich, with lots of crunchy lettuce
>
> With curries, roast duck, roast goose, baked ham, grilled shrimp, or grilled chicken
>
> The herb and spice mixture given in the recipe for the pork may also be used as a dry marinade for poultry, veal roasts, or lamb

 ## Prune and Sekel Pear Sauce for Pork Tenderloin

Pork and prunes are a classic and wonderful combination. I've added pears, generously dosed with black pepper, for another taste. If you cannot find Sekel pears, use the smallest Anjou pears you can find.

■ *MARINADE*

M A K E S   3   C U P S

2 cups full-bodied red wine
2 cloves garlic, crushed
1 carrot, sliced
1 stalk celery, sliced
1 onion, sliced
4 whole cloves
2 teaspoons peppercorns
1 teaspoon whole allspice berries
1 piece stick cinnamon, about 1 inch long

S E R V E S   4

2 pounds pork tenderloin

▪ PRUNE AND SEKEL PEAR SAUCE

MAKES 1 ½ CUPS

8 ounces prunes
¾ pound ripe Sekel pears
1 tablespoon unsalted butter
Freshly ground black pepper
Ground allspice
Salt
2 cups stock, veal (page 8) or chicken and veal (pages 5–6)
Oil
1 tablespoon cornstarch (optional)
Parsley for garnish

To make the marinade, combine all the ingredients in a shallow glass or enameled baking dish. Add the pork, roll it in the mixture to coat it, and cover. Refrigerate and marinate the pork for between 12 and 24 hours, turning twice a day.

To start the sauce, soak the prunes in water to cover for 1 hour and drain. Place them on a plate. While the prunes soak, quarter the pears and remove the cores. Leave them quartered if they are very small; cut them into slices if they are larger. The slices should be about ½ inch wide. Heat the butter over high heat in a skillet large enough to hold the pears in 1 layer. The butter needs to be hot so that the pears will brown slightly. Add the pears and cook them for 2 minutes, tossing gently. Remove them to a plate and sprinkle them heavily with the black pepper and lightly with the allspice and salt. Toss the fruit with a rubber spatula to mix in the spices.

When you are ready to cook the meat, remove it from the marinade and pat it dry. Mix the stock and the marinade and bring the liquid to a boil. Reduce until you are left with 1½ cups liquid. Strain the reduction. While the sauce is reducing, heat some oil in a skillet over high heat. Add the pork and brown it well on all sides. Lower the heat and cook until the meat is the palest of pinks inside; about 20 minutes, depending on size and thickness. Press the meat with your finger; when it is done it will no longer be soft but resistant.

Continue making the sauce by adding the prunes and pears to the strained reduction. Simmer them together for 5 minutes. If you would like a thicker sauce, make a slurry (page 359) by mixing the cornstarch with 1 tablespoon cold water. Slowly pour it into the simmering sauce, stirring continuously. Bring the sauce to a boil and remove it from the heat. Season the sauce with salt and pepper and set it aside.

Slice the tenderloin, season it with salt and pepper, and arrange it on plates. Spoon the sauce over the pork and garnish it with parsley.

—— VARIATIONS ——

Use apricots and prunes or an unsweet ingredient, such as celery root, baby Brussels sprouts, cranberries, baby onions, whole shallots, or whole cloves of garlic.
If you would like a slightly sweeter marinade, add port, honey, and lemon juice. Rosemary also adds a distinctive flavor and is a perfect mate for pears.

PRUNE AND SEKEL PEAR SAUCE may be
Served with rabbit, roast duck or chicken, quail, squab, or braised lamb

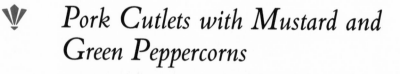

Pork Cutlets with Mustard and Green Peppercorns

This is another sauce in which reduced stock is used. A supply of this ingredient prepared ahead of time will allow you to finish the sauce very quickly.

SERVES 3 OR 4

1/2 tablespoon oil
1 pound pork cutlets

▮ MUSTARD AND GREEN PEPPERCORN SAUCE

M A K E S   A B O U T   ³/₄   C U P

1 cup reduced stock (page 13) veal stock (page 8) or chicken
  and veal stock (pages 5–6)
1 tablespoon grainy Dijon-style mustard
1 tablespoon smooth Dijon-style mustard
1 tablespoon drained green peppercorns, rinsed and drained again
1 tablespoon heavy cream
Salt

Heat the oil over high heat in a skillet large enough to hold the pork in 1 layer. Pan-fry the cutlets for about 2 or 3 minutes on each side, depending on their thickness. They will be pink inside. Remove the cutlets to plates and keep them warm in a low oven with the door ajar.

Deglaze the pan with the stock, scraping up the brown bits. Bring the liquid to a boil and reduce it to ³/₄ cup. Lower the heat to simmer and whisk in the mustards. Add the peppercorns and heavy cream and season the sauce with salt if desired. Slide the cutlets back into the pan to rewarm them and coat them with the sauce.

▮

MUSTARD AND GREEN PEPPERCORN SAUCE may be
  Used with chicken, turkey, beef, veal, or liver
  Used on smoked turkey, chicken, pheasant, or duck
  Spooned on slices of grilled potato
  Tossed with egg pasta

▼ *Pork Chops with Beet Dressing*

Serve this brightly colored dish with asparagus and steamed potatoes.

▮ BEET DRESSING

M A K E S   1 ¹/₂   C U P S

1 beet, weighing about 5 or 6 ounces
¹/₄ cup balsamic vinegar

³/₄ cup orange juice
1 strip orange zest, ¹/₂ inch wide and 3 inches long, chopped
1 large clove garlic, quartered
³/₄ cup oil, such as sunflower, safflower, or a light olive oil
¹/₂ teaspoon salt
Freshly ground black pepper

▪ *PORK CHOPS*

S E R V E S   4

Oil
4 pork chops, trimmed of excess fat
1 to 2 tablespoons scissored fresh chives

Preheat the oven to 350 degrees F. Prick the beet with a fork and bake it on the oven rack about 1 hour or until it is tender. Cool the beet, peel it, and cut it in half. Coarsely chop half the beet and place it in a blender. Dice the remaining half and place that in a bowl. Add the vinegar, ¹/₄ cup of the orange juice, the zest, and garlic to the blender and blend until the mixture is smooth. Add the oil in a stream. Season with salt and pepper and set the dressing aside.

Heat the oil in a skillet over high heat and brown the chops well on both sides. Lower the heat and cook until they are pale pink inside. Remove the chops to warm plates and sprinkle them with salt and pepper if desired. Raise the heat to high, add the remaining ¹/₂ cup orange juice to the pan and deglaze it, scraping up the brown bits. Boil the liquid until it has reduced to a glaze of 2 to 4 tablespoons. This will take about 3 to 5 minutes, and what you want is a nice syrupy glaze. Spoon some glaze over each chop and top with the reserved diced beet. Spoon the dressing over them and sprinkle with the chives.

▪

BEET DRESSING may be
> Used for a potato and asparagus salad, steamed potatoes with dill instead of chives, or over a baked potato
> Spooned over roast duck or chicken
> Used with mint for an apple or Waldorf salad instead of the classic mayonnaise
> Used in a red flannel salad made with corned beef, steamed potatoes, sliced beets, and hard-cooked eggs

Served over slices of cold roast beef or lamb

Spooned over baked onions

Used as a coleslaw dressing for cabbage and grated apple

Used for a salad of cucumbers, cooked chicken, and mint, or a salad of grated raw beets, cucumber slices, grated carrot, and apple or orange sections

Used as a marinade for poultry, pork, beef; omit the diced half beet

❦ Roast Pork with Cranberry and Dried Cherry Sauce

I'm not sure how this sauce came into being. I wanted to make something with cherries and maple syrup for a savory dish. Cranberries add just enough tartness to balance the sauce. Use tart dried cherries if they are available, although sweet dried cherries work as well. For side dishes try baked onions, winter squash, broccoli, celery root, baked sweet or white potatoes, or mashed potatoes.

SERVES 6

¼ cup sunflower seeds (optional)
1 boneless pork roast, weighing about 3 pounds
Freshly ground black pepper
1 cup maple syrup and 1 tablespoon for the pork
1 cup orange juice and 1 tablespoon for the pork
½ cup stock (pages 4–10)
12 ounces (1 package) fresh cranberries
6 ounces dried, pitted tart or sweet cherries
Salt

Preheat the oven to 350 degrees F. Spread the sunflower seeds in a baking pan and toast them for between 5 and 7 minutes, until they are lightly golden. Set them aside and lower the oven to 325 degrees F.

Sprinkle the pork with pepper. Mix 1 tablespoon each of maple syrup and orange juice in a small bowl and brush the mixture over the meat. Place the meat on a rack in a pan and roast it to an internal temperature of 145 to 150 degrees F.; between 1 and 1½ hours. Let the pork rest for 10 minutes before slicing it. Pour off the fat from the roasting pan and deglaze the pan with stock, scraping up the brown bits. Bring the liquid to a boil and reduce it to a glaze.

While the meat roasts, place the remaining maple syrup and orange juice in a saucepan and bring the mixture to a boil. Add the cranberries and cherries and bring the sauce back to a boil. Lower the heat and cook the sauce at a gentle boil for 5 minutes, stirring occasionally. Pour the sauce into a bowl and cool to room temperature.

To serve, slice the pork and sprinkle it with salt and pepper. Drizzle the glaze over the pork slices. Serve the sauce on the side topped with the reserved, toasted sunflower seeds.

VARIATIONS

Replace the sunflower seeds with ½ cup chopped, toasted hazelnuts (page 54). Sauté a Spanish onion or leeks in a bit of oil over low heat until they are browned and caramelized. Season with salt and pepper and add them to the sauce to make it thicker, more like chutney in consistency.

∎

CRANBERRY AND DRIED CHERRY SAUCE may be
    Used for roast turkey or chicken
    Served on game, such as venison, pheasant, or pigeon, roast duck, pan-fried quail, or sautéed rabbit
    Served chilled on the side with a *pâté* or terrine
    Spooned into baked acorn squash, baby pumpkins, or other winter squashes
    Served as a topping for sweet potatoes
    Served on wedges of baked onions, with a splash of vinegar
    Served on vanilla ice cream (my father could not stop eating this)
    Used as a topping for crisp waffles; drizzle warm maple syrup over the top

Pork Tenderloin with Sweet and Sour Caraway Sauce

The inspiration for this dish came from a Polish sauerkraut salad containing carrots and apples. The sweetness of the cooked, browned apples combines with the carrots to balance the tart lemony broth.

This recipe requires reduced stock, so allow extra time for making it.

▍ SWEET AND SOUR CARAWAY SAUCE

M A K E S   A B O U T   2   C U P S

4 thin carrots, cut into ¼-inch-thick slices on the diagonal
Salt
2 apples, Granny Smith or other firm, tart apple, quartered, cored, and peeled
1 tablespoon unsalted butter
1¼ teaspoons caraway seeds
1 teaspoon sugar
¼ teaspoon salt
Freshly ground black pepper
⅓ cup Reduced Stock (page 13)
⅓ cup lemon juice

S E R V E S   4

1 tablespoon oil
1½ pounds pork tenderloin

Bring a large pot of water to a boil. Add the carrots and salt. Bring the water back to a boil and cook the carrots for 5 minutes. Drain and rinse them under cold water. Drain again and set them aside.

Cut the apple quarters into 3 or 4 slices, then cut the slices in half crosswise. Melt the butter in a large skillet over high heat. Add the apples and toss to coat them with butter. Brown the apples, stirring frequently, then lower the heat to medium or medium-low. Cover the pan and cook the apples until they are soft, about 5 minutes. Add the carrots and ¼ teaspoon of the caraway, cover the pan, and cook for 2 more minutes. Transfer the mixture to a bowl and set it aside. Wipe out the pan and set it aside.

Place the remaining 1 teaspoon caraway seeds, the sugar, salt, and a small quantity of pepper in a small bowl. Add the stock and lemon juice and stir the mixture to dissolve the sugar.

Heat the oil in the reserved pan over high heat. Add the tenderloin and brown it on all sides. Lower the heat to medium-high and continue cooking until the pork is pale pink, between 10 and 20 minutes, depending on the thickness of the meat. Press the meat with your fingertip; when it is done it will no longer feel soft, but resistant. Remove the pork to a plate to rest. Add the carrot mixture to the pan and toss to reheat it. Reduce the heat to low and pour in the sauce. Heat the sauce, scraping the pan to deglaze it.

Cut the pork in ½-inch-thick slices on the diagonal and arrange them on plates. Season with salt and pepper and spoon the sauce over the meat.

■

SWEET AND SOUR CARAWAY SAUCE may be
    Made in the same way for veal or for boneless chicken breasts
    Served on pasta, particularly wide egg noodles
    Served on rice, white or brown
    Served on steamed, mashed, or baked potatoes
    Mixed into hot sauerkraut to accompany sausages and smoked pork
      chops

 Marinated Pork and Citrus Skewers

The pork here is simply left to steep with whole shallots and the two are then broiled. The garnish of broiled citrus wedges is both unusual and colorful. Serve this over rice noodles.

The pork and shallots must marinate overnight to develop a full flavor.

▮ MARINATED PORK

S E R V E S   4

24 small shallots, peeled
1½ pounds pork tenderloin, cut in 1-inch chunks

▮ CITRUS MARINADE

M A K E S   A B O U T   1   C U P

½ cup orange juice
¼ cup lemon juice
¼ cup chopped fresh coriander
2 tablespoons olive oil
1 tablespoon balsamic vinegar
2 teaspoons grated orange zest
1 teaspoon grated lemon zest

▮ GARNISHES

2 oranges
1 large lemon
¼ cup toasted almonds (page 54), chopped
4 sprigs coriander

Blanch the shallots in boiling water for 5 minutes. Drain and rinse them under cold water. Place them on 8 skewers alternating them with the cubes of pork.

Mix the orange and lemon juice, coriander, olive oil, vinegar, and orange and lemon zest in a bowl. Place the skewers in a shallow pan and pour the marinade over them. Turn the skewers to coat them well, cover the pan, and marinate them for between 24 and 48 hours in the refrigerator, turning them twice a day.

Just before cooking, prepare the garnish. Cut the oranges and the lemon into eight wedges each. Remove any seeds and skewer the fruit, alternating the colors, on 4 skewers. Set them aside.

Preheat the broiler. Remove the pork from the marinade, dry it, and discard the marinade. Broil the meat skewers for about 5 minutes on each side. Broil the fruit skewers for about 1 to 2 minutes on each side. Place 2 pork skewers on each of 4 plates. Place 1 skewer of the fruit in between the 2 of pork. Remove the skewers and sprinkle the meat and fruit with toasted almonds. Garnish with fresh coriander sprigs and serve.

—————— VARIATION ——————

If you would like to serve the skewers with a dipping sauce, simmer Fresh Tomato Sauce (pages 19–20) with fresh coriander and orange and lemon juice. Top individual bowls of the dipping sauce with the toasted almonds.

CITRUS MARINADE may be
Used for poultry, seafood, or lamb

▼ *Pork Tenderloin Stir-Fry*

The tastes in this dish are at once sweet, sour, and spicy; the textures are crisp. Prepare all the ingredients before you start cooking as the dish cooks quickly once you begin. Serve this over rice.

SERVES 4

▪ GARNISHES

2 tablespoons sesame seeds
2 scallions, trimmed and cut into ⅛-inch slices on the bias
¼ cup toasted walnuts or almonds (page 54), chopped (optional)

▪ VEGETABLES

1 tablespoon peanut oil
1 yellow summer squash, trimmed, halved lengthwise, and cut into
   ¼-inch slices

1 large red pepper, trimmed and cut in ¼-inch slices
¼ pound sugar snap or snow peas, trimmed
¼ pound fresh shiitake or portobello mushrooms, trimmed
    and thinly sliced
Salt
Freshly ground pepper

∎ MEAT

1 tablespoon dark sesame oil
1 pound pork tenderloin, cut in strips
2 large cloves garlic, minced

∎ SAUCE

6 tablespoons rice vinegar
2 tablespoons soy sauce
2 tablespoons dark sesame oil
2 tablespoons currants
¼ teaspoon red pepper flakes
2 tablespoons chopped fresh parsley

Toast the sesame seeds in a dry skillet over medium-high heat, stirring them constantly, until they are golden and fragrant. Transfer to a plate and set aside for garnish.

To cook the vegetables, place the peanut oil in a wok or large skillet and heat it over high heat. Add the squash and pepper and cook for 1 minute. Add the peas and cook for 1 more minute. Add the mushrooms and cook for 2 minutes. Remove the vegetables to a bowl and season them with salt and pepper.

For the meat, heat the sesame oil in the wok, and add the pork strips and garlic, and cook them for 2 minutes. Transfer them to the bowl with the vegetables, season with salt and pepper, and toss.

To make the sauce, add the vinegar and soy sauce to the wok, bring the liquid to a boil, and add the sesame oil and the currants. Reduce the sauce to concentrate its flavors. It will become slightly syrupy. Pour the sauce over the meat mixture, add pepper flakes and parsley, and toss all the ingredients together. Sprinkle the top with scallions,

nuts if you are using them, and the toasted sesame seeds. Serve in
bowls.

 ## Ham Steak with Apple and Garlic Compote

This recipe requires reduced cider in both the compote and in cooking
the ham steak. You can easily make it ahead and store it in the refrigerator. The compote may be eaten right away or set aside at room
temperature to mellow. It keeps well for about two weeks in the
refrigerator.

▮ APPLE AND GARLIC COMPOTE

MAKES ABOUT 4 CUPS

¼ cup raisins
1 whole head garlic, cloves separated and peeled
4 tablespoons unsalted butter
¾ pound Spanish (mild) onions, sliced ¼-inch thick
Salt
Freshly ground black pepper
½ cup Reduced Cider (page 15)
2 apples, Granny Smith or other firm, tart apple, quartered,
  peeled, and cored
Pinch sugar
½ to 1 tablespoon cider vinegar (optional)
2 tablespoons chopped fresh parsley

▮ HAM STEAK

SERVES 4

½ tablespoon unsalted butter

1 ham steak, 1/2- to 1-inch thick, weighing about 1 1/4 pounds, fully
    cooked, smoked if available
Freshly ground black pepper
1/4 cup Reduced Cider (page 15)

To make the compote, put the raisins in a bowl and add enough water
to cover them. Set them aside to soak. Bring a pot of water to a boil.
Add the garlic cloves, blanch them for 2 minutes, and drain.

Melt 2 tablespoons of the butter in a skillet and add the onions and
blanched garlic. Season them with salt and pepper and toss them.
Cook the onions and garlic over medium heat, stirring often, until
they are nicely browned and the vegetables are tender, between 20 and
30 minutes. Add 1/4 cup of the reduced cider and heat the mixture
through. Remove the vegetables to a bowl and save the pan.

Thinly slice each apple quarter crosswise. Melt the remaining 2
tablespoons butter in the pan in which the onions were cooked and
add the apples. Sprinkle them with a bit of sugar and toss the apples to
coat them. Cook them over medium to medium-high heat to brown
and soften the apples but do not cook them until they are falling apart.
Drain the raisins and add them to the apples along with the remaining
1/4 cup reduced cider. Toss the mixture, heat it through, add it to the
onions, and toss well. Season the compote with salt and pepper and the
cider vinegar if you wish to sharpen the flavor. Sprinkle the compote
with chopped parsley and set it aside.

To cook the ham, melt the butter in a skillet over medium-high
heat, add the ham and brown it well on both sides, about 3 to 5
minutes per side. Remove the ham to a plate and sprinkle it with
pepper. Pour off all the fat from the pan and deglaze it with the
reduced cider, scraping up the brown bits. Bring the liquid to a boil
and pour it over the ham. Serve the ham with the compote on the
side.

■

APPLE AND GARLIC COMPOTE may be
    Served with calves' liver, smoked meats, cold sliced meats, baked ham,
        roast pork, poultry (especially duck), and sweet- or white-potato
        pancakes, and baked sweet or white potatoes
    Served as a vegetable

◆ *Baked Ham with Garnet Sauce*

This sauce is my interpretation of a traditional English Cumberland sauce. Serve it with a potato gratin and a fennel and green bean salad. For a more elaborate meal, start with a mushroom soup.

▪ *BAKED HAM*

S E R V E S   8   T O   1 2

1 ham, smoked, fully cooked, bone in, and weighing between 10
  and 14 pounds
Approximately 1 cup orange juice

▪ *GARNET SAUCE*

M A K E S   A B O U T   1 ½   T O   2   C U P S

2 cups full-bodied red wine
2 cups orange juice
¼ cup red wine vinegar
2 strips orange zest, 1 inch wide and 3 inches long
4 cloves garlic, peeled and crushed with the side of a knife
2 onions, chopped
1 tablespoon mustard seed
½ teaspoon powdered ginger
Pinch ground cloves
Pinch cayenne pepper
1 teaspoon fresh thyme leaves or ½ teaspoon dried thyme
1 small bay leaf
1 tablespoon grated orange zest
1 teaspoon grated lemon zest
½ cup raisins
2 tablespoons cornstarch
¼ cup Grand Marnier liqueur (optional)
2 tablespoons lemon juice
Salt
Freshly ground black pepper

Preheat the oven to 350 degrees F. Place the ham on a rack in a large roasting pan. Make a diamond pattern of 1/2-inch-deep crisscross cuts on the surface of the ham. Brush the ham with some orange juice and place it in the oven. Bake it for between 15 and 20 minutes to the pound or until it is glazed and is hot to the center. While the ham is baking, baste it with the orange juice. When it is done, remove it from the oven, transfer it to a platter, and let it stand for 15 minutes.

While the ham bakes, make the sauce. Combine the wine, orange juice, vinegar, strips of orange zest, garlic, onions, mustard seed, ginger, cloves, cayenne pepper, thyme, and bay leaf in a saucepan. Bring the mixture to a boil, lower the heat, and simmer until the liquid has reduced by half. Strain and return the reduction to the pot. Add the grated orange and lemon zest and the raisins and bring the mixture to a simmer. Make a slurry (page 359) by mixing the cornstarch with the liqueur, or 2 tablespoons water, and the lemon juice. Whisk it into the sauce and, continuing to whisk, bring the sauce to a boil. Lower the heat and cook for 2 minutes. Season with salt and pepper. Remove the sauce from the heat and serve it or set it aside at room temperature until you are ready to serve. To serve, reheat the sauce and slice the ham. Arrange the ham on plates and spoon the sauce over the slices.

∎

GARNET SAUCE may be
> Served on poultry, lamb, rabbit, game, liver, egg noodles, rice, or potatoes

Chapter 8

LAMB

and

ACCOMPANYING

SAUCES

*L*AMB HAS A VERY DISTINCTIVE TASTE, SO IT IS OFTEN PAIRED with strong spices, herbs, and condiments like garlic, rosemary, curry, mustard, or salty olives. Many cultures have left their mark on lamb: the English with mint sauce, the Indians with lamb curry, the Italians and French with garlic and artichokes, and the Moroccans with various spices. These time-honored combinations are all delicious and they will stay with us for years to come. In reverence to these traditional dishes, I've included no "new and exciting" flavors in this chapter. I have, however, mixed traditional ingredients in new ways. The recipe for roasted leg of lamb (pages 251–253) calls for baked and puréed eggplant and garlic to be mixed with stock and heavy cream which makes a savory coating for the roasted meat. Kidney Lamb Chops with *Tapenade* (pages 243–244) is an easy recipe for grilled chops topped with a paste of black olives, garlic, and anchovies. The recipe for Moroccan Lamb Chops (pages 246–248) has two sauces: a compound butter, made of many spices including ginger, allspice, and cardamom, and an essence that is drizzled over the dish to reinforce the flavor of the lamb. There are recipes for marinated lamb, braised lamb shanks with gravies made from pan juices, lamb with red wine hollandaise, and a classic French *Blanquette* of Lamb with Artichokes (pages 256–258). A *blanquette* is a stew in which the meat is not browned first.

Since I cannot conceive of a world without garlic, I have included cooked garlic in three of the recipes here. In one, the garlic is puréed with eggplant, while in the other two the garlic cloves are cooked whole. Many people are surprised at how sweet and mild garlic becomes when it's cooked. If you like lamb, it is worth trying one of these garlic sauces because lamb takes to garlic as naturally as it takes to curry or mint.

Butterflied Leg of Lamb with Honey and Mustard Sauce

For this sauce, you simply need to stir the ingredients together. Although it is so very simple to make, most people still buy it at the store. Homemade honey and mustard sauce tastes fresher, and by making your own you can be certain that the ingredients are of the highest quality. The sauce keeps well for about two weeks.

▮ HONEY AND MUSTARD SAUCE

MAKES ABOUT ³⁄₄ CUP

¼ cup Dijon-style mustard
¼ cup grainy mustard
¼ cup honey
2 tablespoons lemon juice
Freshly ground black pepper

SERVES 4 TO 6

2 pounds butterflied leg of lamb
Olive oil
Salt

Mix the mustards and honey in a small bowl. Add the lemon juice and pepper and stir to combine. Set the sauce aside or refrigerate it until you are ready to use it, bringing it to room temperature before serving it.

Preheat the broiler. Place the lamb on a rack in a pan. Brush the lamb on both sides with olive oil. Cook the lamb, close to the heat source until it is rare to medium rare; about 7 to 10 minutes a side.

Transfer the meat to a board and cut it into thin slices. Arrange the slices on plates and season with salt and pepper. Spoon the sauce over the lamb and serve it.

◻ **NOTE**
The lamb may also be grilled or roasted (see Roasted Lamb Salad with Garlic Dressing and Spring Garnishes, pages 76–78).

———————————————— **VARIATIONS** ————————————————

For the sauce, you can substitute other kinds of mustard; I have tried shallot, herb, fruit-flavored, and green peppercorn mustards.

Freshly grated horseradish or apple or a combination of the two may be added to the sauce.

The addition of Tabasco sauce, cayenne pepper, or minced hot chilies and some garlic for extra savoriness will make the sauce spicier.

The lamb benefits from marination. Try a vinaigrette or wine marinade and leave the meat in it for between 24 and 48 hours, turning twice a day.

∎

HONEY AND MUSTARD SAUCE may be

Served with any of the following, hot or cold: poultry (try making a chicken salad), smoked poultry, ham, rabbit, pork, salmon, or white-fleshed fish

Spread on chicken breasts, boned or not, and marinated for a few hours; bake the chicken in a 400 degree F. oven until it is tender; the sauce forms an appetizing crust

Used as a dip for cooked green beans, apple slices, or other vegetables

▼ *Kidney Lamb Chops with Tapenade*

If you have *tapenade* on hand, all this dish requires is for you to cook the lamb. If not, *tapenade* is quite simple to prepare. Kidney chops are the equivalent of beef porterhouse steaks for they combine the loin with a nugget of the tenderloin.

8 kidney lamb chops, trimmed of all fat and connective tissue
Freshly ground black pepper
1/3 cup Tapenade *(page 44)*

Prepare the grill or preheat the broiler. If they are to be broiled, place the chops on a rack in a pan. Cook the lamb close to the broiler or coals for between 3 and 5 minutes on both sides (depending on their thickness) so that they remain pink inside.

Arrange the chops on plates and season them with pepper. Top each hot chop with a spoonful of *tapenade* and serve.

VARIATION

These chops may also be pan-fried in olive oil. If you have some stock on hand, deglaze the pan after removing the chops, reduce the stock to a syrup, and drizzle it over the meat. Top this with the *tapenade*.

TAPENADE is delightful
Used as a garnish for many foods, especially those of the Mediterranean; for other uses, see the index.

♥ *Buttermilk-Marinated Lamb Chops*

This is an excellent marinade for all cuts of lamb: butterflied leg, chops, steaks cut from the leg or shoulder, or kebab cuts. The acidity in the buttermilk helps tenderize the meat.

▮ LAMB CHOPS

S E R V E S   4

8 kidney or 12 small rib lamb chops, trimmed of all fat
    and connective tissue

▮ BUTTERMILK MARINADE

M A K E S   1   C U P

1 cup buttermilk
8 sprigs fresh rosemary
8 cloves garlic, crushed
1 teaspoon coarsely cracked black peppercorns
Salt
Freshly ground black pepper

Place chops in a nonaluminum baking dish. Pour buttermilk over the
chops, lifting and turning to coat them. Top each chop with a sprig of
rosemary and a clove of garlic. Sprinkle the chops with the peppercorns and let the meat marinate for between 24 and 48 hours, turning
it twice a day. Each time you turn the chops replace the rosemary and
garlic on the meat to flavor it directly.

To cook the chops, prepare the grill or preheat the broiler. Remove
the chops from the marinade and pat them dry. If they are to be
broiled, place the chops on a rack in a pan. Grill or broil them close to
the heat, for between 3 and 5 minutes on each side (depending on
their thickness) so they remain pink inside. Transfer them to plates,
season with salt and pepper, and serve.

VARIATIONS

Mix the buttermilk with horseradish and chopped dill. You could also add
    mustard, with or without the horseradish.
Try other herbs such as tarragon, chives, dill, mint, oregano, or basil.

Try tossing and marinating cooked artichokes in the buttermilk, adding mustard and using tarragon in place of rosemary.

∎

BUTTERMILK MARINADE may be
> Used for chicken, pork, veal chops, or seafood
>
> Flavored with chopped garlic and rosemary and used as a dressing over slices of cold lamb, beef, pork, seafood, or poultry, or in mashed potatoes in place of milk
>
> Used as a marinade for cooked vegetables such as potatoes, carrots, cauliflower, green beans, or *cannellini* beans; add the marinade to the vegetables while they are still hot

▼ *Moroccan Lamb Chops*

Moroccans use a spice mixture called *ras-el-hanout* in which countless spices and herbs may be combined. For this dish I borrowed the idea of *ras-el-hanout* but used just a few of the many seasonings. The butterless lamb essence is drizzled over the spicy compound butter and the chops. You may simplify this elegant dish by serving it with the compound butter alone or with the compound butter and a little reduced stock. My favorite accompaniment is simply cooked broccoli, green beans, or carrots.

The essence and butter will keep in the refrigerator for up to three days or they may be frozen.

∎ *MOROCCAN SPICE BUTTER*

MAKES ABOUT 6 TABLESPOONS

6 tablespoons unsalted butter, softened
1 large clove garlic, minced
2 tablespoons chopped fresh mint
1 tablespoon chopped fresh parsley
¾ teaspoon ground ginger
¼ teaspoon ground allspice

1/4 teaspoon ground nutmeg
1/4 teaspoon ground cardamom
1/4 teaspoon ground cinnamon
1/4 teaspoon freshly ground black pepper
1/8 teaspoon ground coriander
Pinch ground cloves
Pinch cayenne pepper
1/4 teaspoon salt

▮ *ESSENCE*

1/2 recipe lamb essence, omitting butter (pages 16–17) made with veal or
chicken and veal stock (pages 5–6, 8)

▮ *LAMB CHOPS*

S E R V E S   6

2 tablespoons olive oil
18 small rib lamb chops, trimmed of all fat and connective tissue
Salt
Freshly ground black pepper
Mint sprigs for garnish
Lemon slices for garnish, seeds removed

To make the spice butter, place the unsalted butter in a small bowl, mix in the garlic, mint, parsley, ginger, allspice, nutmeg, cardamom, cinnamon, pepper, coriander, cloves, cayenne pepper, and the salt. Cover and set the compound butter aside at room temperature to allow the flavors to blend.

Make the essence without the butter enrichment and set it aside.

Just before serving, heat the olive oil in one or two skillets over high heat. Sear the lamb quickly on both sides. Lower the heat to medium-high and continue cooking until the chops are rare to medium-rare, about 1 or 2 minutes. Remove them to a platter. Season the chops with salt and pepper and place a dollop of the spice butter on each. Pour off the fat from the pan, deglaze it with the essence, bring the liquid to a boil, and spoon it over the chops.

▮

MOROCCAN SPICE BUTTER may be
Served on any rice, grain, or potato dish
Served with lobster, shrimp, or poultry

❧ *A Red Pepper Dip for Lamb Nuggets*

This dish makes an original hors d'oeuvre, appetizer, or platter for a buffet table. The Red Pepper Purée is flavored with basil and a hint of orange zest. The nuggets are ground lamb that has been pan-fried in finger shapes. Both the sauce and the lamb mixture can be made ahead, the sauce a day or two, the lamb in the morning.

▌ *ORANGE AND RED PEPPER DIP*

MAKES ABOUT 1 CUP

³/4 cup orange juice
¹/2 cup lemon juice
1 strip lemon zest, ¹/2-inch wide and 2 inches long
1 strip orange zest, ¹/2-inch wide and 2 inches long
2 cloves garlic, crushed
1 recipe Red Pepper Purée (page 46)
¹/4 cup chopped fresh basil
2 tablespoons plain olive oil or basil oil (see Emerald Oil, page 35)
1 tablespoon red wine vinegar (optional)
¹/4 teaspoon cayenne pepper or red pepper flakes (optional)
Salt
Freshly ground black pepper

▌ *LAMB NUGGETS*

MAKES ABOUT 36 NUGGETS

1 pound ground lamb
1 small red onion, finely chopped
2 cloves garlic, finely minced

2 large eggs
½ cup fresh bread crumbs
2 tablespoons chopped fresh parsley
2 tablespoons chopped fresh basil
½ teaspoon grated orange zest
Small pinch cinnamon
½ teaspoon salt
Freshly ground black pepper
Approximately 2 tablespoons olive oil
Orange wedges
Basil sprigs

To make the dipping sauce, combine the orange and lemon juice and zest and the garlic in a saucepan. Heat and reduce the mixture to ⅓ cup liquid. Remove the zest and garlic and mix in the red pepper purée. Add the basil, oil, and, if using, the vinegar and cayenne or red pepper flakes. Mix well and season with salt and pepper. Set the sauce aside for the flavors to blend.

To make the nuggets, mix the lamb, onion, garlic, eggs, bread crumbs, parsley, chopped basil, zest, cinnamon, salt, and pepper in a bowl, combining them thoroughly. Place the oil in a skillet and heat it over medium-high heat. Shape walnut-sized pieces of the mixture (1 to 2 tablespoons) into fingers and fry them, turning them gently so that they brown all over, for about 5 to 10 minutes. Test one nugget; when cooked it should be pink, not red, inside. Drain the nuggets on paper towels and season with salt and pepper.

While the lamb nuggets finish cooking, reheat the sauce. To serve, arrange the nuggets on plates or a platter and garnish them with the orange wedges and basil sprigs. Place the sauce in little bowls for each person.

∎

ORANGE AND RED PEPPER DIP may be
  Served on any type of lamb preparation or with salmon, chicken or turkey breasts, or duck
  Used as a dipping sauce for sautéed shrimp, scallops, or veal
  Served on vegetable custards, terrines, or timbales
  Tossed with pasta

A Sour Cream Dipping Sauce for Lamb Kebabs

This dish incorporates Middle Eastern flavors into an all-purpose sauce. Serve on top of couscous or egg noodles along with a vegetable salad.

▪ LAMB KEBABS

SERVES 4

3 pounds lamb, cut in chunks
Approximately 4 tablespoons olive oil
1 teaspoon paprika
Cayenne pepper

▪ CUMIN AND SOUR CREAM DIPPING SAUCE

MAKES 1 CUP

1 cup sour cream or Drained Yogurt (page 49)
1 teaspoon paprika
Cayenne pepper
1 clove garlic, minced
1 teaspoon tomato paste
1/2 teaspoon ground cumin
1/4 teaspoon ground allspice
Salt
Freshly ground black pepper

Divide the lamb among 8 skewers. Place the skewers on a rack in a pan. Mix the olive oil with 1 teaspoon of the paprika and some cayenne to taste. Brush the oil over the lamb on all sides and set it aside to marinate and come to room temperature. This takes about 1 hour.

In a small bowl, mix the sour cream or drained yogurt with the paprika and some cayenne to taste. Add the garlic, tomato paste, cumin, allspice, salt, and pepper and set aside to allow the flavors to infuse the cream.

Prepare the grill or preheat the broiler. If they are to be broiled, place the skewers on a rack in a pan. Cook the lamb for 2 or 3 minutes and turn it over. Cook for 2 more minutes for rare or 3 minutes for medium-rare. Place 2 skewers on each plate and remove the meat from the skewers. Season with salt and pepper. Taste the dipping sauce for seasoning and adjust if necessary. Divide it among 4 small bowls or pile a spoonful on each plate.

—————————— VARIATIONS ——————————

Mix the sour cream or drained yogurt with between 1 and 4 tablespoons of herbs and spices. Try freshly chopped basil and garlic; scallions, thyme, and cracked black pepper; mint, garlic, a pinch of sugar, and cider vinegar; tomato and orange; curry powder, minced raisins, and toasted, chopped almonds; rosemary and minced artichoke hearts.

∎

CUMIN AND SOUR CREAM DIPPING SAUCE may be
Served with chicken, either baked or pan-fried breasts, on roasted turkey breast cut into thick slices, pan-fried turkey breast *scaloppine*, pan-fried duck breast, veal of all types, or grilled rabbit
Used on potatoes, rice, or mixed with wide egg noodles

▼ *Creamy Eggplant Sauce on a Roast Leg of Lamb*

This comforting sauce is enhanced by the sweet flavor of baked garlic. It is so delicious that you will want to add some croutons and eat it as soup. Serve this recipe with grilled red peppers and zucchini.

∎ *CREAMY EGGPLANT SAUCE*

MAKES ABOUT 3 CUPS

1 eggplant, weighing between 1 and 1½ pounds
14 cloves garlic, unpeeled

Approximately 1 to 2 teaspoons olive oil
2 cups stock, chicken (page 7) or chicken and veal (pages 5–6)
1 cup heavy cream
Salt
Freshly ground black pepper

▮ ROASTED LEG OF LAMB

SERVES 6 TO 8

1 leg of lamb, or half a leg of lamb cut from the sirloin end, weighing
about 5 to 6 pounds
Olive oil

Preheat the oven to 400 degrees F. Prick the eggplant and place it in a baking pan. Place the garlic cloves in another pan, sprinkle them with some of the oil and toss to coat. Bake both vegetables until they are soft when pierced with a knife; the garlic will take about 30 minutes, the eggplant between 45 minutes and 1 hour. Allow them to cool enough so you can handle them. Remove the skin of the eggplant and scrape the pulp into a food processor. Peel the garlic and add the cloves to the processor. Purée until the mixture is smooth, leaving some texture. Transfer the mixture to a bowl and set it aside. (If you do not have a processor, use a potato masher to purée the vegetables.)

To roast the meat, remove the fat from the lamb and rub the lamb with olive oil. Place it on a rack in a pan and roast it at 400 degrees F. for about 1 hour and 15 minutes or until the internal temperature registers 135 degrees F. on a thermometer; about 15 minutes per pound.

While the meat roasts, continue making the sauce. Reduce the stock to ⅓ cup, add the cream, and mix until smooth. Add the reserved eggplant purée and bring the mixture to a boil. Lower the heat and simmer it gently to combine the flavors. If the purée is a bit thin, continue simmering to reduce it slightly. Season with salt and pepper and remove it from the heat.

When the lamb is cooked, let it rest for 15 minutes while you reheat the sauce slowly. Cut the meat in slices and arrange them on plates. Season the slices with salt and pepper, spoon the sauce over the lamb, and serve.

Replace the eggplant with butternut or buttercup squash and serve on roast
chicken.

∎

CREAMY EGGPLANT SAUCE may be
>   Served on poultry, veal, potatoes, grains, rice, or pasta
>   Mixed with pasta, topped with grated Parmesan cheese, and baked

❦ *Braised Lamb Shanks with Orange and Garlic*

The braising juices in this dish are thickened with a *Beurre Manié* (page
357), a mixture often used with stews. If you prefer a gravy without
butter, use a slurry—a mixture of pure starch (cornstarch, for example)
and a liquid—for thickening instead. Serve the lamb over cracked
wheat with a salad of spinach, cucumbers, and red onions.

SERVES   6

Oil
6 lamb shanks
1 onion, sliced
2 large cloves garlic, crushed with the side of a knife
4 branches fresh rosemary
½ cup chopped fresh parsley stems
1½ teaspoons fresh thyme leaves or ½ teaspoon dried thyme
1 bay leaf
4 oranges
2 tablespoons cognac (optional)
4 cups stock, veal (page 8) or chicken and veal (pages 5–6)
3 whole heads garlic, separated into cloves
Salt
Freshly ground black pepper

3 tablespoons flour (optional)
3 tablespoons unsalted butter (optional)

Preheat the oven to 325 degrees F. In a large casserole heat a small amount of oil over medium-high heat. Brown the lamb well all over and remove the shanks to a plate. Add the onion, the 2 crushed garlic cloves, 3 branches of the rosemary, the parsley stems, thyme, and bay leaf and cook for between 3 and 5 minutes until lightly browned. With a vegetable peeler, remove two strips of zest from one of the oranges and add it to the pot. Add the cognac and let it evaporate. Squeeze the partially zested orange and add the juice to the pot with 3 cups of the stock. Bring the liquid to a boil and add the lamb shanks. Cover the pan with a large piece of tin foil that has been smoothed closely over the meat and up the sides of the pan. Top with the lid. Place the pan in the oven and braise the lamb for 1 hour. Turn the lamb shanks over, cover again, and continue cooking for another hour, or until the tip of a knife goes in and out of the meat easily, meeting no resistance.

While the meat cooks, prepare the garnishes. Peel the garlic cloves and leave them whole. In a pot bring the remaining cup of stock to a boil with the garlic cloves. Simmer the garlic until the cloves are soft when pierced with a knife. They should be almost glazed with the stock. Set aside. Peel the remaining three oranges with a knife, removing all the peel and white pith. With a sharp paring knife, remove the orange sections from in between the membranes. Do this over a bowl to catch the juices. Remove any seeds and set the sections aside, covered. Remove the leaves from the remaining branch of rosemary, chop them finely, and set them aside.

When the meat is cooked, remove it to a heatproof serving dish and keep it warm in a low oven. Strain the liquid into a pot, add the reserved rosemary and any orange juice in the bowl, and bring it to a boil. Season with salt and pepper. Reduce the braising liquid over medium heat until it is tasty. Thicken the gravy if you wish, by mixing the butter and flour together with a fork to make a *beurre manié*, adding it to the liquid and bringing the mixture to a boil, stirring constantly. The gravy should be slightly thicker than heavy cream. Add the reserved garlic and orange sections to the sauce. Correct the final seasoning and pour the gravy over the lamb shanks. Serve the lamb from the dish.

Lamb with Red Wine and Persillade Hollandaise

A *persillade* is a combination of minced garlic and parsley and is usually used as a garnish.

Serve this lamb with artichokes or asparagus and any rice.

▌ LAMB

S E R V E S   6   T O   8

1 leg of lamb, weighing between 5 and 6 pounds, excess fat removed
Olive oil

▌ RED WINE AND PERSILLADE HOLLANDAISE

M A K E S   A B O U T   1 ½   T O   2   C U P S

3 cloves garlic, minced
¼ cup chopped fresh parsley
1 cup unsalted butter
½ cup dry, heavy-bodied, French red wine (Côtes-du-Rhone–type)
¼ cup lemon juice
¼ cup balsamic, red wine, or cider vinegar
6 shallots, chopped
½ cup chopped fresh parsley stems
Salt
Freshly ground black pepper
3 large egg yolks

Preheat the oven to 400 degrees F. Rub the meat generously with olive oil and set it on a rack in a roasting pan. Roast until the meat reaches an internal temperature of 135 degrees F.; about 1 to 1¼ hours, depending on weight (about 15 minutes per pound).

While the meat cooks, prepare the sauce. With the side of a knife, crush the minced garlic to a purée by pressing and flattening the garlic several times. Mix the garlic with the chopped parsley. Set this *persillade* aside, covered, in a small bowl. Melt the butter in a pan and set it aside to cool. In a heavy pot, place the wine, lemon juice, vinegar, shallots, parsley stems, and a pinch of salt and pepper. Bring the mixture to a boil, lower the heat to simmer, and reduce the liquid until you have only about 2 or 3 tablespoons left. This will take between 10 and 15 minutes, depending on the size of the pot. Strain the mixture and allow it to cool slightly. Whisk in the egg yolks. Place the mixture over low heat and whisk it constantly to form a thick, foamy mass; about 5 minutes. When it has increased in volume, lightened in color, and thickened so that you can see the bottom of the pan while you are whisking, remove the mixture from the heat. Starting drop by drop and whisking constantly, add the melted butter gradually. When all the butter is absorbed, add the reserved garlic and parsley mixture. Keep the sauce over a pot of barely warm water, off the heat, to prevent curdling. If the sauce should separate and pools of butter appear on the surface, add a little water. Correct the seasoning with salt and pepper. When the lamb is cooked, let it rest for 15 minutes. Cut the meat in slices and arrange on plates. Serve the hollandaise over the slices of lamb.

▮

RED WINE AND PERSILLADE HOLLANDAISE may be
> Served on beef, poultry, fish, eggs, or skinless and boneless duck breasts

❦ *Blanquette of Lamb with Artichokes*

A *blanquette* is a stew made with a cream-enhanced broth. The meat (this dish may also be made with veal or chicken) for a *blanquette* is not browned and is usually cooked, like a sauté or fricassée, on top of the stove, not in the oven, The gravy is thickened with a *roux* after the meat has cooked. Serve this dish on a cooked grain or over egg noodles, with a leafy salad on the side.

▮ *BLANQUETTE OF LAMB*

S E R V E S   6

3 pounds lamb shoulder, cubed
3 cups chicken stock (page 7)

1 onion, sliced
1 carrot, sliced
2 cloves garlic, crushed with the side of a knife
¼ cup chopped fresh tarragon
1 lemon
½ cup chopped fresh parsley stems
1½ teaspoons fresh thyme leaves or ½ teaspoon dried thyme
1 bay leaf

∎ GARNISHES

8 artichokes
4 tablespoons unsalted butter
Salt
Freshly ground black pepper
3 tablespoons flour
½ cup heavy cream
2 tablespoons sliced scallions, green part only
2 tablespoons chopped fresh parsley

Place the lamb in a pot, add the stock, and bring it slowly to a boil. Add the onion, carrot, garlic, 1 tablespoon of the tarragon, a strip of lemon zest, parsley stems, thyme, and bay leaf. Simmer the lamb for 1 hour, uncovered.

While the meat cooks, grate the remaining lemon zest and set it aside. Clean the artichokes by removing all the leaves and the choke right down to the heart. (Discard the choke, but steam and chill the leaves for another meal.) Rub the artichoke hearts with the lemon to prevent them from discoloring. Blanch the artichoke hearts in boiling water for 10 minutes, drain them, and cut them into wedges. Melt 2 tablespoons of the butter in a large skillet and sauté the artichokes gently. Season with salt and pepper, add the reserved grated lemon zest, and the remaining tarragon. Toss well, leave them in the pan, and set it aside off the heat.

When the meat is done, remove it from the pot and add it to the artichokes. Strain the cooking liquid into a bowl. Melt the remaining butter and whisk the flour into the pot. Cook the *roux* for 5 minutes. Add the cooking liquid and bring it to a boil, whisking. Simmer the sauce for about 15 minutes. Add the heavy cream and continue to cook until the gravy coats the spoon, between 5 and 10 minutes. Season the gravy with salt and pepper and pour it over the artichokes and meat. Heat through and serve the *blanquette* sprinkled with the scallions and parsley.

❦ Braised Lamb Shanks with Whole Garlic and Mint Sauce

In this dish the sauce is a reduction of the pan juices; it is not thickened with a starch. The shanks are braised and the meat is removed from the bones. The meat melts in your mouth, the gravy adds a rich taste and texture, and the cooked garlic cloves are a creamy surprise. Serve the dish with a refreshing salad of sliced oranges drizzled with olive oil, a steamed green vegetable, and a loaf of warmed bread or egg noodles, potatoes, or a grain to absorb the extra sauce.

SERVES 4

2 whole good-sized heads garlic
2 tablespoons olive oil
Salt
Freshly ground black pepper
4 lamb shanks, weighing between 1 and 1½ pounds each
2 to 3 cups stock, veal (page 8) or chicken and veal (pages 5–6)
¼ cup chopped fresh mint

Preheat the oven to 350 degrees F. Peel the garlic cloves, place them in a small pan, drizzle with 1 tablespoon of the olive oil, and toss them well. Sprinkle the garlic with salt and pepper and bake for between 25 and 30 minutes, tossing every 10 minutes, until the cloves are golden and soft when pierced with the tip of a knife. When cooked, set the garlic aside and lower the oven to 325 degrees F.

Heat the remaining oil in a casserole, stew pot, or Dutch oven large enough to hold the shanks in one layer. The bones can overlap. Brown the shanks well all over. Add enough stock to come halfway up the shanks and bring it to a boil. Cover the shanks with a sheet of foil that has been smoothed tightly over the meat and up the sides of the pan. Top with the pot lid. Place the pot in the oven and braise the lamb for 1 hour. Turn the shanks over and continue to braise them for another hour or until a knife slides in and out of the meat without resistance. Transfer shanks to a plate.

Strain the cooking juices into a saucepan, bring them to a boil, and reduce them to about ¾ cup. The amount does not need to be exact, but the gravy should be slightly sticky and very flavorful with a texture like that of heavy cream.

While the gravy reduces, remove all the meat from the bones and arrange it on 4 plates. Season with salt and pepper if desired and place the meat in a low oven to keep warm.

When the gravy has reduced, add the reserved garlic and heat through. Correct the seasoning with salt and pepper and add the mint. Spoon the gravy over the lamb and serve.

∎

Leftover WHOLE GARLIC AND MINT SAUCE may be
Served on thick slices of toasted Italian bread drizzled with olive oil
Spooned on poached or over-easy eggs
Served on any type of pasta, potato, couscous, grain, or rice

Chapter 9

■ ■ ■ ■ ■

VEAL, BEEF,
and
ACCOMPANYING SAUCES

*S*AUCES FOR BEEF AND VEAL ARE AS VARIED AND PLENTIFUL AS the cuts offered at butcher shops and supermarkets. Brown sauces are the most popular, and those included in this chapter are based on reduced stock or an essence (see pages 13, 16–17). In brief, an essence is a magnificent, silky, rich sauce that is the result of multiple reductions of stock mixed with browned meat. The strengthened stock provides a consistency and taste unobtainable from plain stock. You may use this same technique with other meats such as lamb, poultry, and game. This type of sauce has to a large extent replaced the classic French *espagnole* and *demi-glace* sauces, which contained flour and fat (*roux*) and were considerably more elaborate and time-consuming.

In this chapter I've included three recipes for dishes with essences that demonstrate the basic technique, but the finished sauce, and subsequently the whole character of the dish, can easily be altered by substituting flavorings and garnishes. Veal *Scaloppine* Marsala (pages 268–269), for instance, can be changed by adding wild mushrooms, garlic, prosciutto, or citrus fruit, or by using reductions of white or red wine instead of the mushrooms and Marsala. Reductions of wine have been added to two of the essence-based sauces, but you may add other sauces or reductions—tomato purée for example—to these essences. In short, my recipes will give you a starting point for experimentation.

In addition to essences, many other sauces are suitable for veal and beef. Cream sauces, for instance, are delicious, particularly with veal, while compound butters (pages 41–43) offer quick solutions for last-minute meals. If you are concerned about fat, sauces and relishes made of vegetables and fruits are healthy, interesting alternatives, as are the lighter sauces made with yogurt, soy sauce, lemon juice, unreduced stock, or fortified wines.

In addition to some of the recipes mentioned above, I have included recipes for a cold beef dish with sour cream and horseradish sauce, for braised beef, and for poached brisket. They taste best the next day when all the flavors have mingled with the meat.

❧ Veal Chops in Hazelnut and Artichoke Cream

This is a rich, delectable sauce. Toast the nuts, reduce them with the cream, and prepare the artichokes ahead of time. The dish can then be easily assembled and cooked in about fifteen minutes.

▪ HAZELNUT AND ARTICHOKE CREAM

MAKES ABOUT 2 CUPS

1 cup toasted hazelnuts (page 54)
1 cup heavy cream
2 large or 3 medium artichokes
2 tablespoons unsalted butter
Salt
Freshly ground black pepper

SERVES 4

4 veal chops, each about 1 inch thick, trimmed of all fat

To make the sauce, chop up ¼ cup of the nuts and set them aside for the garnish. Grind the remaining nuts in a blender and combine them with the heavy cream in a saucepan. Reduce the mixture (pages 13–14) until about ⅔ of a cup of cream is left and strain. Discard the nuts.

Cut the stems off the artichokes and steam them until they are tender when they are pierced with a knife through the bottom. Let the artichokes cool and remove the leaves, saving them for another use. Remove the choke and discard it. Cut the artichoke hearts into irregular pieces. Melt 1 tablespoon of the butter in a skillet over medium heat, sauté the artichoke hearts for 2 minutes, and season them with salt and pepper. Pour the strained, reduced cream over the artichokes and set the sauce aside. It can be made up to one day ahead. Keep refrigerated.

Heat the remaining butter over medium-high heat in a skillet. Cook the chops, browning them well on both sides, for about 3 to 5 minutes per side. The chops should be pale pink. Remove the chops to plates and season with salt and pepper. Add the cream mixture to the pan and reheat it. Scrape the pan to deglaze it while you are reheating the cream. Spoon the sauce over the chops and sprinkle them with the reserved chopped hazelnuts.

■

HAZELNUT AND ARTICHOKE CREAM may be

> Served with lamb chops, pork tenderloin, chicken breasts, or a nonoily white fish
>
> Spooned into a baked potato, served with any egg pasta, or mixed with wild, brown, or *basmati* rice
>
> Served with poached, baked, or coddled eggs
>
> Poured over cooked zucchini that have been layered in a gratin or baking dish; bake until bubbly

▼ *Veal Chops with Cider and Rosemary Butter*

This compound butter can be made ahead, cut in two portions, and frozen or kept in the refrigerator.

▮ *CIDER AND ROSEMARY BUTTER*

MAKES ABOUT ½ CUP

½ cup unsalted butter, softened
¾ teaspoon chopped fresh rosemary

1 clove garlic, minced
½ teaspoon salt
Freshly ground black pepper
6 tablespoons Reduced Cider (page 15), cooled

S E R V E S   4

1 tablespoon olive oil
4 veal chops, each about 1 inch thick, trimmed of all fat

To make the compound butter, cream the butter, rosemary, garlic, salt, pepper, and 2 tablespoons of the reduced cider in a small bowl. Taste for seasoning and set it aside or refrigerate.

When you are ready to cook the chops, remember to remove the cider and rosemary butter from the refrigerator so that it will have softened by the time you plan to serve the dish.

To cook the chops, heat the oil over medium-high heat in a skillet large enough to hold the chops in 1 layer. Cook the chops, browning them well on each side, for about 3 to 5 minutes per side. The chops should be pale pink. Transfer them to plates, season with salt and pepper, and place a spoonful of the cider and rosemary butter on each chop. Deglaze the pan with the remaining 4 tablespoons reduced cider. Scrape the pan well to dissolve the caramelized meat juices. Drizzle the hot cider over the finished chops and serve.

■

CIDER AND ROSEMARY BUTTER may be
Served on pan-fried lamb chops, roast leg of lamb, or pork chops
Spooned on steamed vegetables, such as cauliflower, and tossed to coat
Placed on poached or browned chicken breasts

❖ *Roast Veal with a Very Lemony Sauce*

You have to be a lemon lover to enjoy this tart, yet creamy sauce. Serve this dish with rice and brightly colored vegetables.

Olive oil
1 boneless veal roast from the leg or loin, weighing about 3 pounds, tied
1 carrot, coarsely chopped
1 small onion, coarsely chopped
1 stalk celery, coarsely chopped
3 cloves garlic, sliced
Salt
Freshly ground black pepper
½ cup white wine
3 or 4 lemons
1 cup heavy cream

Preheat the oven to 325 degrees F. On the stove, heat the oil in a baking dish, casserole, or Dutch oven. Brown the veal well on all sides and remove it to a plate. Add the vegetables, season with salt and pepper, and cook them for 2 or 3 minutes. Add the wine and scrape the pan to deglaze it. Bring the wine to a boil, lower the heat and reduce the liquid until it is almost gone. Return the veal to the pan and roast it for between 1 and 1½ hours or until the internal temperature reaches 140 degrees F.

While the veal roasts, remove the zest from one of the lemons. Cut the lemon zest crosswise into very thin strips and then chop the strips. Set the zest aside in a small bowl. Squeeze the zested lemon and as many of the remaining lemons as you need to obtain ½ cup juice. Set the lemon juice aside.

When the meat is done, remove it to a platter and allow it to rest for 15 minutes, keeping it warm. Strain the juices from the roasting pan into a saucepan and add the lemon juice. Bring the mixture to a boil and reduce it to ¼ cup. Add the cream and the reserved, chopped zest and reduce the liquid to 1 cup. Season the sauce with salt and pepper. Slice the meat and arrange it on plates or on a platter. Season the slices with salt and pepper and spoon the sauce over the meat.

∎

Leftover VERY LEMONY SAUCE may be
    Served on noodles, rice, or potato slices
    Spooned over roasted or boneless chicken or turkey breast

Mixed with cooked vegetables, such as green beans, asparagus, artichokes, spinach, carrots, beets, broccoli, or cauliflower

▼ *Veal Scaloppine Marsala*

The veal in this classic dish is smothered in mushrooms. Accompany it with cooked carrots tossed with strips of prosciutto.

S E R V E S   6

*½ recipe veal essence (pages 16–17), without the added butter, or ½ cup
    Reduced Stock (page 13) made with veal or chicken and veal stock
    (pages 8, 5–6)*
8 tablespoons unsalted butter
1½ pounds cultivated mushrooms, thinly sliced
Salt
Freshly ground pepper
1½ pounds thinly sliced veal scaloppine
2 to 4 tablespoons Marsala

Make the essence or reduce the stock and set it aside.

Heat 2 tablespoons of the butter in a large sauté pan over medium heat and add the mushrooms. Season with salt and pepper and toss the mushrooms to coat them with butter and seasonings. Cover the pan and let the mushrooms cook until the juices have been drawn out. Uncover the pan, drain off the juices, and save them. Let the mushrooms brown for a bit in the pan then remove them to a bowl and set the pan aside unwashed. Add the mushroom juices to the reserved essence, bring the mixture to a boil, and reduce to the original thickness of the essence or stock before the mushroom juices were added. Set the sauce aside.

Flatten the veal *scaloppine* with a meat pounder or the heel of your hand. In the mushroom pan heat 2 tablespoons of the butter over high heat and quickly pan-fry the veal until it is brown on both sides. This will take about 1 or 2 minutes a side. Place the *scaloppine* on a platter and keep them warm. Deglaze the pan with 2 tablespoons of Marsala, scraping up the brown bits. Add the reserved sauce and bring to a boil. Whisk the remaining 4 tablespoons of the butter into the boiling sauce. Lower the heat, add the mushrooms, and heat through. Correct the seasoning with salt and pepper and add more Marsala if needed. Season the veal with salt and pepper and spoon the sauce over the *scaloppine*.

VARIATIONS

Substitute turkey, chicken, or beef for the veal.

■

Leftover MUSHROOM AND MARSALA SAUCE may be
    Served over rice, grains—especially barley—potatoes, or pasta
    Spooned over poached, baked, or coddled eggs

 Tenderloin of Beef with Essence and Red Wine

This sauce combines an essence and a reduction of red wine. The addition of fresh tarragon, chervil, and parsley makes this a very aromatic dish.

    You can make the essence (omitting the butter until just before serving) and the wine reduction one or two days ahead to simplify the preparation at serving time.

S E R V E S   6

*½ recipe beef essence (pages 16–17) without the butter added, or ½ cup
    Reduced Stock (page 13) made with veal, veal and beef, or chicken
    and veal stock (pages 8, 7, 5–6)
4 shallots, chopped*

1 cup full-bodied red wine
1 tablespoon red wine vinegar
2 tablespoons chopped fresh tarragon
2 tablespoons chopped fresh chervil
4 tablespoons chopped fresh parsley
3 pounds beef tenderloin, trimmed of fat
1 tablespoon olive oil
4 tablespoons unsalted butter
Salt
Freshly ground pepper

Make the beef essence or reduced stock and set it aside.

Place the shallots, wine, vinegar, 1 tablespoon of the tarragon, 1 tablespoon of the chervil, and 2 tablespoons of the parsley in a saucepan. Bring the mixture to a boil, lower the heat, and simmer until the liquid is reduced to ⅓ cup. Strain the wine reduction and mix it with the beef essence or reduced stock. Set the mixture aside at room temperature or refrigerate it until you are ready to serve.

To finish the dish, preheat oven to 400 degrees F. Rub the beef with olive oil and place it on a rack in a roasting pan. Roast the meat for between 30 and 35 minutes or until a thermometer reads 125 degrees F; the meat will be rare. If you prefer your meat medium-rare, cook it to an internal temperature of between 135 and 140 degrees F. Remove the beef from the oven and let it rest for 5 minutes.

Deglaze the roasting pan with the reserved essence and reduction, scraping up any brown bits. Strain the liquid into a clean saucepan, bring it to a boil, and add the butter, 1 tablespoon at a time, whisking until the sauce is smooth and emulsified. Remove the sauce from the heat, season it with salt and pepper, and add the remaining chopped herbs.

Slice the beef and arrange it on plates or a platter. Season the beef with salt and pepper and spoon the sauce over the slices.

VARIATIONS

This is a superb sauce for lamb, duck, or chicken; when making the essence, use the appropriate fresh meat.

Beef with a Crunch and a Bite

This is a dish of cold beef sauced with a mixture of sour cream and cream cheese. The crunch comes from the cucumbers and the bite from horseradish.

SERVES 6

▮ BEEF

1 tablespoon oil
6 tenderloin steaks, each weighing about 6 ounces

▮ CREAM CHEESE WITH HORSERADISH SAUCE

MAKES 1 1/2 TO 2 CUPS

1/2 cup cream cheese
1 cup sour cream
5 to 6 tablespoons prepared horseradish without liquid, or
    3 to 5 tablespoons freshly grated horseradish
2 tablespoons chopped fresh dill
3/4 teaspoon salt
Lots of freshly ground black pepper
1 European seedless cucumber

Heat the oil in a skillet over high heat. Pan-fry the steaks until they are rare or medium-rare, as you like. The time will depend on the thickness of the steaks. Remove the steaks to a plate or platter large enough to hold them in one layer and allow them to cool.

Beat the cream cheese, add the sour cream a little bit at a time, and mix on low speed until smooth. Change to a spoon and stir in the horseradish (if you are using fresh horseradish, add it to taste—it is more pungent), dill, salt, and pepper. Do not use the mixer, which would make the sauce too thin. Taste for seasoning and keep refrigerated until ready to serve.

Peel and quarter the cucumber lengthwise. Slice each quarter into thin, diagonal slices. Place the cucumber in a bowl and keep it refrigerated.

To serve, slice the meat and arrange it on plates. Spoon the sauce over the slices and top with a generous serving of cucumber.

VARIATION

Replace the horseradish with ½ cup finely diced red onion and ⅓ cup rinsed capers. Serve with beef tenderloin or any of the foods suggested below.

■

CREAM CHEESE WITH HORSERADISH SAUCE may be

Served on smoked salmon accompanied with dark, thin pumpernickel rounds or on cold poached salmon

Substituted for the aïoli in the recipe for Seafood with Aïoli (pages 74–76), or served with any cold fish

Served with other smoked foods, such as trout, turkey, chicken, or game

 Sweet and Sour Beef and Cabbage

This winter dish is a combination of a typical Chinese pot roast and sweet and sour red cabbage. Serve with an unadorned stir-fry of snow peas and Chinese noodles or rice on the side.

S E R V E S   6

2 tablespoons oil
Approximately 4 pounds beef chuck, in one piece
1 tablespoon minced ginger, about ½ ounce
4 good-sized cloves garlic, minced
1 small head red cabbage, weighing about 2 pounds, quartered, cored,
*   and cut crosswise into wide strips*
Salt
½ cup cider vinegar

3 tablespoons soy sauce
1 teaspoon sugar
2 whole star anise
2 cups of stock, chicken, chicken and veal, or veal and beef (pages 5–7)
1 tablespoon cornstarch
Freshly ground black pepper

Preheat the oven to 325 degrees F. Heat the oil in a 3- or 4-quart Dutch oven or stew pot over medium-high heat. Brown the beef well all over and remove it to a plate. Add the ginger and garlic to the pan and toss them for 1 minute. Add the cabbage slices, season well with salt, toss these ingredients together, and cook them for 2 minutes. Add ¼ cup of the vinegar and stir. Cook for about 2 minutes. Add the soy sauce, sugar, anise, and stock. Bring the liquid to a boil, return the beef to the pot, and press it down, spooning the liquid and cabbage over the beef. Cover the meat with a sheet of foil, smoothing it tightly over the meat and up the sides of the pan. Top with the pot lid. Place the pot in the oven and braise the meat for 1 hour. Then turn the meat over, cover it with cabbage again, and continue braising it for between 1 and 1½ hours more. Check for doneness: A knife should go in and out of the meat with no resistance. When it is done, remove the meat to a plate. With a slotted spoon transfer the cabbage to a platter. Keep the meat and cabbage warm in the oven that has been shut off.

Add the remaining ¼ cup vinegar to the pan juices and reduce them until the flavor is sharp and concentrated, about 1½ cups. Mix the cornstarch with a bit of water, enough to form a smooth paste. Add it to the gravy, whisking well, and bring the liquid to a boil to thicken it. Remove the gravy from the heat. Cut the meat into thick slices and arrange them over the cabbage. Sprinkle with salt and pepper. Spoon some gravy over the meat and serve. Pass the remaining gravy separately.

VARIATIONS

This method also works very well with boneless pork loin, skinless duck legs, or a whole chicken, quartered.

Entrecôte Marchand de Vin

An *entrecôte* is a steak cut from the rib. In America it is sold as a rib eye and perhaps as a Delmonico steak, although that name is rarely used today. The classic *marchand de vin* sauce, which is French, is a reduction of red wine and shallots. In this recipe the sauce is made with an essence, which gives it more texture and flavor. A quicker version can be made by reducing two cups of stock to half a cup, and using that to deglaze the pan. When deglazing, reduce the stock further to a glaze, add the wine reduction, and then whisk in the butter.

Without the butter and herbs, the sauce may be made up to two days ahead. Gently reheat the sauce and add the butter and herbs just before serving.

▌ *MARCHAND DE VIN SAUCE*

MAKES ABOUT 1 TO 2 CUPS

½ pound shallots
3 tablespoons unsalted butter
Salt
Freshly ground black pepper
2 cups of full-bodied red wine
1 tablespoon lemon juice
1 sprig thyme or ¼ teaspoon dried thyme
Half a bay leaf
½ recipe mixed veal and beef essence (pages 16–17) without the added
    butter, or ½ cup Reduced Stock (page 13) made with veal, veal and
    beef, or chicken and veal stock (pages 5–8)

▌ *STEAKS*

SERVES 4

4 rib eye steaks, weighing about 6 to 8 ounces each, trimmed of all fat
1 tablespoon olive oil
1 tablespoon chopped fresh parsley (optional)
1 tablespoon scissored fresh chives (optional)

Peel and cut the shallots lengthwise in quarters if they are small, sixths if they are medium, or eighths if they are large. Heat 1 tablespoon of the butter in a wide skillet. Sauté the shallots with salt and pepper over moderate heat for 5 minutes. Add the wine, lemon juice, thyme, and bay leaf. Bring the mixture to a boil, lower the heat, and reduce it until 1/2 cup liquid remains. It will be nice and syrupy, coating the shallots. Discard the bay leaf.

While the wine reduces, make the essence or reduced stock and then combine it with the wine reduction and simmer them together for 10 minutes. Bring the mixture to a boil and add the remaining 2 tablespoons of butter, whisking until smooth. Season with salt and pepper and set the sauce aside.

Grill, broil, or pan-fry the steaks in oil over high heat. Sear the beef on both sides until it is well-browned; about 1 or 2 minutes. Lower the heat if you are pan-frying, lower the rack if you are broiling, or move the steaks to the outer edge of the grill and continue cooking until done. This will depend on the thickness of the steaks. Remove the steaks to plates and season them with salt and pepper. Add the optional herbs to the sauce and spoon it over the steaks.

--- **VARIATION** ---

Whisk cream or butter into the wine reduction, omit the essence, and serve on fish such as ocean perch fillet, salmon, flounder, or haddock.

∎

MARCHAND DE VIN SAUCE may be

Served on poached chicken breasts, veal chops or *scaloppine*, pork chops, pork tenderloin, pork cutlets, roast duck or duck legs, or roast turkey breast or legs

Spooned on poached eggs

Served with egg noodles, rice, or potatoes

♥ *Flank Steak with Tangerine Marinade*

This dish is meant to be served hot, but it is also excellent when served cold as a salad over a bed of rice and shredded lettuce or chicory.

▮ *TANGERINE MARINADE*

MAKES 1½ TO 2 CUPS

2 tangerines
4 scallions
¼ cup soy sauce
¼ cup dark sesame oil
¼ cup vegetable oil
3 tablespoons balsamic vinegar
1 tablespoon honey
2 small dried hot red chiles, seeded (optional)
2 cloves garlic, peeled and crushed
*2 tablespoons Mandarin Napoleon (tangerine liqueur), Grand Marnier
    liqueur, or sherry*

▮ *FLANK STEAK*

SERVES 4 TO 6

2 pounds flank steak

Set aside 1 tangerine and 2 scallions for garnish. Remove the zest in strips from the remaining tangerine. Cut the zest into ½-inch pieces and place them in a small saucepan. Squeeze the tangerine to obtain ¼ cup juice and add that to the saucepan. Trim the remaining 2 scallions, cut them into 1-inch pieces, and add them to the saucepan. Add the soy sauce, oils, vinegar, honey, chilies if you are using them, and garlic to the saucepan. Bring the mixture to a boil, remove it from the heat, cover, and allow it to cool to room temperature. Add the liqueur and stir well.

Place the meat in a 2- or 3-quart baking dish. Pour the marinade over the meat and coat it well on both sides. Cover and refrigerate the meat for between 12 and 48 hours, turning twice a day.

To make the garnish, peel and remove all the membrane from the reserved tangerine and separate the segments. Cut each segment in half crosswise and remove any seeds. Place the tangerine in a small bowl. Trim and slice the reserved 2 scallions thinly on the bias and toss them with the tangerine sections. Cover and set the garnish aside in the refrigerator until an hour before serving, then take it out of the refrigerator and allow it to come to room temperature.

When you are ready to cook, drain and dry the meat. Discard the marinade. Grill the flank steak until it is done; rare or medium-rare is best. This steak can also be broiled. Broil it close to the heat.

To serve, cut the beef in thin slices, between 1/8- and 1/4-inch wide, across the grain at a very slight angle. Top the slices with the reserved garnish and any pan juices if the steak was broiled.

∎

TANGERINE MARINADE is
Delicious when used for duck or chicken breast, either whole or cut into strips for a stir-fry
Very complementary to pork tenderloin or cutlets, skewered
Good with fish

❦ *Beef Tenderloin with Stilton, Walnuts, and Port*

One of the finest constellations of flavors is that of Stilton cheese, toasted walnuts, and a glass of rich port. The sauce here is based on those flavors with the addition of watercress for a slight bite. This sauce may be served over roast tenderloin of beef instead of the pan-fried tenderloin steaks used in this recipe.

∎ *STILTON, WALNUT, AND PORT SAUCE*

1 cup Reduced Stock (page 13), made with veal or veal and beef stock (pages 7–8)
1 tablespoon unsalted butter, softened
2 ounces Stilton cheese, about 1/2 cup

Freshly ground pepper
2 tablespoons toasted walnuts (page 54), chopped
2 tablespoons chopped fresh watercress
2 tablespoons tawny or ruby port

▌ *BEEF TENDERLOIN*

S E R V E S   4

Oil
4 tenderloin steaks
Salt

Place the reduced stock in a small sauce pan, reduce it further to ½ cup, and set it aside. On a small plate, cream the butter and 1 ounce of the cheese until smooth. Season the mixture well with pepper and set it aside. On a separate plate, crumble the remaining ounce of cheese and mix it with the walnuts and watercress. Set that garnish mixture aside.

Heat the oil in a skillet large enough to hold the steaks without their touching. Pan-fry the steaks over high heat to make a nice crust. Cook the meat to the degree that you like, though rare or medium-rare works best. Season the steaks with salt and pepper and arrange them on plates.

Divide the nut, cheese, and watercress garnish into 4 portions and scatter on each steak. Keep the meat warm.

Pour off the fat from the pan and deglaze the pan with the reserved, reduced stock, scraping up the browned bits. Bring the liquid to a boil and remove it from the heat. Add the Stilton butter and whisk to blend. Add the port, correct the seasoning, and spoon the sauce over the steaks.

▌

STILTON, WALNUT, AND PORT SAUCE, with toasted walnuts and watercress may be

Served on poached eggs, browned chicken breasts, or sautéed or grilled pork tenderloin

♥ *Braised Beef with Italian Flavors*

For this dish I wanted all the flavors of an Italian pot roast, but I wanted the gravy made in such a way that it could be served on a steak or with roast beef. So I made a separate wine sauce, braised the beef alone in stock, then combined the wine and stock to finish the dish. Serve with risotto or wide egg noodles sprinkled with grated Parmesan cheese.

▎ *BRAISED BEEF*

SERVES 4

1 tablespoon oil
Approximately 2½ to 3 pounds chuck, in one piece
2 cups stock, veal (page 8), veal and beef (page 7), or chicken and veal
    (pages 5–6)
A small handful of fresh thyme sprigs or 1 teaspoon dried thyme
1 bay leaf

▎ *PORCINI MUSHROOM AND RED WINE SAUCE*

MAKES ABOUT 2 CUPS

1 ounce dried porcini *mushrooms*
¼ pound pancetta, *cut into ¼-inch-thick slices and diced*
1 carrot, chopped
1 stick celery, chopped
1 small onion, chopped
3 large cloves garlic; 2 chopped, 1 minced
2 cups Chianti or other red wine, such as Côtes du Rhône
1 teaspoon tomato paste
½ teaspoon black peppercorns
1 tablespoon unsalted butter
2 tablespoons chopped fresh parsley

To braise the beef, preheat the oven to 325 degrees F. Heat the oil in a Dutch oven or casserole just large enough to hold the meat. Brown the meat thoroughly all over and transfer it to a plate. Pour off any excess oil and add the stock. Bring the liquid to a boil, scraping the pan, and add the meat and the herbs. Cover the pan with foil smoothed tightly over the meat and up the sides of the pan. Cover with the lid and braise the meat in the oven for between 2 and 3 hours, or until a knife passes in and out of the meat easily without meeting any resistance.

While the meat cooks, make the sauce. Soak the mushrooms in warm water to cover for 20 minutes. Strain the liquid into a cup through a fine strainer or cheesecloth and set it aside. Rinse the mushrooms under running water to remove any grit, chop them coarsely, and set them aside. Brown the *pancetta* in a wide skillet over medium heat and transfer it to a bowl. Pour off the fat, leaving 1 tablespoon in the pan. Add the carrot, celery, onion, and the 2 chopped cloves of garlic, and cook the mixture for 2 or 3 minutes. Add the wine, the reserved mushroom liquid, the tomato paste, and the peppercorns. Whisk to smooth out the tomato paste. Bring the liquid to a boil, lower the heat, and reduce the mixture until you have about 3/4 cup liquid left. Strain and set it aside.

Melt the butter in a small skillet and sauté the chopped *porcini* mushrooms for a minute or two to dry them out. Add the remaining clove of minced garlic and cook for 2 or 3 minutes, stirring, to brown the mixture slightly. Transfer it to the bowl with the *pancetta*, add the parsley, and mix.

When the meat is done, remove it to a platter and keep it warm. Pour the braising liquid into a saucepan and reduce it to 1/2 cup. Add the reserved wine reduction and cook the mixture for between 5 and 10 minutes over medium heat to blend the flavors. Add the *pancetta* and mushroom mixture and reheat. Cut the meat into wide slices and season them with salt and pepper. Spoon the sauce over the meat and serve.

VARIATIONS

To serve Porcini Mushroom and Red Wine Sauce on a roast or on steaks, reduce the 2 cups of stock called for in the braising recipe to between 1/4 and 1/2 cup. Proceed with the recipe.

Porcini Mushroom and Red Wine Sauce is excellent
Served over poached eggs, roast chicken, calves' liver, grilled Italian
sausages, duck, rabbit, veal, rice, pasta, or potatoes

❖ *Poached Brisket with a Caper Sauce*

This recipe can also be made with top of the round, bottom of the
round, or a round roast. The brisket is moister and has a softer texture
than the rounds, but they are all well flavored. You may cook the meat
one or two days ahead if you like since it improves with age. Serve the
dish with *bruschetta*: large slices of grilled Italian bread rubbed with
garlic and brushed with olive oil.

▮ *POACHED BRISKET*

SERVES 4 TO 6

2 to 3 pounds first-cut brisket
2 quarts stock, veal (page 8), chicken and veal (pages 5–6),
*   or veal and beef (page 7)*

▮ *CAPER SAUCE*

MAKES ³/₄ TO 1 CUP

1 tablespoon cider vinegar
2 tablespoons Dijon-style or grainy mustard
¼ cup olive oil
3 tablespoons drained capers, rinsed and drained again
Freshly ground black pepper
2 tablespoons chopped fresh parsley (optional)

Place the brisket in a large pot. Cover it with stock and bring the
liquid to a boil. Lower the heat and simmer the meat for 3 to 4 hours,
adding water as needed to keep the meat submerged. Leave the meat
in the pot to keep warm while you make the sauce. (If you are serving

it on another day, remove the meat to a plate, cool the stock to avoid overcooking the meat, return the meat back to the cooled stock, and refrigerate.)

To make the sauce, remove 2 cups of stock and place it in a saucepan. Bring the stock to a boil and reduce it to ¼ cup of glaze. Remove the glaze from the heat and add the vinegar, which will thin the glaze. Transfer the glaze to a bowl and whisk in the mustard. Slowly pour in the oil, whisking all the while. Finally, add the capers, pepper to taste, and the optional parsley. Serve the sauce warm or at room temperature.

To serve, slice the brisket across the grain and arrange the slices on plates or a platter. (If it has been refrigerated, simmer the meat until it is heated through.) Spoon a bit of the stock from the pot over the meat to moisten it and top with the sauce. Pass extra sauce on the side.

VARIATIONS

This brisket may be served with many dipping sauces. Try aïoli (pages 74–76) or green peppercorn sauce (page 118).

■

CAPER SAUCE may be
Served with poultry, beef, veal, sausages, ham, and smoked meats or poultry

 # Hot and Sweet Rib Steaks

I like the combination of yellow raisins and green peppercorns so much that I could not stop trying it on new foods. My family is more discriminating, so now I only use this mixture with a few outstanding dishes. This is one of them—a grilled rib eye steak.

Make the compound butter a day ahead so that there is time for the butter to be infused with the flavor of the raisins and green peppercorns. Bring the butter to room temperature before serving; freeze any extra.

▮ YELLOW RAISIN AND GREEN PEPPERCORN BUTTER

MAKES ABOUT ½ CUP

1 tablespoon, packed, yellow raisins
1 tablespoon cognac
½ cup stock, veal (page 8), veal and beef (page 7), or chicken and veal
    (pages 5–6)
1 tablespoon drained green peppercorns, rinsed and drained again
4 tablespoons unsalted butter, softened
Salt
Freshly ground black pepper

▮ RIB STEAKS

SERVES 4

4 rib eye steaks
Salt
Freshly ground pepper

Soak the raisins in cognac for 30 minutes. Place the stock in a small saucepan, reduce it to 1 tablespoon, and transfer it to a small bowl to cool. When the raisins have soaked, drain the cognac into the bowl with the reduced stock. Chop the raisins and green peppercorns together and add them to the bowl along with the butter. Cream the ingredients together until the mixture is smooth. Taste for seasoning and add salt and pepper as desired. Set the compound butter aside (preferably for 24 hours) to allow the flavors to blend.

Prepare the grill and cook the steaks until they are rare or medium-rare. (The steaks may also be broiled or pan-fried in oil.) Remove the meat to plates and season it with salt and pepper. Spread a spoonful of the butter over the whole surface of each steak.

▮

YELLOW RAISIN AND GREEN PEPPERCORN BUTTER may be
    Served on browned, boneless chicken breasts
    Served on poached salmon steaks or fillets
    Spooned on roast leg of lamb
    Used to top roasted turkey breast
    Spooned on sautéed calves' liver or chicken livers

Steak au Poivre

Steak *au Poivre* is a classic steak and pepper dish. Make the steaks as hot and peppery as you want by increasing the amount of peppercorns. Serve this with a crisp stir-fry of snow peas and carrots.

SERVES 2

2 sirloin strip steaks, weighing about 6 to 8 ounces each, trimmed of all
    fat, at room temperature
2 teaspoons black peppercorns, coarsely cracked
1 tablespoon oil
Salt
1 tablespoon cognac
¼ cup Reduced Stock (page 13), using veal (page 8), veal and beef
    (page 7), or chicken and veal stock (pages 5–6)
¼ cup heavy cream
2 tablespoons scissored fresh chives or chopped fresh parsley

Place the steaks on a sheet of waxed paper and sprinkle ½ teaspoon of the peppercorns over each. Press the peppercorns into the meat with your hands. Turn the steaks over and press in the remaining peppercorns. Place the steaks on a rack or jelly-roll pan or other pan and allow them to marinate for between 30 minutes and 1 hour.

Place the oil in a skillet and heat it over high heat. Add the steaks and brown them quickly on both sides. Lower the heat and continue cooking until the steaks are done as you like, being careful not to burn the pepper. Season the meat with salt and remove it to plates.

Add the cognac to the pan and turn the heat back up to high. Add the stock, deglaze the pan, and bring it to a boil. Add the cream and mix well. Cook the sauce for a minute or two until it is reduced to a coating texture, season with salt, and add the chives or parsley. Spoon the sauce over the steaks and serve.

A Dark Mushroom Sauce on Beef Slices

The inspiration for this dish comes from my good friend and colleague Kathy Gunst. The heated sauce is a light, yet flavorful topping, the addition of browned mushrooms contributing a caramelized taste. The dish can be made very quickly as the sauce takes only about five minutes to cook. Serve with rice and stir-fried radish slices.

▌ DARK MUSHROOM SAUCE

MAKES ABOUT ³/₄ CUP SAUCE *without mushrooms*

1 tablespoon oil
1 pound cultivated mushrooms, sliced
Salt
Freshly ground black pepper
3 tablespoons soy sauce
¼ cup lemon juice
¼ cup sherry
½ tablespoon minced fresh ginger

▌ BEEF SLICES

SERVES 4

1 tablespoon oil
4 tenderloin steaks, each about 1 inch thick, trimmed of all fat

To make the sauce, warm the oil in a large skillet over medium heat. Add the mushrooms and season with salt and pepper. Toss them well and cover the pan until the juices have been extracted, about 3 to 5 minutes. Toss the mushrooms once or twice during this step. Uncover the pan, pour off the juices into a saucepan, and return the skillet to the heat. Raise the heat to medium-high and, tossing the mushrooms, brown them well. Remove the mushrooms to a plate and set them aside.

Place the saucepan with the mushroom juices over medium-high heat. Reduce the juices to 2 tablespoons. Lower the heat, add the soy sauce, lemon juice, sherry, and ginger, and heat gently without boiling to blend the flavors; about 5 minutes.

When you start heating the sauce, cook the steaks. Heat 1 tablespoon oil in a skillet over high heat. Pan-fry the steaks until they are rare or medium rare. Remove the meat to plates and add the mushrooms to the pan to reheat them. Slice the steaks in ½-inch strips, season with salt and pepper if desired, top with mushrooms, and spoon on the sauce.

∎

DARK MUSHROOM SAUCE (mushrooms included) may be
> Served on salmon, halibut, swordfish, or other white fish such as flounder, haddock, tile fish, cusk, and scrod
> Served on rice of any color or potatoes
> Served with poultry, pork, or veal
> Served, at room temperature, over steamed vegetables, such as carrots, broccoli, green beans, or cauliflower
> Used as a marinade

Chapter 10

■ ■ ■ ■

DESSERTS

and

SAUCES

*D*ESSERT IS NOT SOMETHING THAT I EAT OFTEN, BUT WHEN I do, I really like it to be complemented by a sauce. In fact, I could eat a sauce on almost any dessert, with the exception of a baked custard.

In this chapter I wanted to provide a range of dishes with superb sauces or toppings without limiting the selections to chocolate, custard, or butterscotch. Not all the sauces in this chapter are gooey, rich, and fattening. Some are light; a few have more calories than anyone needs. Both the Chocolate Soufflé with Pistachio *Crème Anglaise* (pages 323–324) and Creamy Caramel Sauce for Warm Apple Crisp (pages 326–328) make wondrous endings to light meals. The Apricot Sherbet with Sliced Strawberry Sauce (page 299) or any of the recipes for fruit desserts, such as Rhubarb and Strawberry Compote (pages 303–304), will round out a meal without adding heaviness or extra fat. When you are feeling adventurous, try the Meringue Shells with Strawberries and Gingered Apricots (pages 307–308) or the Sweet and Sour Berry Sauce for Angel Food Cake (pages 318–320). Here are two desserts that are substantial but low in fat.

There is something for everyone in this chapter. Desserts are so much a part of our culture and yet we are very health conscious now. Both those who want a rich dessert and those who want something lighter should be able to enjoy the pleasure of eating dessert at the end of a meal.

♥ *Lemon Heart Tart with Mocha Sauce*

This sauce coats nicely yet is thinner than a fudge or chocolate sauce made with cream. Because it is made with coffee, to prevent bitterness it should not be boiled. Remove the sauce from the heat as soon as the chocolate is melted.

To bolster the taste of citrus, add some grated zest to the filling.

SERVES 6 TO 8

▮ *PASTRY CRUST*

MAKES AN 8- TO 9-INCH CRUST

¹/₂ cup butter, softened
¹/₃ cup sugar
¹/₄ teaspoon salt
¹/₃ cup ground almonds
³/₄ cup flour

▮ *LEMON FILLING*

¹/₂ cup sugar
¹/₄ teaspoon salt
2 tablespoons unsalted butter, melted
3 large eggs
¹/₃ cup lemon juice

▮ *MOCHA SAUCE*

MAKES ABOUT ³/₄ CUP

¹/₂ cup strong black coffee
3 tablespoons sugar
Pinch salt
3 ounces bittersweet chocolate, broken in pieces

To make the crust, preheat the oven to 350 degrees F. Butter an 8- to 9-inch, tin or porcelain, heart-shaped or round tart pan. Using a mixer, cream the butter, sugar, and salt until smooth, about 2 minutes. Add the almonds and mix to combine. Gently mix in the flour. Spread the dough with the back of a spoon, pressing it evenly into the prepared tart pan. Prick the pastry all over with a fork. Bake the crust for between 25 and 30 minutes until the pastry is just cooked and pale golden. Lower the oven heat to 300 degrees F.

Just before the crust is finished baking, make the filling. Mix the sugar and salt in a bowl and add the melted butter, whisking the mixture until the sugar absorbs the butter. Add the eggs and beat well until the mixture is smooth. Gradually pour in the lemon juice, whisking continuously. Pour the filling into the just-cooked crust and bake the tart at 300 degrees F. for between 10 and 15 minutes longer, or until the filling is set. Remove the tart from the oven and allow it to cool to room temperature.

While the tart is cooling, make the sauce. Mix the coffee, sugar, and salt in a small saucepan. Place the pan over medium heat and stir the mixture to dissolve the sugar. Add the chocolate and whisk until the chocolate is melted and the sauce is smooth. Remove the pan from the heat and transfer the sauce to a pitcher or bowl.

To serve, cut wedges of tart and spoon the sauce over them.

VARIATIONS

You can change the flavor of this tart to orange or tangerine, using the same
     quantity of juice.
The sauce may be varied with the flavorings of *café brûlot,* an after-dinner coffee
     to be found in New Orleans: add a strip of lemon zest, a pinch of
     cinnamon, a generous pinch of ground cloves with the chocolate, and
     a spoonful of cognac at the end.

∎

MOCHA SAUCE may be
     Served over any dish that is complemented by a chocolate sauce, such
          as ice cream, cake, a tart, bread pudding, crêpes, or a soufflé

Rhubarb Tart with Orange Caramel Sauce

I am crazy about rhubarb, and the combination of rhubarb and caramel is a particularly enjoyable one. Make this sauce ahead of time—it keeps well in the refrigerator for ten days.

SERVES 6 TO 8

∎ PASTRY CRUST

MAKES A 9- TO 10-INCH
LATTICE-TOPPED CRUST

2 cups sifted flour
1 tablespoon sugar
³/₄ teaspoon salt
14 tablespoons cold unsalted butter
Approximately 3 to 5 tablespoons ice water

∎ ORANGE CARAMEL SAUCE

MAKES ABOUT 1 ¹/₂ CUPS

1 recipe Caramel Sauce (pages 51–52), made with ²/₃ cup orange juice

∎ RHUBARB FILLING

2 pounds rhubarb
³/₄ cup sugar
1 tablespoon cornstarch
1 teaspoon ground ginger
Pinch salt

To make the pastry, combine the sifted flour, sugar, and salt in a bowl. Cut the butter into pieces the size of a tablespoon and add them to the bowl. Coat the butter with flour and work the mixture to a coarse meal. Add 3 tablespoons of the water and mix to form a loose ball. If the pastry seems to be very dry, sprinkle on more water, using

1 tablespoon at a time. Form the dough loosely into a ball and then flatten it into a cake. (The dough may look a little ragged, but it will come together when rolled out.) Wrap the dough in plastic and refrigerate it for at least 30 minutes.

While the dough chills, make the caramel sauce, flavoring it with orange juice. When it is cool, set the sauce aside, at room temperature.

To make the tart, preheat the oven to 375 degrees F. Lightly butter a 9- to 10-inch quiche or pie pan. Cut the dough into 2 pieces, one slightly smaller than the other. Roll out the larger piece and gently fit it into the prepared pan. Trim the edges and place the pan in the refrigerator to rest the dough. Roll out the second piece and cut it into 3/4-inch-wide strips. Place the strips on a lightly floured cookie sheet and refrigerate them.

Make the filling while the pastry chills. Trim the rhubarb and cut it on the diagonal into 1/2-inch-long pieces. Place the pieces in a bowl. Combine the sugar, cornstarch, ginger, and salt in a bowl and mix them with a fork. Add that mixture to the rhubarb and toss everything together. Remove the pastry shell from the refrigerator and fill it with the rhubarb. Arrange the pastry strips over the filling in a lattice pattern and trim the edges. Bake the tart for about 45 minutes, or until the pastry is golden and the filling is tender when pierced with the tip of a knife. Let the tart cool and serve it in wedges with the caramel sauce, which may be served at room temperature or slightly warmed.

VARIATION

Replace the ground ginger in the tart with 1 to 2 tablespoons minced fresh ginger or fresh ginger julienne. Cut the julienne in fine angel-hair threads.

∎

ORANGE CARAMEL SAUCE is delicious
On pancakes, French toast, waffles, poached pears, baked apples, ice cream, fresh figs, sliced oranges, sliced pineapple, peaches, and fruit tarts (especially cherry)

Nectarine Tart with Sour Cream Sauce

Whipped cream is served on many desserts, but for a change you can try this sauce, which blends whipped cream with sour cream for an edge of tartness. You may make this sauce about two hours ahead. If it should separate, whisk it until it is smooth and homogenized. This sauce will keep in the refrigerator for two days.

SERVES ABOUT 8

▮ *NECTARINE TART*

MAKES A 9- TO 10-INCH TART SHELL

¹/₂ recipe pastry crust (pages 292–293)
8 ripe nectarines
Juice of half a lemon
¹/₂ cup ginger conserve or preserves, warmed

▮ *SOUR CREAM SAUCE*

MAKES ABOUT 1 ¹/₂ CUPS

2 tablespoons honey
1 teaspoon vanilla extract
¹/₂ cup sour cream
¹/₂ cup heavy cream

Preheat the oven to 375 degrees F. Lightly butter a 9- to 10-inch quiche or pie pan. Roll out the pastry and fit it into the pan. Trim the edges and refrigerate the shell for at least 20 minutes.

Just before baking, prepare the fruit. Leaving the peel on, cut the nectarines into between 8 and 12 slices, depending on their size. Toss the slices in a bowl with the lemon juice and warmed conserve or preserves. Pour the fruit into the crust and bake the tart for about 45 minutes, until the fruit is tender and golden and the pastry has browned. Allow the tart to cool until it is warm or at room temperature.

While the tart bakes, make the sauce. Place the honey in a bowl and mix in the vanilla. Add the sour cream and whisk until the mixture is smooth. In a separate bowl, beat the heavy cream until it forms soft peaks. Add it to the sour cream and beat again until the sauce forms soft peaks. Serve the tart with the sauce spooned over it.

VARIATIONS

If you want a more intense ginger flavor, replace the honey in the sauce with ginger conserve.

For a lighter sauce, use Drained Yogurt (page 49) in place of the sour cream.

For desserts with flavors other than nectarine, vary the flavorings of the sauce to complement them: use cinnamon for apple, pear, or chocolate dishes; add grated lemon zest and cinnamon for coffee *granita* or sherbet.

▮

SOUR CREAM SAUCE may be
Served on any dessert instead of whipped cream
Served on coffeecake or chocolate cake—add a pinch of cardamom
Used as a topping for any fruit shortcake

❧ *Pear Tart with Chocolate Cream Sauce*

This is not a dark, shiny chocolate sauce; it is light in color and does not have an intensely chocolate taste, yet it is very creamy and velvety. The *mascarpone* cheese is what makes this sauce a bit different. The sauce keeps well in the refrigerator for several days.

SERVES 6 TO 8

▮ *PEAR TART*

MAKES A 9- TO 10-INCH TART SHELL

½ recipe pastry crust (pages 292–293)

¹/₄ cup water
¹/₄ cup sugar
2 tablespoons pear or apricot jam
6 Anjou or Comice pears
1 tablespoon lemon juice
Black pepper
Mace
1 tablespoon cold unsalted butter

▮ CHOCOLATE CREAM SAUCE

M A K E S   A B O U T   ³/₄   C U P

1¹/₂ ounces bittersweet chocolate
2 tablespoons water
1 tablespoon sugar
Pinch salt
¹/₂ cup mascarpone *cheese*
¹/₂ teaspoon vanilla extract or ¹/₂ tablespoon liqueur

For the tart, butter a 9- to 10-inch quiche or pie pan. Roll out the pastry and fit it into the pan. Refrigerate the tart shell while you prepare the glaze and the pears.

Preheat the oven to 375 degrees F. Combine the water and sugar in a small saucepan, bring the mixture to a boil, remove it from the heat, and whisk in the jam. Transfer this glaze to a bowl and set it aside to cool.

Quarter, peel, and core the pears. Toss them gently in a bowl with the lemon juice. Arrange the pears on the pastry in one layer. (They may be arranged like spokes on a wheel with the center filled with more pears, or in any other design that you like.) Sprinkle the pears with black pepper and mace and spoon the glaze over them so that each pear is covered. The glaze should be at room temperature or, if it has been taken from the refrigerator, warm it slightly over low heat. If it is too hot and has thinned out, it will not coat the pears. Cut the tablespoon of butter into 8 pieces and scatter them over the pears. Bake the tart for between 50 and 60 minutes, or until the pears are tender and the pastry is browned and cooked.

To make the sauce, melt the chocolate and water together in a bowl over warm water on low heat. Add the sugar and salt and stir for 1 minute until they are dissolved. Whisk in the cheese until it is smooth and add the vanilla. Remove the sauce from heat. Serve the warm sauce drizzled over the tart. To rewarm the sauce, place the bowl back over warm water. Stir until the sauce is warm; do not allow it to become hot.

∎

CHOCOLATE CREAM SAUCE may be
Served with pound cake of any flavor, crêpes, angel food cake, steamed puddings, ice cream, or poached pears

❦ *Lemon Cheesecake with Blueberry Sauce*

This is the kind of cheesecake that, like a mousse, does not require baking. In the sauce, whole berries are combined with a purée. The fresh taste of the uncooked berries adds a tartness that balances the rich filling.

SERVES 10 TO 12

∎ *CHEESECAKE CRUST*

MAKES A 10-INCH CRUST

12 graham crackers
1 cup sliced almonds, toasted (page 54)
6 tablespoons unsalted butter, melted
1 tablespoon sugar

∎ *LEMON FILLING*

1/2 cup heavy cream
1 pound cream cheese
3/4 cup sugar
1/4 teaspoon salt
1/2 cup lemon juice
2 tablespoons grated lemon zest
1 cup sour cream

▌ BLUEBERRY SAUCE

MAKES 3 TO 4 CUPS

1 cup water
½ cup sugar
2 pints blueberries

To make the crust, place the graham crackers and toasted nuts in a food processor and grind them. Add the butter and sugar and process to blend. Transfer the mixture to a 10-inch springform or deep pie pan. Press the crumbs evenly over the sides and bottom of the pan. Set the crust aside.

To make the filling, beat the cream until soft peaks form and then set it aside, refrigerated. Combine the cream cheese, sugar, and salt, beating until the mixture is light. Add the lemon juice and zest and beat until smooth. Gently mix in the sour cream by hand. Fold in the softly beaten cream and pour the filling into the prepared crust. Refrigerate until the filling is firm and cold, at least 6 hours.

While the cheesecake chills, make the sauce. Place the water and sugar in a saucepan. Bring the mixture to a boil over medium heat and boil it for 5 minutes. Add 1 pint of the blueberries and cook them for 3 minutes, stirring a few times. Place the remaining pint of berries in a bowl. Set a strainer over the bowl. Remove the cooked berries with a slotted spoon to the strainer and purée by pushing on the berries with the back of the spoon. Scrape the purée off the outside of the strainer, add it to the uncooked berries, and mix well. Over high heat reduce the sugar syrup to ½ cup and pour it over the berry and purée mixture. Stir well to combine and chill the sauce until you are ready to serve it. Because of the pectin in the berries, the sauce will jell slightly. Stir the sauce with a spoon to loosen it before serving.

To serve, cut wedges of cheesecake and spoon the sauce across the middle of each wedge.

▌

BLUEBERRY SAUCE may be
> Spooned over ice cream, sherbet, lemon Bavarian cream, meringues filled with fresh fruit, angel food cake, waffles, pancakes, French toast, lemon tart, bread pudding, pound cake, or slices of fresh honeydew melon or peaches

Apricot Sherbet with Sliced Strawberry Sauce

The blend of strawberries and apricots is both striking to the eye and refreshing to the palate. For the idea of combining the two fruits, I thank Jim Dodge, a wonderful pastry and dessert chef. The idea came from his book, written with Elaine Ratner, called *The American Baker* (New York: Simon & Schuster, 1987).

▌ SLICED STRAWBERRY SAUCE

MAKES ABOUT 3 TO 4 CUPS

2 pints fresh strawberries, rinsed, dried, and hulled
1 to 2 tablespoons sugar
1 teaspoon lemon juice

▌ APRICOT SHERBET

SERVES 6 TO 8

2 pounds fresh apricots, pitted
½ cup sugar
½ cup water
Pinch of salt

To make the sauce, place 1 pint of the strawberries in the blender or food processor and purée them. Thinly slice the second pint of berries. Combine the two in a bowl and mix in 1 tablespoon of the sugar and the lemon juice. Stir the mixture and let the sugar dissolve. Taste and add more sugar if desired. Cover the sauce and set it aside in the refrigerator.

To make the sherbet, purée the apricots in a blender or a food processor and pour them into a bowl. Place the sugar and water in a small saucepan and bring the mixture to a boil. Lower the heat and simmer the syrup for 5 minutes. Pour the syrup into the apricot purée, add the salt, and whisk to blend. Cover the sherbet and chill it in the refrigerator. When the sherbet is cold, freeze it in an ice cream machine according to the manufacturer's directions. Transfer to a container and freeze.

To serve, scoop spoonfuls of sherbet into dishes and ladle the strawberry sauce over the top or spread a pool of sauce on a plate and set the sherbet on it.

VARIATION

Reverse the flavors by making a strawberry sherbet and an apricot sauce. Cook the apricots in sugar syrup (sugar and water brought to a boil together) for about 10 minutes. Purée or leave them chunky and then chill the sauce.

■

SLICED STRAWBERRY SAUCE may be
Served with angel food cake, lemon or pound cake, cheesecake, lemon soufflé, other fruit or berry sherbets, fresh fruits, and ice cream

▼ *Dad's Chocolate Sauce with Butterscotch-Praline Ice Cream*

This sauce is the type that gets sticky when poured over ice cream. The stickiness and the degree to which it hardens depend on how long it is cooked. Adjust the cooking time to your own taste. This recipe was given to me by my father who, as a young boy, learned it from his mother.

Butterscotch is a mixture of butter, brown sugar, and lemon juice. Usually encountered as a sauce, butterscotch is superb as a flavoring for ice cream, particularly when a crunchy pecan praline is folded in.

■ *PRALINE*

¹/₂ cup pecans, about 2 ounces, toasted (page 54)

½ tablespoon unsalted butter, softened
½ cup sugar
¼ cup water
Few drops lemon juice

∎ BUTTERSCOTCH-PRALINE ICE CREAM

S E R V E S   6   T O   8

1 cup dark brown sugar
3 tablespoons unsalted butter
¼ cup water
¼ cup fresh lemon juice
1 cup light cream
8 large egg yolks
Pinch salt
1 cup heavy cream
1 teaspoon vanilla extract

∎ DAD'S CHOCOLATE SAUCE

M A K E S   A B O U T   1   C U P

1 cup sugar
½ cup powdered cocoa
½ cup milk
2 tablespoons unsalted butter
½ teaspoon salt
1 teaspoon molasses
1½ teaspoons vanilla extract

To make the praline, have the nuts toasted and ready. Butter a jelly-roll pan and set it aside. Place the sugar, water, and lemon juice in a saucepan and set the pan over low heat so that the sugar dissolves slowly. When the sugar has dissolved, bring the liquid to a boil and cook until you have a deep, dark caramel; between 5 and 10 minutes. Add the nuts and immediately pour the mixture onto the prepared jelly-roll pan. Let it cool completely and then break the praline up into chunks. Process the chunks in a blender or food processor until they are coarsely chopped. Set the praline aside.

To make the ice cream, heat the brown sugar, butter, water, and lemon juice in a saucepan. Bring the mixture to a boil and boil it gently for about 10 minutes, until it is syrupy and reduced slightly. Remove the syrup from the heat and slowly whisk in the light cream. Mix the egg yolks in a bowl and whisk into them a ladleful of butterscotch. Whisk the egg yolk mixture back into the butterscotch mixture. Cook the custard until it has thickened and will coat the back of a spoon. Do not let the mixture boil or it will curdle. Remove the custard from the heat, strain it, and whisk it until it is cool, adding a pinch of salt. Chill the custard until cold. Add the heavy cream and vanilla. Churn the ice cream until it is firm, but still soft enough to fold in the praline. Put the ice cream in a cake pan or bowl and fold in the reserved praline. Cover the pan with plastic wrap, smoothing it directly on the surface of the ice cream and freeze it until you are ready to serve.

Just before serving, make the sauce. In a heavy pot, mix the sugar and cocoa. Whisk or stir in the milk. Bring the mixture to a boil and add the butter and salt. Lower the heat and boil the sauce gently for about 6 minutes. It you want a thicker, stickier sauce, cook it for a bit longer. Remove the sauce from the heat and stir in the molasses and vanilla. Serve hot or warm.

∎

DAD'S CHOCOLATE SAUCE may be

Served over ice cream of other flavors, especially ginger, coffee, or peppermint stick

Poured over soufflés, nut tarts, pound cake, or other cakes served with or without ice cream

Used to top an ice cream cake roll—a childhood favorite of mine was the ice cream cake roll with chocolate sauce served at Howard Johnson's

Rhubarb and Strawberry Compote

In this unusual spring dish, red wine complements the poached rhubarb and fresh strawberries. The sauce is made by reducing the poaching liquid to a syrup, which intensifies the flavors of the spices. This sauce keeps for several days in the refrigerator.

SERVES 4

1/2 cup heavy cream
1 cup sugar
1 cup red wine
2 strips lemon zest, measuring 3 inches long by 1 inch wide
1/2 teaspoon allspice berries
1/4 teaspoon black peppercorns
1 pound rhubarb
1 pint strawberries

Beat the cream until soft peaks begin to form. Keep the whipped cream refrigerated until you are ready to serve.

Combine the sugar, wine, zest, allspice, and peppercorns in a saucepan. Bring the mixture to a boil, lower heat, and simmer for 3 minutes.

While the syrup cooks, trim the rhubarb and cut it on the bias into pieces about 1/2 inch wide and 2 inches long. Poach the rhubarb in syrup in 2 batches for between 3 and 5 minutes each until it is tender when pierced with the tip of a knife, but not falling apart. With a slotted spoon, remove the rhubarb to a plate. Return the lemon zest and spices to the pan if they were removed with the rhubarb. When all the rhubarb is cooked, raise the heat to high and reduce the syrup to 1/2 cup. Strain it and set it aside at room temperature.

Hull the strawberries and cut them in half lengthwise.

Just before serving, heat the syrup gently until it is just warm.

Arrange the strawberries around the edges of 4 plates. Place a portion of rhubarb in the middle of the plate and drizzle the strawberries and rhubarb with the warm syrup. Beat the whipped cream briefly to homogenize it and spoon it over the fruit.

For a low-fat topping, serve the compote with a dollop of Drained Yogurt (page 49) instead of the cream.

∎

RHUBARB AND STRAWBERRY COMPOTE may be
> Served over cakes, steamed puddings, French toast, pancakes, or waffles
> Leftover syrup may be mixed with sparkling water

▼ Crusted Pears in a Cream Sauce

This heavenly dish requires reducing both pear juices and cream. The reduced pear juices are drizzled over the fruit, which is then served with flavored reduced cream. Use Comice pears if they are available.

∎ CRUSTED PEARS

S E R V E S   4

4 ripe Comice, Bartlett, or Anjou pears
1 lemon, cut in half
1/4 cup water
2 tablespoons sugar

∎ CREAM SAUCE

M A K E S   A B O U T   3/4   C U P

1 cup heavy cream, reduced (pages 13–14) to 1/2 cup
2 tablespoons sour cream
1 to 2 tablespoons Drambuie or Grand Marnier liqueur, Scotch whisky
*   mixed with 1 teaspoon honey, preferably heather honey, or orange*
*   juice*
1/4 cup dark brown sugar

Preheat the oven to 350 degrees F.

Butter an 8-inch-square baking dish or other dish just large enough to hold the pears. Peel the pears, rubbing each one as you peel it with the cut lemon to prevent its browning, and core them from the bottom with a melon baller. Place the pears in the baking dish. Pour the water around the pears and sprinkle them with the sugar. Cover the dish with foil and bake the fruit for between 45 minutes and 1 hour, depending on the variety used and ripeness of the pears, or until they offer no resistance when pierced with the tip of a sharp knife. Remove the pan from the oven and pour the juices into a small saucepan. Leave the pears in the baking dish. Reduce the juices over high heat until you have 2 tablespoons left, about 2 minutes.

Place the reduced cream in a bowl and whisk in the sour cream and the liqueur. Set the cream aside at room temperature.

Preheat the broiler.

Sift the brown sugar evenly over the pears and broil them just until the sugar is melted and bubbly. Place each pear on a plate. Drizzle the reduced pear cooking juices over the hot pears, pour the reduced cream around them and serve.

∎

CREAM SAUCE may be
Served with baked apples, over cakes, over other stewed or poached fruits, or poured into the slits of baked fruit pies

▼ *Poached Pears in Ginger Syrup with Chocolate Drizzle*

Ginger and chocolate are doubly aphrodisiacal when offered with gently poached pears. The pears can be made ahead of time and chilled overnight in the cooled, reduced syrup. The next day, gently heat the pears and syrup together before serving.

4 firm ripe Bosc or Anjou pears
1/2 cup lemon juice
1 ounce fresh ginger in 1 piece
2 cups orange juice
1 cup sugar
3 ounces bittersweet chocolate

Peel the pears, cut them in half, and remove the cores and stems with the small end of a melon baller. Toss the pears in a bowl with the lemon juice. Peel the ginger, slice it, and cut the slices into thin julienne strips.

Combine the orange juice and sugar in an 8- or 9-inch sauté pan with deep sides. Bring the mixture to a boil. Add the ginger and pears with all the lemon juice. Bring the liquid back to a boil, lower the heat, and simmer the fruit for 10 minutes. Turn the pear halves over and simmer them for another 10 minutes or just until they are tender when pierced with the tip of a sharp knife. (If the pears still feel hard, turn them over again and continue simmering them until they are tender, about 5 to 10 minutes more.) With a slotted spoon, remove the pears to a serving platter. Raise the heat to high and boil the syrup and ginger until the liquid is reduced to 1 cup, about 10 minutes.

While the syrup is being reduced, melt the chocolate. To serve, spoon the syrup and ginger over the pears. With a teaspoon, drizzle melted chocolate over the syrup and serve the fruit warm.

VARIATIONS

Replace the pears with apples, peaches, or nectarines—results are equally delicious.

∎

Leftover GINGER SYRUP may be
> Served over pancakes, waffles, or French toast, baked apples, cakes, crêpes filled with a sweet compound butter (page 43) or fruit, mixed berries, grapes, melon, pineapple, mango or papaya, or fruit tarts

Meringue Shells with Strawberries and Gingered Apricots

Crisp meringue nests are filled with sliced fresh berries and topped with a pungent ginger and apricot sauce. This sauce must be made with fresh ginger.

SERVES 6

▪ MERINGUE SHELLS

MAKES 6 SHELLS

3 large egg whites
6 tablespoons superfine sugar
1/2 teaspoon vanilla extract
1/4 teaspoon ground ginger
Pinch salt

▪ GINGER AND APRICOT SAUCE

MAKES 1 1/2 TO 1 3/4 CUPS

1 pound fresh apricots; 5 or 6 large or 8 to 12 small fruits
1/4 cup sugar
1/4 cup water
1/2 ounce fresh ginger, peeled and minced; about a scant
    2 teaspoons minced ginger

▪ FILLING

1 pint fresh ripe strawberries, rinsed and dried, hulled and sliced

To make the meringue shells, preheat the oven to 225 degrees F. Anchor a piece of parchment paper to a cookie sheet with a little butter and then butter the parchment. Set the pan aside.

Place the egg whites in a bowl and beat until they are foamy. Add 2 tablespoons of the sugar and all of the vanilla, ginger, and salt. Beat until the whites are firm and hold a peak, but are not dry. Fold in the remaining sugar. Place 6 scoops of meringue, spaced apart, on the prepared pan. Using the back of a spoon, hollow each scoop to make a nest. Bake the meringues for 1 hour and 15 minutes or until dry. Because of the vanilla and ginger, they will be golden, not white. Remove the paper to a rack and cool the meringues. When they are cool, peel off the paper and place the meringues in an air-tight container until you are ready to serve. Meringues can be made 1 or 2 days in advance if the weather is dry. Otherwise, plan to serve them as soon as they are cool.

While the meringues bake, make the sauce. Pit the apricots, slice them, and cut the slices in half crosswise. Place the apricots in a small saucepan with the sugar, water, and minced ginger. Bring the mixture to a boil, lower the heat, and simmer the apricot pieces for 10 minutes, stirring frequently, until they are soft, but still intact in the syrup. Try not to crush the apricots while they are cooking. Remove the sauce to a bowl and let it cool to room temperature. This sauce may be served warm or chilled.

To serve the dessert, arrange the berries in the shells and spoon the sauce over the fruit.

■

GINGER AND APRICOT SAUCE may be

Spooned over any ice cream or sherbet, lemon Bavarian cream, crêpes, lemon, angel food, toasted almond, or pound cake, roast duck or goose, or almond-coated pan-fried pork tenderloin

Spooned over Double Gingerbread (pages 314–315) instead of the lemon cream

▼ Sliced Pineapple with Butterscotch Sauce

This classic butterscotch sauce will keep for a week or two in the refrigerator, so it gives you the time and flexibility to make quick desserts.

SERVES 6 TO 8

1 large pineapple, peeled, eyes removed, and quartered lengthwise

▎ *BUTTERSCOTCH SAUCE*

M A K E S   A B O U T   1 ¹/₄   C U P S

3 tablespoons unsalted butter
3 tablespoons lemon juice
1 tablespoon water
1 cup light brown sugar
¹/₂ cup heavy cream

Core the pineapple quarters and cut each quarter crosswise into slices roughly ¹/₄- to ¹/₂-inch thick. Pile the slices into a bowl, cover it, and set it aside. The fruit is at its best when served at room temperature, so if you prepare it ahead and need to refrigerate it, take it out ahead of time so that it may warm up.

To make the sauce, melt the butter in a heavy, medium-size saucepan. Add the lemon juice and water and mix. Add the sugar and stir until it is dissolved. Bring the mixture to a boil, stirring occasionally, and boil it gently for 7 minutes. Remove the pan from the heat and let it sit for a couple of minutes until the syrup has stopped boiling. Whisk in the cream until the mixture is smooth and pour the sauce into a bowl or pitcher. Butterscotch sauce may be served warm or at room temperature.

Spoon the pineapple into bowls and pour the sauce over it.

VARIATIONS

Replace the pineapple with oranges, bananas, papaya, grapes, peaches, or nectarines or mix the fruits in any combination you like.

▪

BUTTERSCOTCH SAUCE may be
Served with baked apples, crêpes filled with fruit or ice cream, chocolate-pecan, rhubarb, or pear tart, lemon, sponge, or pound cake, steamed pudding (it is particularly good with cranberry-orange steamed pudding), and ice cream, especially vanilla

Pineapple Marinated in Honey and Fennel Syrup

This is another dish inspired by Jim Dodge, maker of wonderful fruit desserts. Allow two to four hours for the fruit to marinate before serving it. Accompany the dish with crisp *tuiles*, the thin, French tile-shaped cookie made with almonds.

SERVES 4

1 pineapple, peeled, eyes removed, and quartered lengthwise
1 lemon, sliced paper thin, seeds removed

▮ HONEY AND FENNEL SYRUP

MAKES ABOUT 1 1/2 CUPS

1 cup honey
1/2 cup water
1 tablespoon fennel seeds, crushed

Core and slice pineapple quarters crosswise into 1/4-inch pieces. Place them in a bowl, add the lemon slices, and gently toss together.

Bring the honey, water, and fennel seeds to a boil. Pour the mixture over the fruit, toss it well, and let the fruit steep until the marinade has cooled to room temperature. Cover the dish and marinate the fruit in the refrigerator for between 2 and 4 hours, tossing 2 times an hour. Serve in bowls with the syrup. Top with whipped cream (pages 50–51), Sour Cream Sauce (pages 294, 295), or Drained Yogurt (page 49) if you like.

▮

HONEY AND FENNEL SYRUP may be
Used to marinate other fruit, such as slices of peeled oranges, peaches, nectarines, apricots, plums, cherries, or grapes
Poured hot over a mixture of dried fruit such as pears, prunes, apples, cranberries, cherries, peaches, apricots, or figs

Spooned over lemon cake, or used as a syrup in which to soak a *savarin* cake or *babas*

Poured cold over fresh mixed berries

Fresh Melons with Coconut and Yogurt Sauce

In this light dessert, Drained Yogurt (page 49) is used as the basis of the sauce. The coconut may be toasted first by placing it on a jelly-roll pan and baking it for fifteen or twenty minutes, tossing it often, in a 350 degree F. oven. Unsweetened coconut is available at health food stores.

▌ *COCONUT AND YOGURT SAUCE*

M A K E S   A B O U T   1 ½   T O   2   C U P S

1½ cups Drained Yogurt (page 49)
¾ cup unsweetened shredded coconut
½ cup sliced almonds, toasted (page 54)
1½ tablespoons sugar
1½ teaspoons vanilla extract

S E R V E S   6

1 small honeydew melon
1 small cantaloupe
1 pint strawberries

To make the sauce, place the yogurt, coconut, almonds, sugar, and vanilla in a bowl. Mix well and set aside in the refrigerator.

Quarter, seed, and peel the melons. Cut the quarters into thin slices. Arrange the melon on 6 plates, alternating the colors. Scatter a few whole, unhulled strawberries over the melon. Place a spoonful of the sauce to the side of the fruit and serve.

<hr>

VARIATIONS

Serve Coconut and Yogurt Sauce with mango and papaya or peaches and nectarines; toss the fruit with lemon juice before serving with sauce.

■

COCONUT AND YOGURT SAUCE may be
> Served over pancakes, waffles, or French toast with maple syrup
> Used to top slices of lemon, pound, or upside-down fruit cakes, crisps, cobblers, or gingerbread
> Used as a topping for shortcake, replacing whipped cream
> Served over poached fruit or fresh mixed berries

 # *Baked Apples with Cardamom Cream*

Cardamom cream is a stunning, luxurious sauce with a haunting flavor. The recipe makes enough for about six servings. It keeps very well in the refrigerator for about a week.

■ *BAKED APPLES*

SERVES 6

6 tart apples (Granny Smith or Gravenstein)
6 teaspoons light brown sugar
2 tablespoons unsalted butter
Ground cinnamon
Ground cardamom

▪ CARDAMOM CREAM

M A K E S   A B O U T   1   C U P

¾ cup reduced heavy cream (pages 13–14), cooked with
*   1 teaspoon ground cardamom*
1 to 2 tablespoons Calvados

Preheat the oven to 350 degrees F. Cut a thin slice from the top of each apple. Using a melon baller or grapefruit spoon, remove the core, leaving between ¼ and ½ an inch of solid apple at the bottom. Place 1 teaspoon sugar and 1 teaspoon butter in each apple and sprinkle them liberally with cinnamon and cardamom.

Butter a baking pan and arrange the apples in it. Cover the pan with foil and bake the apples for between 45 minutes and 1 hour or until they are tender when pierced with the tip of a sharp knife. Slide a metal spatula under the apples to transfer them to plates. Serve the apples warm or at room temperature.

While the apples bake, reduce the cream with the cardamom. Pour the reduced cream into a bowl or pitcher, add the Calvados, stir, and serve warm, spooned over the apples.

VARIATIONS

Change the flavorings for the cream to suit your mood and what you have in your cupboard: citrus zest, honey, raisins, toasted nuts, different spices, rum, Benedictine, or Grand Marnier liqueur. All work well.

▪

CARDAMOM CREAM may be
Served on fruit pies or tarts: change the spice to complement the dish
Spooned over steamed pudding, cobblers, crisps, poached fruit, upside down cake, bread pudding, and crêpes filled with poached fruit

Double Gingerbread with Lemon Cream

This cream sauce includes *mascarpone*, a very rich Italian cream cheese available at most gourmet shops.

The sauce keeps well for two or three days in the refrigerator. To reheat it, place the sauce over very low heat, in a double boiler, or in a bowl over water and gently warm it, whisking often.

▮ *DOUBLE GINGERBREAD*

MAKES 1 LOAF

¼ *cup unsalted butter*
½ *cup molasses*
2 *cups unsifted flour*
1½ *teaspoons baking soda*
½ *teaspoon salt*
2 *tablespoons ground ginger*
1 *teaspoon ground cinnamon*
¼ *teaspoon ground cloves*
¼ *teaspoon ground nutmeg*
⅛ *teaspoon freshly ground black pepper*
½ *cup water*
½ *cup buttermilk*
2 *large eggs*
1 *cup, packed, dark brown sugar*
2 *ounces fresh ginger, peeled and minced*

▮ *LEMON CREAM*

MAKES ABOUT 2 CUPS

1 *recipe Basic* Crème Anglaise *(pages 52–54): increase the sugar to* ½
    cup, replace the milk or cream with ½ *cup lemon juice, and omit the
    vanilla*
2 *tablespoons unsalted butter*
2 *teaspoons grated lemon zest*
1 *cup* mascarpone *cheese*

Preheat the oven to 350 degrees F. Butter a 9¼-inch by 5-inch loaf pan and set it aside. If your loaf pan is slightly smaller or larger, merely adjust the cooking time accordingly. This cake may also be baked in a square or round cake pan. Check the cake after it has been cooking for 35 minutes and continue baking it if it is not done.

Melt the butter, mix in the molasses, and set the mixture aside to cool. Combine the flour, soda, salt, and spices, including the pepper, in a large bowl. Make a well in the dry ingredients and add the water, buttermilk, eggs, sugar, butter and molasses mixture, and fresh ginger. Gently mix the ingredients with a whisk to combine them. Pour the batter into the prepared pan and bake the cake for between 40 and 45 minutes. Let the cake cool in the pan on a rack for 20 minutes, unmold it onto the rack, and allow it to cool completely.

While the gingerbread bakes, make the sauce. Make the *crème anglaise* and, when the custard is done, remove it from the heat and whisk in the butter, 1 tablespoon at a time. Strain the custard into a bowl. Add the zest and mix well. Whisk in the *mascarpone* until the sauce is smooth and serve it warm over the gingerbread.

To serve the dish, slice the gingerbread ½-inch thick. Cut each slice into 2 triangles. Overlap the triangles on a plate and spoon the sauce over them.

VARIATIONS

This makes excellent picnic fare when served as a loaf or when sandwiches are made by filling two triangles with the chilled sauce. The gingerbread may be served with Ginger and Apricot Sauce (pages 307–308) or with slightly warmed pineapple slices and whipped cream.

∎

LEMON CREAM may be
Served on toasted almond, pound, blueberry, or fruit upside-down cake, fresh fruit such as peaches, nectarines, orange slices or orange and banana slices, berries of any type, especially blueberries, fruit tarts, bread pudding, and chocolate soufflé

Chocolate Cake with Spiced Cherries

This cake combines the richness of a brownie with the moistness of a French cake. It is a lush dessert with a deep chocolate flavor that comes from unsweetened chocolate. To keep it moist, the center should be slightly undercooked. It is best served the next day, but if you cannot wait, at least make sure it is absolutely cool before cutting it.

▌ CHOCOLATE CAKE

MAKES A 9-INCH CAKE

4 ounces bittersweet chocolate
4 ounces unsweetened chocolate
1 cup unsalted butter
1 cup plus 1 tablespoon sugar
1/2 teaspoon salt
1 tablespoon vanilla extract
4 large eggs, separated
1/4 teaspoon cream of tartar (omit if you are using a copper bowl)
1/2 cup sifted cake flour

▌ SPICED CHERRY SAUCE

MAKES ABOUT 2 TO 3 CUPS

1 cup sugar
2 cups water
1 teaspoon black peppercorns
1/2 teaspoon whole allspice berries
1 strip lemon zest, 1/2 inch wide and 3 inches long
1 1/2 pounds fresh sweet cherries, pitted

To make the cake, preheat the oven to 350 degrees F. Heavily butter a 9-inch springform pan.

Melt the chocolate and the butter in a large bowl set over warm water on low heat. Remove the bowl from the heat and add 1 cup sugar and the salt and stir to combine. Add the vanilla and stir for 1 minute. Mix in the egg yolks, one at time. Set the mixture aside.

Beat the egg whites and a pinch of salt. When the whites are foamy and just beginning to mound softly, add 1 tablespoon sugar and the cream of tartar. Continue beating until the egg whites are firm, but not dry. Slide the beaten egg whites on top of the chocolate mixture. Sift the cake flour again, this time over the egg whites. Using a large balloon whisk (a utensil I find more helpful than a spatula when starting to fold the ingredients) gently fold the whites and flour into the chocolate mixture until you cannot see any more particles of flour. However, the mixture should not yet be homogeneous. Exchange the whisk for a large rubber spatula and continue to fold until the batter is well mixed and smooth, making sure to scrape the sides and bottom of the bowl as you fold. Pour the batter into the prepared pan and bake it for 30 minutes; the cake will be moist and soft in the center when tested with a knife or toothpick. Cool the cake in the pan on a rack for 30 minutes and then remove the outer rim. Allow the cake to cool completely.

While the cake bakes, make the sauce. Combine the sugar and water in a pan. Place the peppercorns and allspice berries in a piece of cheesecloth and tie the cloth to make a pouch, or place the spices in a tea ball. Add the spices to the pan along with the lemon zest and bring the mixture to a boil. Lower the heat and simmer the syrup for 2 minutes. Add the cherries, bring the liquid back to a boil, lower the heat, and simmer the fruit for 3 minutes, stirring frequently. Using a slotted spoon, transfer the cherries to a plate, placing them in 1 layer. Bring the syrup with the spice bag and lemon zest to a boil and reduce the liquid to about 1 cup. Discard the spices and zest and pour the syrup into a bowl to cool. When it is cool, add the cherries.

You can serve the cake right from the springform bottom onto plates or transfer it to a plate or platter. To disengage the cake from the pan, not an easy task as the cake is so moist and heavy, slide a long metal spatula under the entire bottom of the cake, pressing down as you slide it around. Then take another spatula and slide that under the cake at right angles to the first. Lift up the cake and place it on a plate or platter.

To serve, cut the cake in wedges and spoon the cherries with their syrup over the top.

This chocolate cake is equally delicious with a *Crème Anglaise* (pages 52–54).

∎

SPICED CHERRY SAUCE may be
>   Served on hazelnut-chocolate, pound, toasted almond, or lemon cake,
>   lemon cheesecake (fabulous), chocolate soufflé, or ice cream
>   Served on grilled quail, duck, or goose

 Sweet and Sour Berry Sauce for Angel Food Cake

This recipe offers a nice way to serve angel food cake in fall or winter, but you may want to make it year-round. To do so, you'll need to buy cranberries in the fall and freeze them for use through the winter. Be sure to have all the ingredients measured and ready before you start making the cake.

SERVES 8 TO 10

∎ *ANGEL FOOD CAKE*

MAKES A 10-INCH CAKE

1¼ cups sugar
1 cup sifted cake flour
1½ cups egg white; 10 to 12 large eggs
1 teaspoon cream of tartar
½ teaspoon salt
2 teaspoons vanilla extract
2 tablespoons lemon juice

▮ SWEET AND SOUR BERRY SAUCE

MAKES ABOUT 2 ½ CUPS

1 cup water
½ cup sugar
8 ounces fresh cranberries
1 bag (12 ounces) frozen blueberries, not thawed, or
    1 pint fresh blueberries
2 tablespoons cassis or Chambord liqueur (optional)

To make the cake, preheat the oven to 375 degrees F. In a small bowl, mix ½ cup of the sugar with the flour and set it aside.

Place the egg whites in a large mixing bowl and beat them slowly, low to medium speed, until they are loose and frothy. Add the cream of tartar and salt. Slowly pour in the vanilla and lemon juice. Turn the mixer up to high and beat until the whites just begin to hold their shape. Start adding the remaining ¾ cup sugar, 2 tablespoons at a time, pouring slowly. Continue beating until the whites are forming soft peaks and are very shiny. They should not be stiff but should mound and make peaks, the tips of which fall slightly.

Place the flour and sugar mixture in a sifter or strainer and sift one-third into the egg whites. Using the largest wire whisk you have, fold the flour mixture in. Working quickly and gently, add the rest in two batches. Use a spatula to scrape the sides of the bowl and finish with a fold or two just to smooth the mixture. (If you do not have a large wire whisk, use a rubber spatula for all the folding.)

Pour the batter into a large, ungreased angel food cake pan or other tube pan and bake the cake for 30 minutes. The cake will crack. Test by inserting a knife in one of the cracks and counting to 10 before removing the knife, which should be hot and dry. Take the cake out of the oven and invert it on a counter to cool for 1 hour. If the pan has no feet, invert it over the neck of a bottle, so the cake doesn't touch the counter. After 1 hour, run a knife around the outer and inner sides of the pan and unmold the cake. Allow the cake to cool completely on a rack.

While the cake cooks, make the sauce. Combine the water and sugar in a medium-size saucepan. Bring the mixture to a boil over medium heat, turn the heat to high, and boil the syrup for 5 minutes. Add the cranberries and cook them over high heat for 5 minutes, stirring often. Add the frozen blueberries and cook them for 3 minutes, still over high heat. Cook fresh berries for 2 minutes. Remove the mixture to a bowl, allow to cool, and add the liqueur if you are using it. Serve the sauce warm or at room temperature over the cake.

VARIATIONS

In the spring, serve angel food cake with stewed rhubarb and perhaps sliced fresh strawberries or with Sliced Strawberry Sauce (page 299). In the summer for a topping make a nectarine and ginger compote by cooking chopped ginger and slices of not-too-ripe nectarine slices in a sugar syrup until they are tender or serve the cake with a Mango and Lime Sauce (pages 321–322). In the winter, try an apple and lemon sauce: Cook slices of firm apple in a sugar syrup with fine strips of lemon zest and a little spice such as mace, nutmeg, or cinnamon. This cake may also be served with a raspberry purée made with or without fresh blueberries or other berries added to the purée.

■

SWEET AND SOUR BERRY SAUCE may be

Served on ice cream, fruit sherbets, almond sponge, toasted almond, or pound cake, lemon cheesecake, crêpes, slices of fresh fruit such as melon, papaya, or mango, fresh mixed berries, any type of quick bread, such as cranberry, nut, poppy seed, or orange, pancakes, French toast, or waffles with yogurt, meringue shells, and lemon or orange Bavarian cream

Orange and Lime Cake with Mango and Lime Sauce

This sauce is both refreshing and creamy rich. The lime brings out the deep flavor of the mango.

■ ORANGE AND LIME CAKE

SERVES 8 TO 12

1 cup unsalted butter, softened
3 cups sifted flour
¾ teaspoon baking powder
½ teaspoon baking soda
1½ cups sugar
½ teaspoon salt
1 tablespoon grated orange zest
1 tablespoon grated lime zest
3 large eggs
2 tablespoons orange juice
2 tablespoons lime juice
¾ cup buttermilk

■ MANGO AND LIME SAUCE

MAKES ABOUT 3 CUPS

2 mangoes
1 lime
½ cup lime juice
½ cup sugar

To make the cake, preheat the oven to 350 degrees F. Butter a large Bundt or tube cake pan.

Mix the flour, baking powder, and soda in a small bowl. In a separate bowl, cream the butter, sugar, salt, and citrus zest until the mixture is light; about 2 minutes with a mixer. Scrapes the sides of the bowl once. Add the eggs, one at a time, beating well after each addition. Add the citrus juices and blend the batter well, scraping the sides of the bowl.

Place the flour mixture in a strainer and sift one-third of it over the batter. Gently blend the ingredients on the low speed of the mixer or with a rubber spatula. Add half of the buttermilk and mix it in gently. Add half of the remaining flour, the remaining buttermilk, and then the rest of the flour, mixing gently between each addition. Spoon the mixture into the prepared pan, place roughly a fourth of the batter in 4 different places in the pan. This makes it easier to spread the batter evenly in the pan without overworking it. Smooth the top of the batter and bake the cake for between 40 and 45 minutes, or until a knife comes out hot and dry after a count of 10. Cool the cake, still in the pan, on a rack for 10 minutes, then unmold it and allow it to cool completely.

While the cake bakes, make the sauce. Peel the mangoes, cut into irregular slices or chunks, then set them aside on a plate. Using a vegetable peeler, remove the zest from the lime being careful not to remove any bitter white pith. Squeeze the peeled lime and add the juice to the ½ cup of lime juice that has already been measured out.

Combine lime juice and sugar in a heavy, medium-sized saucepan and bring the mixture to a boil. Add the lime zest and boil for 5 minutes. Add the mango and bring the liquid back to a boil. Gently boil the sauce for 2 minutes and immediately pour it into a bowl to cool. When the liquid is cool, remove the zest. Serve the sauce at room temperature or cold on slices of the cake.

VARIATIONS

You can change the citrus flavors in this cake from orange and lime to lemon and lime, lemon, tangerine, orange and grapefruit, or any combination you like. I would leave the lime in the sauce and change the flavor of the cake only.

This cake can be served with many other fruit sauces such as those made with cherries, blueberries, peaches, apricots, stewed rhubarb, or with dried fruit compotes. Try also creamy sauces, such as custard, butterscotch, or caramel sauce (pages 52–54, 309, and 51–52) topped with toasted nuts.

∎

MANGO AND LIME SAUCE may be

Served with ice cream, particularly ginger or vanilla, sherbets or fruit *granitas*, particularly lemon *granita*, fresh fruit, particularly pineapple, strawberries, or melon, as a filling for crêpes topped with whipped cream, on waffles, pancakes, or French toast with yogurt on the side, on pound cake, particularly on slices that have been toasted, in a meringue shell, on cooked or uncooked cheesecake, on a mango shortcake topped with whipped cream or sweetened yogurt, or as a condiment for lamb or chicken curry or for pork and duck dishes

Chocolate Soufflé with Pistachio Crème Anglaise

A chocolate soufflé is good with any custard sauce. The combination of pistachio and chocolate in this sauce is different and wonderful. Make the *crème anglaise* ahead and bring it to room temperature—or heat it gently over a pan of warm water—before serving.

▮ PISTACHIO CRÈME ANGLAISE

MAKES ABOUT 1 TO 1 ½ CUPS

1 recipe Nut Crème Anglaise *(pages 52–54), made with 4 large egg yolks, milk, 1 cup shelled and toasted (page 54) pistachios, and vanilla or 1 or 2 tablespoons pistachio-flavored liqueur, Grand Marnier, or Mandarin Napoleon liqueur*

▮ CHOCOLATE SOUFFLÉ

SERVES 6

6 ounces bittersweet chocolate
2 ounces unsweetened chocolate
6 large eggs, separated, plus 1 extra egg white
⅓ cup sugar
Pinch salt
1 tablespoon vanilla extract
1 tablespoon water

To make the sauce, measure and chop 2 tablespoons of the nuts and set them aside for garnish. Make the nut *crème anglaise* using the remaining pistachios. Let the sauce cool slightly and add the vanilla or liqueur. Set the sauce aside at room temperature while you make the soufflé.

Preheat the oven to 400 degrees F. Butter a 6-cup soufflé dish. Sprinkle the bottom and sides of the dish with sugar and shake out the excess. Set the dish aside. Melt the chocolate and set it aside to cool. Place the egg yolks, sugar, and salt in a bowl and beat the mixture with a whisk or mixer until it is thick, pale yellow, and falls in folds from the beaters if they are lifted up. Add the cooled chocolate, the vanilla, and the water and blend.

Beat the egg whites until they are firm, but not dry, and stir a spoonful into the chocolate mixture. Fold the remaining egg whites into the chocolate mixture until no white remains visible. Spoon the batter into the prepared dish and smooth the top. Bake the soufflé on the lowest rack of the oven for about 20 minutes. Test with a knife or skewer. The center should be soft and creamy and moist pieces should be clinging to the knife or skewer. The outer edges of the soufflé will be cooked and a skewer inserted there will be dry. Immediately spoon the soufflé onto plates and pour pistachio sauce over the servings. Sprinkle the top with the reserved chopped pistachios.

VARIATION

The *crème anglaise* may be flavored with other types of nuts, all of which will complement a chocolate soufflé.

▪

Pistachio Crème Anglaise may be
Served over apricot, lemon, pound, or chocolate cake
Spooned over a poached winter compote of dried fruits such as figs, apricots, and prunes

❦ *Lemon Soufflé with Raspberry Purée*

Lemon and raspberry make a very refreshing combination. There is just enough sweetness in raspberries to provide a counterpoint to the acidity of lemon. The sauce is simple to make and, because you can use frozen berries, it can be made year round. The finished sauce freezes well. Serve this dish with thin, crisp cookies.

▮ *RASPBERRY PURÉE*

M A K E S   A B O U T   1   C U P

1 recipe Basic Fruit Purée (pages 48–49), made with raspberries
Lemon juice or water to thin, if necessary

▮ *LEMON SOUFFLÉ*

S E R V E S   4

⅓ cup sugar
2 tablespoons flour
¼ teaspoon salt
5 tablespoons light cream
3 tablespoons fresh lemon juice
1 tablespoon grated lemon zest
4 large eggs, separated, plus 1 additional egg white

Make the raspberry purée and thin it with the water or lemon juice if necessary. Cover the purée and set it aside to be served at room temperature.

To make the soufflé, preheat the oven to 400 degrees F. Butter a 6-cup soufflé dish. Sprinkle the bottom and sides of the dish with sugar and knock out the excess. Set the dish aside.

Mix the sugar, flour, and salt in a small, heavy saucepan. Whisk in the cream and then the lemon juice and place the pan over medium heat. Bring the mixture to a boil and whisk until it has thickened. Remove the pan from the heat and place the mixture in a large bowl. Add the lemon zest. Cool the mixture for a few minutes and then add the egg yolks, one at a time.

Beat the egg whites until they are firm but not dry and stir a spoonful into the lemon mixture. Fold the remaining whites into the lemon mixture until no white remains visible. Spoon the batter into the prepared dish and bake the soufflé on the lowest rack of the oven for about

15 minutes. Test with a knife or skewer. The center should be soft and creamy and moist pieces should be clinging to the knife or skewer. The outer edges of the soufflé will be cooked and a skewer inserted there will be dry. Immediately spoon the soufflé onto plates and pour the raspberry sauce, which should be at room temperature, over the servings.

VARIATION

Add 1 pint of fresh blueberries to the sauce.

■

RASPBERRY PURÉE is extremely versatile and may be
> Served with rice pudding, poached fruit, especially pears or peaches, cakes, especially chocolate, angel food, or pound, ice cream, sorbets, slices of fruit, especially melon, orange, peaches and nectarines, and mixed berries, cake with fresh fruit arranged on top, pancakes, French toast, waffles, apple or other fruit fritters, and fruit upside-down cakes

❦ *Creamy Caramel Sauce for Warm Apple Crisp*

Creamy Caramel Sauce is different from an ordinary caramel because the addition of cream makes it a thicker, silky, and rich sauce. This sauce may be made one or two days ahead.

Any of the recommended varieties of apple may be used alone, but the flavor of the crisp will be improved if you use a combination of them—for example, if you use the sweeter apples, mix a tart apple in with them.

■ *CREAMY CARAMEL SAUCE*

MAKES 1 TO 1 ½ CUPS

1 recipe Caramel Sauce (pages 51–52), made with 1 cup heavy or light cream

■ *APPLE CRISP*

S E R V E S   8

6 apples (Granny Smith, Baldwin, Russet, Northern Spy, Cortland, or
    Golden Delicious), quartered, peeled, and cored
2 tablespoons fresh lemon juice
1 teaspoon white sugar
1/2 teaspoon ground cinnamon
Allspice
Mace
1 cup flour
1/3 cup light brown sugar
1/2 cup cold unsalted butter

Make the caramel sauce and set it aside.

To make the crisp, preheat the oven to 375 degrees F. Cut apple quarters into 3 or 4 slices depending on their size. The slices should not be too thin. Sprinkle the apple with the lemon juice, the white sugar, 1/4 teaspoon of the cinnamon, and a pinch each of allspice and mace. Toss the apples to coat them with the mixture and place them in a shallow 2-quart baking dish.

Combine the flour, brown sugar, remaining cinnamon, and a pinch each of allspice and mace in a bowl with a pastry cutter or in a food processor. Cut in the butter and mix the ingredients until they resemble coarse meal. Sprinkle the mixture over the apples and bake for about 45 minutes or until the topping is browned and the apples are tender.

To reheat the sauce, place it over low heat and stir often until it is warmed, but not hot.

VARIATIONS

You can also make this crisp with a mixture of apples and pears or toss in a handful of cranberries, fresh or dried, or raisins, or both. If you like nuts in your crisp topping, try walnuts, pecans, or hazelnuts.

CREAMY CARAMEL SAUCE may be

> Served with gingerbread, lemon, chocolate, or pound cake, tarts, especially pear, apple, cranberry, and chocolate-nut, ice cream, poached fruit, especially pears, a winter compote of dried fruits, bread pudding, and fruit upside-down cakes

Chocolate Bread Pudding with Orange Crème Anglaise

This dish combines three of my favorite flavors: chocolate, cinnamon, and orange. Bread pudding is at its best if the bread is allowed to soak in the custard before baking.

▪ CHOCOLATE BREAD PUDDING

SERVES 8 TO 12

1 pound cinnamon-raisin bread
2 cups light cream
1 cup milk
2 ounces unsweetened chocolate
4 large eggs
2/3 cup sugar
1 teaspoon vanilla extract
1 teaspoon ground nutmeg
Pinch ground cinnamon
Pinch salt

▪ ORANGE CRÈME ANGLAISE

MAKES ABOUT 1 1/2 CUPS

1 recipe Basic Crème Anglaise (pages 52–54)
1 tablespoon grated orange zest
2 tablespoons Grand Marnier liqueur (optional)

To make the pudding, preheat the oven to 350 degrees F. Lightly butter a shallow, 2-quart baking dish. Cut the bread into 1-inch dice, and place it in the prepared pan. Scald the cream and milk and remove them from the heat. Add the chocolate and whisk until it has melted. Set the mixture aside to cool slightly.

In a bowl, beat the eggs, sugar, vanilla, nutmeg, cinnamon, and salt together, then slowly pour in the chocolate milk. Strain the custard over the bread cubes in the pan. Push the bread down so that it absorbs some of the custard. Let the bread sit for 10 minutes to soak, pushing it down once or twice. Bake the pudding for between 35 and 45 minutes until the custard is set.

While the pudding bakes, make the *crème anglaise*, strain it, add the orange zest, and whisk to cool. When the sauce is cool, add the optional liqueur. Serve the sauce either warm or cold over the pudding, which may also be served warm or cold.

VARIATION

The pudding may be served with a caramel sauce.

∎

ORANGE CRÈME ANGLAISE is almost a universal dessert sauce and may be
  Served on a soufflé, particularly chocolate, or on fruit tarts such as
    rhubarb, pear, peach, nectarine, or plum, on any of the cakes in this
    book, fruit upside-down cakes, or on fresh fruit such as peeled and
    sliced oranges

Chocolate Filled Crêpes with Anise-Maple Sauce

These crêpes are intensely flavored; mysterious, my father commented. The combination of chocolate, cardamom, anise, and maple may sound like a flavor war, but the results are magnificent.

It is best to fill and sauce the crêpes immediately when they come out of the pan. If that is impractical, make all the crêpes, stack them on a plate covered with a towel to keep them warm, then fill, sauce, and serve. The crêpe batter, filling, and sauce can all be made ahead. Bring all the components to room temperature before cooking and filling the crêpes.

SERVES 4 TO 6

▪ CRÊPES

MAKES ABOUT 12 CRÊPES

½ cup flour
1 teaspoon sugar
¼ teaspoon salt
½ cup milk
1 large egg
1 tablespoon unsalted butter

▪ CHOCOLATE FILLING

MAKES ABOUT ¾ CUP

½ cup unsalted butter, softened
½ cup sifted confectioner's sugar
1 tablespoon light cream
1 teaspoon vanilla extract
¼ teaspoon ground cardamom
Pinch salt
2 ounces bittersweet chocolate, melted and cooled

▪ ANISE-MAPLE SAUCE

MAKES 1 CUP

½ cup maple syrup
½ cup orange juice
1 teaspoon ground cardamom
1 teaspoon anise seeds

To make the crêpe batter, place the flour, sugar, and salt in a small bowl and make a well. Add the milk and egg and whisk them together. Gradually gather in the flour to make a batter. Set the batter aside to rest for between 20 minutes and 1 hour.

While the crêpe batter rests, make the filling and sauce. For the filling, cream the butter and sugar in a small bowl. Add the cream, vanilla, cardamom, and salt and mix. Pour in the cooled chocolate and blend well. Set the filling aside.

Make the sauce just before you start cooking the crêpes. Combine the maple syrup, orange juice, cardamom, and anise seeds in a saucepan and warm the mixture for about 5 minutes over medium-low heat. Set aside until you are ready to serve.

When you are ready to cook the crêpes, heat a 6-inch crêpe pan, cast-iron, or other heavy skillet over medium-high heat. Add the tablespoon of butter and allow it to melt. Slowly pour the butter into the batter, whisking constantly.

To cook each crêpe, tilt the pan up and away from you until only the farther edge is still on the burner. Using a 2-tablespoon ($1/8$ cup) measure, stir the batter and scoop up $3/4$ of the measure of batter and pour it into the pan. Quickly tilt the pan back and forth to spread the batter over the entire bottom of the skillet and form a thin pancake. Cook the batter for a minute or two until it browns in patches, then flip the crêpe over. Cook it for another minute or so and remove it to a plate. Continue making crêpes with the remaining batter.

To assemble the dish, spread a spoonful of the chocolate cream over each warm crêpe and fold it in quarters. Arrange the crêpes on plates, providing 2 or 3 per person. Warm the sauce and spoon it over the crêpes.

■

ANISE-MAPLE SAUCE may be

> Served with fresh cut-up fruit, cakes, fruit upside-down cake, bread or steamed puddings, pancakes, French toast, waffles, fruit tarts, ice creams, and even shortcake

■ ■ ■ ■ ■

A List of

SAUCES

by

CHAPTER

Chapter 2
SALADS, SAUCES, AND DRESSINGS

Chapter 3
VEGETABLES AND SAUCES

Chapter 6
POULTRY AND ACCOMPANYING SAUCES

Chapter 7
PORK AND ACCOMPANYING SAUCES

Pork Medallions *Agrodolce*   218–219
Pork Chops with a Caper and Tomato Sauce   219–220
A Peach and Basil Chutney for Roast Pork   220–222
Prune and Sekel Pear Sauce for Pork Tenderloin   222–224
Pork Cutlets with Mustard and Green Peppercorns   224–225
Pork Chops with Beet Dressing   225–227
Roast Pork with Cranberry and Dried Cherry Sauce   227–228
Pork Tenderloin with Sweet and Sour Caraway Sauce   229–230
Marinated Pork and Citrus Skewers   230–232
Pork Tenderloin Stir-Fry   232–234
Ham Steak with Apple and Garlic Compote   234–235
Baked Ham with Garnet Sauce   236–237

Chapter 8
LAMB AND ACCOMPANYING SAUCES

Butterflied Leg of Lamb with Honey and Mustard Sauce   242–243
Kidney Lamb Chops with *Tapenade*   243–244
Buttermilk-Marinated Lamb Chops   244–246
Moroccan Lamb Chops   246–248
A Red Pepper Dip for Lamb Nuggets   248–249
A Sour Cream Dipping Sauce for Lamb Kebabs   250–251
Creamy Eggplant on a Roasted Leg of Lamb   251–253
Braised Lamb Shanks with Orange and Garlic   253–254
Lamb with Red Wine and *Persillade* Hollandaise   255–256
Blanquette of Lamb with Artichokes   256–258
Braised Lamb Shanks with Whole Garlic and Mint Sauce   258–259

Chapter 9
VEAL, BEEF, AND ACCOMPANYING SAUCES

Veal Chops in Hazelnut and Artichoke Cream   264–265
Veal Chops with Cider and Rosemary Butter   265–266

Chapter 10
DESSERTS AND SAUCES

■ ■ ■ ■

A Cross Reference to

SAUCES

by

TYPE

Stocks and Stock-Reduction Sauces

STOCK
All-Purpose Brown Chicken and Veal Stock (pages 5–6)
Chicken Stock (page 7)
Fish *Fumet* (Fish Stock) (pages 9–10)
Veal and Beef Stock (page 7)
Veal Stock (page 8)
White Stock (page 7)

REDUCTIONS
Essence (pages 16–17)
Meat Glaze (pages 8–9)
Reduced Stock (page 13)

SAUCES
Braised Leeks in a Tarragon Coat (pages 116–117)
Caper Sauce (pages 281, 282)
Caper and Tomato Sauce (pages 219–220)
Creamy Eggplant Sauce (pages 251–252, 253)
Garlic Sauce (pages 154–155)
Gravy (pages 10–11)
Mustard and Green Peppercorn Sauce (page 225)
Prune and Sekel Pear Sauce (pages 223, 224)
Shallot and Vinegar Sauce (pages 218, 219)
Steak *au Poivre* (page 284)
Stilton and Port Sauce with Walnuts (pages 277–278)
Sweet and Sour Caraway Sauce (pages 229–230)
Woodsy Red Wine Sauce (pages 190–191)
Yellow Raisin and Green Peppercorn Sauce (page 167)

Cream Sauces

Corn Sauce (pages 144–145)
Cream, Dill, and Asparagus Sauce (pages 203–204)

Cream Dressing (pages 71, 72)
Creamy Eggplant Sauce (pages 251–252)
Feta Cream Sauce (pages 133–134)
Ginger Cream (page 112)
Gorgonzola Cream (pages 139, 140)
Hazelnut and Artichoke Cream (pages 264–265)
Mushroom and Cardamom Cream Sauce (pages 177–178)
Ravigote Cream Sauce (pages 100–102)
Reduced Cream (pages 13–14)
Sage Cream (pages 128, 129, 130)
Shrimp Sauce (pages 171–172)
Very Lemony Sauce (pages 266–267)

DESSERT SAUCES
Cardamom Cream (page 313)
Cream Sauce with Pears (pages 304, 305)
Lemon Cream (pages 314, 315)
Whipped Cream (pages 50–51)

Wine Sauces

Bacon and Wine Sauce (pages 164–165)
Essence and Red Wine Sauce (pages 269–270)
Garnet Sauce (pages 236, 237)
Marchand de Vin Sauce (pages 274, 275)
Porcini Mushroom and Red Wine Sauce (pages 279–280)
Prune and Sekel Pear Sauce (pages 223, 224)
Ravigote Cream Sauce (pages 100–102)
Reduced Wine (pages 14–15)
Red Wine and *Persillade* Hollandaise (pages 255–256)
Red Wine Sauce (pages 103–104)
Saffron and Lemon Sauce (pages 172–173, 174)
Woodsy Red Wine Sauce (pages 190–191)

DESSERT SAUCES
Rhubarb and Strawberry Compote (pages 303–304)

Other Reductions

Apple and Garlic Compote (pages 234, 235)
Cider and Apple Sauce with Ginger Threads (page 194)
Cider-Glazed Apple Wedges (pages 122–123)
Cider and Rosemary Butter (pages 265–266)
Fennel and Red Pepper Sauté (page 124)
Orange and Red Pepper Dip (pages 248, 249)
Pineapple Dressing (pages 64–65)
Reduced Cider (page 15)

DESSERT SAUCES
Ginger Syrup (page 306)
Spiced Cherry Sauce (pages 316, 317)

Essences

Essence (pages 16–17)
Essence and Red Wine Sauce (pages 269–270)
Essence of Chicken and Citrus (pages 192–193)
Marchand de Vin Sauce (pages 274, 275)
Marsala Sauce (pages 268–269)
Moroccan Spice Butter with Essence (pages 246–247)

Beurre Blanc Sauces (White Butter Sauces)

Beurre Blanc (White Butter) (pages 17–18)
Lime and Mint Butter (pages 168–169)
Saffron and Lemon Sauce (pages 172–174)

Gravies Made from Pan Juices

Blanquette of Lamb with Artichokes (pages 256–258)
Braised Leeks in a Tarragon Coat (pages 116–117)
Caper Sauce (pages 281, 282)
Cider-Braised Chicken with Marjoram (pages 204–206)
Cream, Dill, and Asparagus Sauce (pages 203–204)
Orange and Garlic Sauce (pages 253–254)
Porcini Mushroom and Red Wine Sauce (pages 279–280)
Sweet and Sour Sauce (pages 229–230)
Very Lemony Sauce (pages 266–267)
Whole Garlic and Mint Sauce (pages 258–259)

Tomato Sauces

Caper and Tomato Sauce (pages 219, 220)
Dill-Tomato Sauce (page 107)
Fresh Tomato Sauce with Variations (pages 19–20)
Ginger Barbecue Sauce (pages 195–196)
Grapefruit and Tomato Compote (page 183)
Hazelnut and Tomato Sauce (pages 137–138)
Honeyed Tomato Sauce (pages 102, 103)
Ragù (pages 146–147)
Rigatoni all'Amatriciana (page 135)
Sherry Vinegar Dressing (pages 67, 68)
Shrimp Cocktail Sauce (pages 179–180)
Shrimp Sauce (pages 171–172)
Tomato and Cinnamon Sauce (pages 141, 142)
Winter Tomato Sauce with Variations (pages 20–22)

Marinades

Beet Dressing (pages 225–226)
Buttermilk Marinade (pages 245, 246)

DESSERT MARINADES

Vinaigrettes and Salad Dressings

Compound (Flavored) Butter

Mustard-Thyme Butter (pages 150, 151, 152)
Red Pepper Butter (page 115)
Spice Butter (page 131)
Stilton Butter (pages 277–278)
Tapenade (page 44)
Yellow Raisin and Green Peppercorn Sauce (page 167)

DESSERT BUTTER
Chocolate-Cardamom Butter (page 330)

Noisette Butter (pages 208, 209, 210)

Fruit Sauces

Apple and Garlic Compote (pages 234, 235)
Avocado Sauce (pages 99–100)
Cherry Tomato Salsa (pages 176, 177)
Chunky Pear and Ginger Sauce (page 212)
Cranberry and Dried Cherry Sauce (pages 227, 228)
Curry and Cranberry Sauce (pages 188–189)
Fruit Purées with Variations (pages 48–49)
Grapefruit and Tomato Compote (page 183)
Grape Sauce (pages 132, 133)
Mango Dressing (pages 62–63)
Peach and Basil Chutney (pages 220–221)
Prune and Sekel Pear Sauce (pages 223, 224)
Red Onion and Cranberry Compote (pages 206–207)
Rhubarb and Leek Sauce (pages 210, 211)
Rhubarb-Mustard Sauce (pages 161, 162)

DESSERT SAUCES
Blueberry Sauce (page 298)
Ginger and Apricot Sauce (pages 307, 308)
Mango and Lime Sauce (pages 321, 322)

Raspberry Purée (page 325)
Sliced Strawberry Sauce (page 299)
Spiced Cherry Sauce (pages 316, 317, 318)
Sweet and Sour Berry Sauce (pages 319–320)

Herb Sauces

Fresh Mint Sauce (page 200)
Pesto (page 44)

Vegetable Sauces

Apple and Garlic Compote (pages 234, 235)
Avocado Sauce (pages 99, 100)
Beet Dressing (pages 225–226)
Cherry Tomato Salsa (pages 176, 177)
Corn Relish (pages 198–199)
Creamy Eggplant Sauce (pages 251–252, 253)
Garlic Sauce (pages 154–155)
Grapefruit and Tomato Compote (page 183)
Mushroom and Marsala Sauce (pages 268–269)
Pancetta and Corn Sauce (pages 144–145)
Red Onion and Cranberry Compote (pages 206–207)
Red Pepper Butter (page 115)
Red Pepper Dip (pages 248, 249)
Red Pepper Purée (page 46)
Rhubarb and Leek Sauce (pages 210, 211)
Vegetable Purées with Variations (pages 46–47)

Chutneys, Relishes, Compotes, and Salsas

Apple and Garlic Compote (pages 234, 235)
Cherry Tomato Salsa (pages 176, 177)
Corn Relish (pages 198–199)

Cranberry and Dried Cherry Sauce (pages 227, 228)
Curry and Cranberry Sauce (pages 188–189)
Grapefruit and Tomato Compote (page 183)
Peach and Basil Chutney (pages 220–221)
Red Onion and Cranberry Compote (pages 206–207)
Red Wine Sauce (pages 103–104)
Rhubarb and Leek Sauce (pages 210, 211)
Rhubarb and Strawberry Compote (pages 303–304)

Yogurt and Sour Cream Sauces

Cream Cheese with Horseradish Sauce (page 271)
Creamy Shallot and Balsamic Vinegar Sauce (pages 174–175)
Cumin and Sour Cream Dipping Sauce (pages 250, 251)
Drained Yogurt (Yogurt Cheese) and Variations (pages 49–50)
Feta Sauce (pages 143, 144)
Indian Marinade (pages 201–202, 203)
Leek Topping (pages 153, 154)
Yellow Raisin and Green Peppercorn Topping (page 167)
Raita Yogurt Sauce (pages 189–190)
Waldorf Salad (pages 63–64)
Yogurt-Curry Sauce (pages 98, 99)

DESSERT SAUCES
Coconut and Yogurt Sauce (page 311)
Sour Cream Sauce (pages 294, 295)

Mayonnaise Sauces

Aïoli (pages 74–75)
Basic Mayonnaise with Variations (pages 39–41)
Creamy Shallot and Balsamic Vinegar Sauce (pages 174–175)
Green Goddess Dressing (pages 149, 150)
Green Peppercorn Sauce (page 118)
Hazelnut Mayonnaise (page 60)

Spicy Lemon Aïoli (pages 191–192)
Tartar Sauce (pages 180–181)

Hollandaise

Red Wine and *Persillade* Hollandaise (pages 255–256)

Dipping Sauces

Aïoli (pages 74–75)
Bagna Cauda Dipping Sauce (page 108)
Basic Mayonnaise with Variations (pages 39–41)
Cherry Tomato Salsa (pages 176, 177)
Cocktail Sauce (pages 179–180)
Cumin and Sour Cream Dipping Sauce (pages 250, 251)
Honey and Mustard Sauce (page 242)
Mignonette Dipping Sauce (pages 163, 164)
Orange and Red Pepper Dip (pages 248, 249)
Pesto (page 44)
Raita Yogurt Sauce (pages 189–190)
Red Pepper Dip (pages 248, 249)
Shallot and Vinegar Sauce (pages 218, 219)
Shrimp Cocktail Sauce (pages 179–180)
Spicy Lemon Aïoli (pages 191–192)
Tapenade (page 44)
Tempura Dipping Sauce (pages 110, 111)

Caramel and Butterscotch Sauces

Butterscotch Sauce (page 309)
Caramel Sauce (pages 51–52)
Creamy Caramel Sauce (pages 326–327)
Orange Caramel Sauce (pages 292, 293)

Custard Sauces

Crème Anglaise (Basic Custard Sauce) with Variations (pages 52–54)
Lemon Cream (pages 314–315)
Orange Crème Anglaise (pages 328, 329)
Pistachio Crème Anglaise (pages 323–324)

Chocolate Sauces

Chocolate Cream Sauce (pages 296–297)
Chocolate Drizzle (page 306)
Dad's Chocolate Sauce (pages 301, 302)
Mocha Sauce (pages 290, 291)

Miscellaneous Sauces

Amatriciana Sauce (page 135)
Dark Mushroom Sauce (pages 285–286)
Honey and Mustard Sauce (page 242)
Noisette Butter (pages 208, 209, 210)
Pork Tenderloin Stir-Fry (pages 232–234)
Sweet and Sour Caraway Sauce (pages 229–230)
Tapenade (page 44)
Tuna Sauce (pages 136, 137)

DESSERT SAUCE
Anise-Maple Sauce (pages 330, 331)

■ ■ ■ ■

A Glossary of

INGREDIENTS,

TECHNIQUES,

and

TERMS

Beurre manié   Literally "handled butter," *beurre manié* is a mixture of equal parts of butter and flour used to thicken a gravy or a sauce. For an example, see the recipe for Woodsy Red Wine Sauce on pages 190–191.

Broth   The liquid that results when ingredients such as meat, poultry, fish, game, vegetables, or combinations of those, are cooked in water. They impart their own flavor and body from the natural gelatin they contain. The strained liquid is broth. The words broth and stock are used interchangeably.

Caramel   Sugar cooked in a pan until it becomes a deep, dark brown syrup.

Caramelize   To cook an ingredient so that the natural sugars it contains will brown. For instance, onions, steak, or sugar may be caramelized.

Compote   A stew of fruits flavored with spices and liqueurs, served cold. The fruit is cooked slowly so that it holds its shape. In this book I use the term loosely when referring to vegetables as well as fruit cooked in that fashion.

Condiment   A dish or seasoning (such as soy sauce) used to accompany food. Salt, pepper, chutney, relish, pickles, mustard, ketchup, salsa, jam, jelly, preserves, conserves, fruit butters, piccalilli, and hot pepper sauces are all considered condiments.

Curdle   Egg protein that coagulates and separates from liquid or fat because it has been overheated or been combined with an acid ingredient is said to have curdled. Curdling can happen in a custard sauce or in a hollandaise-type sauce. If your sauce does curdle, you will see bits of cooked egg floating in it. Unlike a sauce in which the egg has merely separated, a curdled sauce cannot be saved. Start over again.

Deglaze   To wash and dissolve any caramelized juices in a pan. Juices that have caramelized during pan-frying or roasting are tremendously flavorful. These bits are like meat glaze in that the juices that escape from a piece of food during cooking reduce, brown, and sometimes harden so that they provide a strong flavor upon which to build a sauce.

Emulsify   To mix together two incompatible ingredients that do not normally blend, such as oil and water. Emulsions may be unstable or stable. Oil and vinegar make an unstable emulsion; one that will separate upon standing. Mayonnaise is a stable emulsion; it will not separate.

Enrichments   Ingredients added to a sauce for flavor, texture, or both. A sauce may be enriched with butter, cream, yogurt, sour cream, *crème fraiche*, a mixture of egg yolks and cream, *mascarpone* cheese, flavored oil, liqueur, a brandy, or fortified wine.

Essence   Stock simmered down in successive batches with browned meat, game, or poultry until it is reduced to a thick glaze. See pages 16–17 for details and the recipe.

Fortified wine   Wine to which brandy has been added to stop fermentation and increase the alcohol content. Port, sherry, Madeira, and Marsala are all fortified wines.

Glaze   A liquid that is very sticky, usually dark in color, and the consistency of thick syrup. See also Meat glaze.

Gravy   A gravy is a sauce made specifically from pan drippings or juices. Roasted meats or poultry, stews, braises, pot roasts, poaching, or a sauté all create the base from which gravies are made.

Infuse   To steep or simmer seasonings in a liquid so that the liquid is flavored. For example, ground nuts may be infused in cream or milk; herbs and vegetables cooked in vinegar or wine result in an infusion.

Liaison   Thickening a sauce. From the French verb *lier* (to bind). The thickening agent may be egg yolks, blood, flour, or starch.

Marinate   To steep a food in a mixture of ingredients to add flavor and somewhat soften the fibers of the food. A marinade may be cooked or uncooked, dry or liquid. See pages 22–27 for details and recipes.

Meat glaze   Stock reduced to a thick, sticky syrup. See pages 8–9 for the recipe.

Mother sauce   A sauce base to which ingredients are added to form a variant of the original. In classic French cuisine, the mother sauces are mayonnaise, hollandaise, béchamel (white sauce), *velouté*, and *Espagnole* (brown sauce).

***Noisette* butter**   Butter cooked until it has the color and smell of hazelnuts (*noisette* is French for hazelnut). The best *noisette* butter is made with whole, not clarified butter, as most of the flavor comes from the milk solids that are removed in the clarifying. Whole butter requires a bit more attention because the browned milk solids fall to the bottom of the pan and may burn. For an example of its use, see the recipe for Turkey *Scaloppine* with Fennel Crumbs and *Noisette* Butter on pages 208–210.

Reduce   To boil or simmer a liquid, decreasing its volume, to concentrate the flavors and thicken the texture.

Ribbon   This refers to beating eggs or egg yolks and sugar together until they are thick, pale, and very aerated. To test, lift the beaters or whisk from the bowl. The batter should fall off the beaters very slowly in a wide band, folding onto itself. It resembles a ribbon that falls onto itself when dropped. The falling batter slowly blends back into the rest of the batter in the bowl. Once this stage is reached, the batter is ready for the next step.

Roux   A mixture of melted fat and flour cooked together and used to thicken sauces. For an example, see the recipe for *Blanquette* of Lamb with Artichokes on pages 256–258.

Separation   In sauces such as a mayonnaise or hollandaise that contain a lot of fat and not much moisture, the oil or fat may separate if enough moisture evaporates. Pools of oil or fat will appear on the surface.

Slurry   A mixture of a starch and a liquid used to thicken a sauce. The starch may be cornstarch, arrowroot, or potato starch, but is usually not flour, although I'm sure there are people who remember watching their mothers shake water and flour in a jar and use it to finish the turkey gravy. For an example, see Sweet and Sour Beef with Cabbage on pages 272–273.

Small Sauce   In classic French cooking, a small, or compound sauce is a mother sauce to which an ingredient has been added that changes its character.

Stock   A liquid made by cooking meat, poultry, fish, game, or vegetables in water. The water gains flavor and body from the ingredients. The strained stock is used primarily for sauces, soups, stews, and braising. The word is used interchangeably with broth.

Thickeners   A variety of starches, proteins, or fats may be used to bind or thicken a sauce. The starches include cornstarch, arrowroot, potato starch, or flour. A sauce may also be thickened with egg yolks, butter (see the recipes for essence and *beurre blanc* on pages 16–18), a mixture of flour and fat, or vegetable purées. Each agent produces a different texture and appearance.

INDEX

Port, macerated cherries in, 28
Potatoes
    baked, with three butters, 150–152
    baked, with vegetables and pesto,
        147–148
    fish and chips, 180–182
    gnocchi with ragù, 146–147
    grilled, with green goddess dressing,
        148–150
    mashed, with garlic sauce, 154–155
    pancakes, with leek topping,
        153–164
Potato Gnocchi with Ragù, 146–147
Potato Pancakes with Leek Topping,
    153–154
Poultry, 185–213
    chicken, broiled, with herb butter,
        196–198
    chicken, cider-braised, with
        marjoram, 204–206
    chicken, grilled, with ginger
        barbecue sauce, 195–196
    chicken, parmesan-baked, with corn
        relish, 198–200
    chicken, roasted, six sauces for,
        188–194
    chicken sauté with cream, dill, and
        asparagus sauce, 203–204
    chicken with fresh mint sauce,
        200–201
    chicken with Indian marinade,
        201–203
    duck, roast, with rhubarb and leek
        sauce, 210–211
    duck legs with pear and ginger sauce,
        212–213
    turkey, roasted, with red onion and
        cranberry compote, 206–207
    turkey and white bean salad with
        cream dressing, 70–72
    turkey salad with mango dressing,
        62–63
    turkey scaloppine with fennel crumbs
        and noisette butter, 208–210
Prune and Sekel Pear Sauce, 223–224

*Prune and Sekel Pear Sauce for Pork
    Tenderloin*, 222–224
Prune Plum Purée, 48
Purées, 43–49
    fruit, 47–49, 324–326
    herb, 44–46
    as marinades, 25–27
    vegetable, 46–47, 102–103

Ragù, 146–147
Raita Yogurt, 50
Raita Yogurt Sauce, 189–190
Raspberry Purée, 325
Ravigote Cream Sauce, 100–102
Red Cabbage à La Grecque, 59
Red Onion and Cranberry Compote,
    206–207
Red Onion Dressing, 91–92
Red Onion Vinaigrette, 31
Red Pepper Butter, 115
Red Pepper Dip, 248–249
Red Pepper Dip for Lamb Nuggets,
    248–249
Red Pepper Purée, 46
*Red Peppers and Peas with Lemon Zest
    Dressing*, 80–82
Reduce, defined, 364
Reduced Cider, 15
Reduced Cream, 13–14
Reduced Stock, 13
Reduced Wine, 14–15
Reductions, 11–18
    apple and garlic compote, 234, 235
    beurre blanc (white butter sauce),
        17–18
    cider, 15
    cider and apple sauce with ginger
        threads, 194
    cider and rosemary butter, 265–266
    cider-glazed apple wedges, 122–123
    cream, 13–14
    defined, 364
    essence, 16–17
    fennel and red pepper sauté, 124
    ginger syrup, 305–306
    meat glaze, 8–9